The Labour Party and the world
VOLUME 2

MANCHESTER
1824

Manchester University Press

The Labour Party and the world

VOLUME 2

Labour's foreign policy since 1951

Rhiannon Vickers

Manchester University Press
Manchester and New York

published exclusively in the USA by Palgrave Macmillan

Published by
Manchester University Press
Oxford Road, Manchester M13 9NR, UK
and Room 400, 175 Fifth Avenue, New York, NY 10010, USA
www.manchesteruniversitypress.co.uk

Distributed exclusively in the USA by
Palgrave Macmillan, 175 Fifth Avenue, New York,
NY 10010, USA

Distributed exclusively in Canada by
UBC Press, University of British Columbia, 2029 West Mall
Vancouver, BC, Canada V6T 1Z2

British Library Cataloguing-in-Publication Data
A catalogue record for this book is available from the British Library

Library of Congress Cataloging-in-Publication Data applied for

ISBN 978 0 7190 6746 4 *hardback*
      978 0 7190 6747 1 *paperback*

First published 2011

Typeset by Helen Skelton, Brighton, UK
Printed in Great Britain
by CPI Antony Rowe Ltd, Chippenham, Wiltshire

In loving memory of my father,
George Vickers, 1926–2008

Contents

Acknowledgements

I would like to thank the following institutions for permission to quote from the documents of which they hold the copyright: the Bodleian Library, Oxford, for the George Brown papers and the Harold Wilson papers; the British Library of Political and Economic Science, London School of Economics, for the use of the following papers: Arthur Bottomley, Antony Crosland, the International Marxist Group, Hugh Jenkins, Peter Shore, George Wigg; Churchill College, Cambridge, for the use of following papers: Patrick Gordon Walker, Neil Kinnock, Michael Stewart; the Modern Records Centre, University of Warwick, for the following archives: Campaign for Nuclear Disarmament, Richard Crossman, the International Marxist Group, Keep Left, TUC and miscellaneous papers; the National Labour History Archive, Manchester, for the Labour Party archive and the Jo Richardson papers; the National Archives (previously known as the Public Record Office), for Foreign Office, Cabinet Office, Prime Minister's Office papers; the US National Archive, College Park, Maryland, for State Department papers; and the National Security Archive at the George Washington University, Washington D.C. In particular, the archivists at the National Labour History Archive, Manchester, and the Modern Records Centre at the University of Warwick were of great assistance, and I thank them. I am also grateful to the British Academy for providing research grant number SG 36705, which enabled me to carry out my archival work. Research in the US was aided by a sabbatical spent at the George Washington University. My thanks also go to the people who kindly agreed to be interviewed by me for this book. They offered invaluable insights as well as encouragement.

I would like to thank friends and colleagues at the University of Sheffield for providing advice and support in the writing of this volume. My particular thanks go to Andrew Mumford for his invaluable research assistance and for his unfailing good humour. I would also like to thank the anonymous reviewers for their comments and suggestions, and everyone at Manchester University Press involved in the publication of this book. I, of course, remain responsible for any errors.

Finally, a few words of explanation are necessary. The writing of these volumes has presented me with the formidable challenge of covering an extensive historical topic, with a vast source of potential archive material and secondary sources, whilst maintaining a sense of clear historical narrative with, I hope, a lucid and coherent argument. I have done this to the best of my abilities under the given circumstances. This second volume presented me with the further challenge of deciding whether to interview the large number of key figures from the Wilson, Callaghan and Blair governments, and those who influenced policy while Labour was in opposition. It became clear to me early on in the writing of this volume that strict limits would have to be placed on the amount of interviews I could carry out if I were ever to finish it. The world, as the Labour Party has always regretted, is not an ideal place, and choices have to be made about what is desirable, and what is achievable. The same is true of the way that I cover the issues and events in this volume.

List of abbreviations

ABM	Anti-ballistic missile
AFL	American Federation of Labor
ANC	African National Congress
ANF	Atlantic nuclear force
BBC	British Broadcasting Corporation
CAP	Common Agricultural Policy (of the EC)
CIA	Central Intelligence Agency
CLPD	Campaign for Labour Party Democracy
CND	Campaign for Nuclear Disarmament
CPGB	Communist Party of Great Britain
CSCE	Conference for Security and Cooperation in Europe
DFID	Department for International Development
EC	European Community
EEC	European Economic Community
EFTA	European Free Trade Association
END	European Nuclear Disarmament
ERM	Exchange Rate Mechanism
EU	European Union
FCO	Foreign and Commonwealth Office
G-8	Group of 8 Industrialised Nations
GNP	Gross National Product
HC Deb	House of Commons Debates (Hansard)
HIPC	Heavily Indebted Poor Countries
ILP	Independent Labour Party
IMF	International Monetary Fund
INF	Intermediate-range Nuclear Forces
ISAF	International Security Assistance Force
LPACR	Labour Party Annual Conference Report

MEP	Member of European Parliament
MLF	Multilateral Force
MOD	Ministry of Defence
MP	Member of Parliament
MRC	Modern Records Centre
NATO	North Atlantic Treaty Organisation
NEC	National Executive Committee (Labour Party)
PLO	Palestinian Liberation Organisation
PLP	Parliamentary Labour Party
PRO	Public Record Office
SALT	I & II Strategic Arms Limitations Talks
SDP	Social Democratic Party
SDR	Strategic Defence Review
START II	Strategic Arms Reduction Treaty
SWAPO	South West Africa People's Organisation
TGWU	Transport and General Workers' Union
TNA	The National Archives (previously known as the Public Record Office)
TUC	Trades Union Congress
TUCR	Trades Union Congress Annual Report
UDI	Unilateral Declaration of Independence (Southern Rhodesia)
UN	United Nations
UNESCO	United Nations Education, Scientific and Cultural Organisation
UNSCOM	United Nations Special Commission
WEU	Western European Union
WMD	weapons of mass destruction
ZANU	Zimbabwe African National Union
ZAPU	Zimbabwe African People's Union

Introduction

This book is the second volume on *The Labour Party and the World*. Volume 1 began by pointing out that foreign policy has been an under-researched area of Labour Party policy and history. Studies of the Labour Party have tended to focus on domestic policy, in particular social and economic policy, both in terms of policy-making and in terms of ideology. None of the major studies of the Labour Party subject Labour's foreign policy to sustained analysis, and the general conclusion was that Labour had failed to provide an alternative foreign policy. This dearth of material occurs despite the fact that foreign policy has always been an area of contention for Labour, providing the arena for some of the most intense tribal warfare within the party; and it has contributed to the myth that Labour has been insular in its outlook, not much interested in international affairs, and has made little in the way of contribution to British foreign policy. This study, therefore, seeks to rectify this gap in the literature on both the political ideology and the history of the Labour Party's foreign policy and to demonstrate that the Labour Party has, from its very beginning, been involved and interested in international policy and with Britain's relations with the rest of the world. International affairs have been a major cause for concern for the Labour Party, not least because of its fundamental understanding that domestic and international politics were part of a whole that could not be treated as mutually exclusive.

Foreign policy under 'New Labour' stimulated a renewed interest in the nature of Labour's approach to the world. What has been particularly interesting is that much of this work has come from International Relations scholars rather than Labour specialists.[1] There have been two main reasons for this renewed interest. First, as was pointed out in Volume 1, Labour governments since 1997 emphasised ideas about a moral dimension to foreign policy, about Britain's membership of an international community, and about the need to think of the international interest and not just the national interest. These were not new ideas; rather, they reflected a particular worldview that has been prevalent throughout the Labour Party's history. However they *appeared* to many commentators at the time to be new. This interest was initially sparked by Robin Cook's much-quoted mission statement at the Foreign and Commonwealth Office in May 1997, in which he made a commitment to an 'ethical dimension' to British foreign policy. Cook declared that he was going to implement a new kind of foreign policy, which 'recognises that the national interest cannot be defined only by narrow realpolitik'. The aim was 'to make Britain once again a force for good in the world'.[2] Cook's comments initiated a debate on the nature of Labour's foreign policy, which was further fuelled by Blair's keynote speech on the 'doctrine of the international community' at the height of the Kosovo conflict in 1999, and his speech to the Labour Party conference in September 2001, when he outlined his aim of reordering the world. The second main reason for this renewed interest was because so much happened in terms of international affairs between 1997 and 2010. Labour politicians did not experience the peaceful, ordered, post-Cold War world that they had expected to encounter when they came to power; instead, British foreign policy was particularly focused on conflict situations and on responding to threats. The Kosovo conflict, the terrorist attacks of 9/11, the wars in Afghanistan and Iraq, inevitably become the focus of academic debate and public interest.

This two-volume study provides a political history of the evolution of Labour's foreign policy, a daunting task given the enormous range of issues and events that could be covered, but nevertheless a fascinating one. Inevitably there have been some events that could have been studied in more depth, and one of the main challenges of this study has been to edit down the coverage of any one issue and to decide to cut out some things all together. This study also constructs a framework through which Labour's foreign policy and its outlook on the world can be analysed and interpreted. It argues that Labour did seek to offer an alternative to the traditional power politics or realist approach of British foreign policy, which had stressed national self-interest, and to provide a version of British foreign policy based on internationalism, which stressed co-operation and interdependence, and a concern with the international as well as the national interest. In this, by far the most important influence on Labour's foreign policy were liberal views of international relations. Thus, Labour sought a reformist rather than a radical or revolutionary approach to foreign policy. This study argues therefore that there has been a discernable Labour Party foreign policy throughout the twentieth century, and this can most helpfully be categorised as 'internationalism'. This approach will be outlined in more detail in the following chapter, before the book continues its historical overview. Volume 1 of this study ended with an assessment of foreign policy under the Attlee governments, and this second volume of *The Labour Party and the World* begins with Labour's 1951 election defeat.

Outline of study

Chapter 1 identifies policies that reflect the six core beliefs at the heart of Labour's foreign policy, which arise from its fundamental internationalist approach to international relations outlined in Volume 1 of this study. These are first, that while states operate in a system of international anarchy, fundamental reform of the system is possible because states have common interests and values. This change is only likely to be secured through the construction of international institutions to regulate economic, political and military relations between states. Second, linked to this is a sense of belonging to an international community, and that each state has a responsibility to work towards the common good of the international system, to work in the 'international' interest rather than purely in what it perceives to be its national interest. Third, that international policy and governance should be based on democratic principles and universal moral norms. Fourth, that collective security is better than secret bilateral diplomatic treaties or balance of power politics, which are self-defeating in terms of generating conflict. Fifth, that armaments and arms races can destabilise the international system, and that the proliferation of arms should be limited, the arms trade regulated, and that disarmament, in principle, is desirable. In addition to these five largely liberal internationalist principles is one additional socialist aspect of Labour's international thought, and this has been a belief in international working-class solidarity and a concern to improve working conditions and to alleviate poverty.

Chapter 2 resumes the historical narrative of this two-volume study and deals with the opposition years of the 1950s when the Labour Party became increasingly divided over the issues of rearmament, nuclear weapons and Britain's role in the world. By the late

1950s, partly due to internal divisions in the party, and partly due to developments in weapons and the perception of the intensification of the nuclear threat, there was a clear split between left and right. While Gaitskell and the right of the party were pushing the party along traditional foreign and defence lines, those on the left wanted the party to take an ethical stance and provide moral leadership by renouncing nuclear weapons altogether. The bitter wrangling gave the party a reputation for division and the focus on unilateral disarmament one of extremism, which did little to help the party electorally, despite the Conservatives' humiliation over Suez. Remarkably, despite the party's inability to produce a coherent defence policy, it recovered sufficiently to win the 1964 general election, and entered the election campaign-with a manifesto largely based on its late-1950s policies.

Chapter 3 examines the foreign policy of the Wilson governments of the 1960s, which were marked by debate about Britain's role in the world. Despite Wilson's unsuccessful bid to join the European Community, the decision that Britain had to withdraw its troops from east of Suez, the impasse over the Smith regime's unilateral declaration of independence in Rhodesia, and the ongoing realisation that Britain's relative economic decline meant that it could not return to the days when Britain was one of the 'Big Three' powers in the world, Wilson continued to present himself as a player on the world stage. Indeed, his attachment to Britain's world role and its imperial legacy prevented him from accepting sooner what many in the Labour Party were arguing, namely that Britain should retreat from its old imperial commitments east of Suez, not only for economic reasons but for ideological ones as well. Indeed, in terms of foreign policy, there seemed to be little remaining of Wilson the former left-wing Labour MP. This was most obviously demonstrated by Wilson's position on Vietnam, as he publicly supported America's intervention, which meant that Britain provided the semblance of international agreement over US policy. While Wilson was successful over Vietnam in that he held out against American demands for him to send British troops, he also did his utmost to avoid even 'dissociating' the British government from specific American actions. It was this issue, more than any other, that drained support for Wilson's foreign policy from Labour Party members and members of the general public, and became part of the lexicon of the left that Wilson had betrayed the party. As soon as Labour lost the 1970 election, the party line changed to one of outright condemnation of US policy in Vietnam.

Chapter 4 turns to the 1970s, when the Labour Party moved to the left in its political programme. This was partly as a reaction against six years in government, and partly in an attempt to recuperate its base inside the trade unions and reconnect with the constituency parties, which had both seen an influx of left-wing members. As a consequence, foreign policy positions also moved leftwards. Over Vietnam, the issue that had caused so much division in the 1960s, the party was pretty much united in condemning the ongoing conflict and urging the withdrawal of American forces. Party divisions over whether Britain should join the EC re-emerged, but the biggest shift was over defence policy and nuclear weapons. Whereas the party had been fairly acquiescent over Britain's nuclear policy during the 1964–1970 Wilson governments, once Labour lost power, its attitude changed. Resolutions passed at the 1972 and 1973 annual conferences advocated the dissolution of NATO, the closure of nuclear bases, and the rejection of a British defence policy based on the threat of the use of nuclear weapons. Labour then developed two conflicting defence policies in the mid to late 1970s. There was the policy of the Labour Party's National Executive Committee, which reflected resolutions passed at conference and the attitudes of the left of the party, and which was based on reducing the reliance on Britain's nuclear deterrent. With the period of détente in the early 1970s, and the success of the Helsinki Conference of the summer of 1975, some in the Labour Party started to view the end of the Cold War as a possibility that could be hastened by the actions of a British government if it were willing to negotiate and to renounce Britain's independent nuclear deterrent. Then there was the policy of the Labour government, which reflected the centre-right of the party, which was firmly committed to bolstering the Anglo-American relationship and to strengthening Britain's nuclear deterrent. That the inconsistencies between the two were not more widely apparent helped the government at the time, but these inconsistencies reflected a battle for the future of Labour's defence policy, which were to reach their peak in the early 1980s when they proved an electoral liability for the party.

Chapter 5 deals with the 1980s when foreign and defence policy became radicalised in Britain with the end of détente and the deepening Cold War. The Conservative Party moved to the right on foreign and defence policy after Thatcher's Falklands victory in 1982, at a time when Labour had moved ideologically to the left on these issues. This combination meant that foreign and defence policy became a political battleground, and, unusually for Britain, increasingly salient to the voters in the 1983 and 1987 elections. The Conservatives successfully labelled Labour as being weak on foreign and defence policy and not to be trusted with the nation's security. At the same time, foreign and defence policy became a key part of the ideological battle within the Labour Party. Labour's shift to the left on foreign and defence policy did the party immense harm electorally, but, somewhat ironically, it left the party better prepared to deal with the immense changes in the international system at the turn of the 1990s with the end of the Cold War. Having already devoted attention to a new, and more modest, understanding of Britain's role in the world, and accepted that Britain was working in an increasingly interdependent world, Labour was well placed to accept the new tenets of globalisation in the 1990s, and to deal with the rise in transnational issues that has been a concomitant part of international relations at the end of the twentieth century.

Chapter 6 deals with foreign policy under the Blair governments. It starts by examining the years immediately preceding the 1997 election and then outlines Robin Cook's mission statement in which he promised an 'ethical dimension' to foreign policy. It suggests why Cook made this commitment, and assesses the extent to which the government has been able to live up to it through an examination of issues and events, in particular arms sales and humanitarian intervention. It then examines Tony Blair's response to the Kosovo crisis, Britain's role in Europe, and an assessment of international development and aid policy The chapter finishes by assessing what was 'new' about New Labour's foreign policy. It argues that during New Labour's first administration there were a number of changes: first, there was some shift away from a more traditional balance of power approach to British foreign policy to a more internationalist stance, which reflected a new understanding of the post-Cold War, globalised world. Second, Labour spearheaded a new approach to foreign policy in terms of opening up both the processes and institutional structures to wider involvement from NGOs and the public. Third, Labour broadened the definition of foreign policy, giving a greater prominence to transnational issues, which transcend the traditional boundaries between domestic and foreign policy, such as the environment, people-trafficking, international organised crime, and the proliferation of small arms.

Chapter 7 begins with the events of September 11, 2001, and goes on to outline Britain's role in the 'war on terror', the invasions of Afghanistan and Iraq, and the way in which Blair staked his legacy on the way that his government responded to a disordered world. This is then contrasted with Gordon Brown's more risk-averse approach to foreign affairs – in tune with concerns felt by the public, which had no appetite for further troop deployments to conflict zones – and a greater awareness of the limitations of what could be achieved through the use of force. One of the defining features of Brown's approach to foreign policy was that he has tended to say very little about it. He perhaps felt that Blair's very public focus on international affairs, his response to Kosovo and to 9/11, distracted him from the domestic agenda and caused divisions in the Labour Party. The optimism of the late 1990s, when there was a renewed confidence in Britain's role in the world, had been replaced by pessimism, lowered expectations, and a lack of debate within the Labour Party about international affairs, an area which was seen as an electoral liability to the party as a result of the wars in Iraq and Afghanistan.

The book concludes by revisiting some of the main themes of this study. Volume 1 argued that Labour never really came to an ideological agreement over how to be internationalist within an international system dominated by nation-states. Labour did not question the existence of a world of sovereign nation-states, but its internationalist perspective led it to look for ways to control relations between states and ameliorate the inherent conflict in the international system: to replace the system of international anarchy with a world order that could create the framework for a world society.[3] The tension between national sovereignty and internationalism lay behind many of the battles over Labour' foreign policy, and the party often found itself unable to transcend national barriers in order to meet its commitment to internationalism. However, in recent years, with the end of the Cold War and the impact of globalisation, support for multilateralism appeared to offer a solution and a way to transcend national barriers in order to meet commitments to internationalism. By the time that Labour came to power in 1997 it had come to the conclusion that on many issues – which were increasingly transnational in nature – what was in the international interest was also in Britain's long-term national interest. However, while Labour's position might have provoked debate about whose interest Britain should act in, and whether it was possible to reconcile national and international interests, one question that has not been sufficiently studied is the problem of knowing what is in the international interest. While Chapter 1 of this volume began by pointing out that the national interest is not self-evident or value neutral, that interests are constructed, exactly the same could be said of the international interest. The Blair and Brown governments of 1997 to 2010 have tended to make the same sort of assumptions about the international interest that earlier governments made about the national interest.

Notes

1 For instance, Mark Curtis, *Web of Deceit: Britain's Real Role in the World* (London: Vintage, 2003); Richard Little and Mark Wickham-Jones, eds, *New Labour's Foreign Policy. A New Moral Crusade?* (Manchester: Manchester University Press, 2000); Nicholas Wheeler and Tim Dunne, 'Good international citizenship: a Third Way for British foreign policy', *International Affairs*, 74:4 (1998), pp. 847–70; Paul Williams, *British Foreign Policy under New Labour, 1997–2005* (Basingstoke: Macmillan, 2005).
2 Robin Cook, 'Mission statement for the Foreign and Commonwealth Office', FCO, London, 12 May 1997.
3 Labour Party, *Problems of Foreign Policy* (London: Labour Party, 1952), p. 2.

Chapter 1

Labour's foreign policy approach

Traditional accounts of British foreign policy emphasise a bipartisan foreign policy consensus, characterised by the major members of the main political parties broadly agreeing with one another as to how foreign policy should be carried out. Any disagreements over policy therefore come from within the parties, for example from back-benchers, or in the case of the Labour Party, from party members as well.[1] While some authors have noted that the motivations of the political parties in foreign affairs were clearly different, they have still argued that their essential objectives were not.[2] Speaking in 1993, Foreign Secretary Douglas Hurd argued that 'British foreign policy exists to protect and promote British interests. Despite all the changes in the world that underlying truth has not changed.'[3] This study, however, works from the perspective that to argue that foreign policy basically stays the same, regardless of which party is in power, is overly deter-ministic, and that actors within the state can have an impact on foreign policy. Both internal and external factors and context are important, and political parties form part of the domestic context. The fact that the motivations of the two main parties are significantly different is in itself important, and has given rise to fundamentally different beliefs about foreign policy and the international system. These have affected the perception of what is in the national interest, as 'State interests do not exist to be "discovered" by self-interested, rational actors. Interests are constructed through a process of social interaction.'[4] As Finnemore has argued, 'That process of defining interests is as intensely political and consequential as our subsequent efforts to pursue those interests'.[5] As a result, it is possible to identify, at various time periods and on a variety of issues, a Labour foreign policy that is distinct from a more traditional foreign policy as advocated by the Conservative Party. This chapter begins by outlining what could be considered a 'traditional' view of British foreign policy, before moving on to outline the constitutive principles of Labour's foreign policy approach.

Traditional British foreign policy

Traditional British foreign policy, Conservatives argued, was based on pragmatism. Conservatives defined international relations in terms of a realist worldview and this became the dominant framework for thinking about British foreign policy in the nineteenth century. They took a Hobbesian approach to relations between states, where there is no overarching authority able to maintain order within the international system, and so relations between states tend towards conflict as states seek constantly to maximise their military, economic and political power and calculate their interests in terms of power and ability to meet military threats. They did not believe in the ability to fundamentally change the international system. Unlike the Labour Party, the Conservatives have never had difficulty in defining the aim of their foreign policy, and that aim has always been to protect and promote the national interest. The national interest was seen as resting on enduring, timeless, geohistorical and geopolitical interests, as ideologically neutral, and, to a large extent, self-evident. In Britain's case, these enduring interests included the geopolitical impact of Britain's location as an island off the continent of Europe, its global reach across the Atlantic, its commercial basis as an island trading nation, and its reliance on naval power as an instrument of military influence.[6] For example, as Britain is an island separate from the rest of Europe it has had an ambivalent relationship with the rest of Europe. This way of thinking of enduring geopolitical interests did not determine foreign policy, but it did affect the way in which foreign policy was thought about. For example, British foreign policy should be based on the protection of British interests, rather than promotion of values. In addition, British foreign policy was seen as the preserve of a policy-making elite, and implemented through the Foreign Office. Despite this agreement over the nature of foreign policy, Conservatives still tended, just like the Labour Party, to disagree about which policy will best meet the ends of protecting the British national interest. For instance, both Europhiles and Eurosceptics have argued that it is in the national interest to follow their respective line on relations with Europe.

Thus, Conservative foreign policy has been based on the pursuit and protection of national interests, rather than in terms of Britain's obligations to the international community. The Conservative Party has not tended to promote its foreign policy as moral or based on ethical principles; as Douglas Hurd commented, foreign secretaries must deal with the world as it is and not how they would like it to be. However, they too have evoked the languages of rights and principles, and have taken the promotion of human rights as part of their international goals. While the Conservatives have worked through international organisations, they have sometimes been less avowedly supportive of them, in particular the United Nations (UN), than their Labour counterparts. The Conservatives have placed a strong emphasis on the Anglo-American relationship and have usually supported US policy, though this has not always been automatic; for instance, Thatcher caused consternation with the US for refusing to support their intervention in Granada in 1983.[7]

Obviously there will be some degree of consensus between the Conservatives and Labour as it is difficult for parties to make a difference when it comes to making foreign policy. Both parties have to deal with the same historical legacy of Britain as a former superpower and the economic and political consequences of Britain's relative economic decline, and the realities of an increasingly interdependent world. Both parties have to make policy in relation to international events and circumstances, in the face of opportunities and pressures brought by the international system, and the network of international organisations, alliances and enmities, of which Britain is a part. Both parties have to make policy within the context of a domestic political system based on Parliamentary scrutiny and opposition. Both parties have to deal with the opposition of their own backbenchers and the influence of powerful interests and pressure groups. Frankel argued that while 'On the fact of it, the British political system carries the risk of discontinuity in foreign policy caused by changes of government', the reality of the committee system on which British government is based means that consensus and continuity has been the basis of British foreign policy.[8] Wallace has noted how foreign policy issues rarely require legislation, 'so that most proposals are spared the process of detailed discussion and possible amendment involved in a bill's passage through Parliament.' This means that domestic interests, including parties, have less impact on foreign policy, and the government's relative freedom from the need to gain parliamentary sanctions limits informed debate and the exercise of political influence.[9]

Despite the convergence at times over Conservative and Labour foreign policy, there have also been fundamental differences between them. If Conservatives worked within the realist tradition of international relations, Labour took a 'transformationalist' view of international relations, believing that it was possible for the context of relations between states to change and hence for the fundamental basis of British foreign policy to change.[10] Labour has been, for much of its history, ideologically opposed to traditional foreign policy. Attlee said that 'There is a deep difference of opinion between the Labour Party and the Capitalist parties on foreign as well as home policy, because the two cannot be separated. The foreign policy of a Government is the reflection of its internal policy.'[11] These differences arose from the fundamental belief that for Labour, there should be congruity been domestic and foreign policy, in particular between a democratic political system and a democratic foreign policy. Linked to this was the need for legitimacy in foreign policy. The Conservatives, however, have tended to see domestic and foreign policy as separate entities, and this is at the heart of the fundamental differences between the analytical framework with which traditional and Labour foreign policies have developed.

The Labour Party, unlike the Conservatives, has always had a problem concerning the fundamental purpose of British foreign policy. As we have seen, the Conservative Party has been content to present foreign policy as the pursuit and protection of British interests, as the playing out of power politics. There might be disagreements over how to implement this, but the underlying values remain the same. While Margaret Thatcher introduced a more ideological stance to Britain's foreign policy with her 'megaphone diplomacy', at the heart of this was the protection of Britain's interests.[12] The Labour Party, however, has historically found this conception of foreign policy problematic, wanting to go beyond it with a call for foreign policy to be based upon moral purpose. This has been for two main reasons.

First, the Labour Party has tended to encompass a wider spectrum of political opinions than the Conservative Party, and, with its emphasis on party democracy, has given greater importance to its extra-parliamentary institutions of policy-making. This has acted as a constraint on the party leadership. As outlined in Volume 1 of this study, given the Labour Party's ideological and representational beginnings, and, particularly in its early years, the belief that the principles guiding domestic policy could be projected on to the international arena, different factions within the party have pulled foreign policy in

different directions. There were five main influences on the early
Labour Party. These were the trade union movement; the Independent
Labour Party; the Social Democratic Federation, a British Marxist
group; the Fabian Society; and radical Liberals, epitomised by the
members of the Union of Democratic Control. Each of these groups
had its own particular influence over the way that foreign policy and
international affairs were thought about. Each had their own particular analytical framework for understanding relations between states,
and each their own way of responding to concrete situations. These
different influences provided a rich source for ideas on international
politics, but also produced impulses towards Labour's appropriate
response to particular foreign policy issues which were sometimes antithetical to each other. This has added to the problems of developing a
typology of the British Labour Party's foreign policy, while also
explaining in part the depth of the some of the intra-party conflict on
international affairs.

For believers in class struggle, the Labour Party's role was to
protect working-class interests, internationally as well as nationally, and
to promote international working-class solidarity and socialist internationalism. The radical Liberals contributed greatly to Labour's liberal
internationalism, including the belief in self-determination, international justice, and in the workings of international organisations such
as the League of Nations and the UN. For the ethical socialists and
Nonconformists, pacifism and anti-militarism were important compo-
nents of their worldview. The Independent Labour Party and the
radical Liberals reinforced each other in their belief that militarism and
secret diplomacy were the causes of war. Some of the radical Liberals
influenced the Marxist perspective on the economic basis of inter-capi-
talist rivalry. These different contributing streams to Labour's foreign
policy often pulled in opposing directions, as evinced by the split over
how to respond to the outbreak of the First World War in 1914, or
debates over rearmament in the early 1930s.[13]

The second main reason for Labour's search for a foreign policy
that involves more than the protection of national interests has been
that, for extensive periods in the twentieth century, Labour's foreign
policy has developed while the party has been in opposition rather than
in power. The Labour Party was born out of domestic political discontent and its policies tended to reflect this. As such, foreign policy developed more as a response to the internal dynamics of the party, the
tensions between left and right factions, rather than as a response to
international events and experience of governance. The result of this

has been that Labour has tended to promise an alternative foreign policy when in opposition, seeking a new formulation of foreign policy based on principles that reflect party opinion with an in-built suspicion of power politics. It then finds that once in government, the opinions of rebellious backbenchers become rather less significant than pressures that governments come under from other nations, international organisations, existing commitments, international events, and the consequences of earlier foreign policy decisions, and so this results in a changed foreign policy stance. This problem even led to the situation during the 1974 to 1979 governments where on issues of defence, the Labour Party ended up with two very different defence policies, the one that was voted for by activists at the annual conference and was contained in the 1974 election manifestos, and the one that was actually implemented by the Labour government.

The tensions over foreign and defence affairs have been apparent throughout the Labour Party's history, and reveal themselves in recurring issues and themes. The main premise has been that Labour should offer an alternative to the traditional, power politics or realist approach of British foreign policy, which had stressed national self-interest. This alternative was internationalism, which stressed co-operation and interdependence, and a concern with the international as well as the national interest. In this, the most important influence on Labour's foreign policy were liberal views of international relations, but Labour's internationalism also arises from certain meta-principles of Labour's ideology, which have influenced Labour's external principles and policies as much as its domestic ones. These are a belief in progress and change, influenced by the Enlightenment tradition with its teleology of progress, and an optimistic view of human nature, which was then extrapolated to the nature of relations between states. This is that human nature is capable of positive, rational, co-operative, fraternal and moral thought and action. Man is naturally sociable, and is capable of solidarity with the rest of mankind, and that this solidarity overcomes national boundaries. If people are capable of behaving rationally and co-operatively, then so too are states as they are governed by such people. These meta-principles, such as a belief in progress and an optimistic view of human nature, reflect an internationalist perspective.

The principles of Labour's foreign policy approach

Developing an overall analytical framework within which to outline a typology of Labour's foreign policy is undoubtedly problematic. The timeframe in question, 1900 to 2010, is extensive, the international context ever-changing, the amount of material that could be included vast. The Labour Party of 1906 or 1945 was very different to the Labour Party of today. Earlier studies focused on developing a typology of whether Labour had a 'socialist' foreign policy. The most interesting attempts to do this were by Michael Gordon in *Conflict and Consensus in Labour's Foreign Policy: 1914–1965*, and Kenneth Miller's *Socialism and Foreign Policy*, which examined the period up to 1931.[14] As Volume 1 of this study argued, as far as foreign policy was concerned, it is not clear that the Labour Party ever had any socialist ideology as such. Sections of the Labour Party did at times offer a socialist critique of some of the liberal internationalist assumptions of the party's foreign policy perspective, which sometimes combined with the more radical liberal critiques, but the socialist standpoint only usually had minority support within the Labour Party, certainly from 1937 onwards with the party's acceptance of rearmament in the face of a rising European fascist threat. While Labour has sought to transform British foreign policy and indeed, relations between states, it has done so through a gradual, reformist approach, and not a revolutionary one. Labour has not rejected the international system as such. Rather, it has embraced internationalism.

With the surge in interest in foreign policy under the Blair governments there have been more recent attempts to outline the extent to which Labour has projected a foreign policy in which Britain acted as a 'good international citizen', or developed a different approach to foreign policy and the role that ethical issues have played in policy formation.[15] The most comprehensive study has been Paul Williams' excellent book on *British Foreign Policy under New Labour*, which argues that Blair had a liberal internationalist foreign approach that resulted in four specific foreign policy commitments. These were multilateralism, with a commitment to finding shared solutions to common international problems; Atlanticism, and the desire to be considered America's closest ally; support for neoliberal principles of political economy; and 'moralism', a rejection of *realpolitik* in favour of a more cosmopolitan approach and a willingness to emphasise the ethical dimensions of foreign policy.[16] In contrast, Mark Curtis has argued New Labour's claims to an 'ethical dimension' or Blair's claims to be 'doing the right thing' are little more than propaganda, and that 'Britain's role remains an essentially imperial one: to act as junior partner to US global power; to help organise the global economy to benefit Western corporations; and to maximise Britain's (that is, British elites') independent political standing in the world and thus remain a "great power".'[17] While many would agree that there has been a great deal of difference between Labour's statements outlining a new foreign policy approach with its moral leadership of the world and the actual impact of the policies that have been implemented, nevertheless, this study argues that not only under New Labour, but throughout its history, the Labour Party has sought to develop an approach that was different from that of the traditional pragmatic British foreign policy with its enduring interests, and that this has not merely been a case of propaganda designed to placate its party activists or to obscure its real foreign policy goals. This approach has been internationalism, and it has been espoused by Labour leaders from Keir Hardie to Tony Blair.

Internationalism, broadly defined, is the desire to transcend national boundaries in order to find solutions to international issues. However, there are different strands of internationalism, and it is not a worldview that is the preserve of the Labour Party. Much of the party's thinking on internationalism was shaped by radical Liberals of the early twentieth century, but it has also been influenced by a Christian-social-ist, Nonconformist streak amongst party members. Indeed, as Leonard Woolf noted, 'Historically, the Labour Party inherited its foreign policy from Cobden and Bright through Gladstonian liberalism'.[18] In addi-tion, internationalism does not necessarily provide clear policy solu-tions in the face of particular policy problems. Internationalism is an impulse that can be used to prescribe non-intervention in the pursuit of peace, or intervention for military or humanitarian means. This is because, as a concept, internationalism is very vague and has some-times meant different things at different times in history. Despite the problems of definition, Volume 1 of this study outlined a framework in order to analyse the nature of Labour's foreign policy through the concept of internationalism. At the heart of this framework is the fundamental belief that while states are sovereign entities, the peace and stability of any one state and the peace and stability of the inter-national system as a whole are inexorably linked.

The Labour Party's own particular brand of internationalism has emphasised six aspects of internationalist thought. These are first, that while states operate in a system of international anarchy, fundamental reform of the system is possible because states have common interests and values. This change is only likely to be secured through the construction of international institutions and laws to mitigate the worst aspects of international anarchy by regulating economic, politi-cal and military relations between states. Second, strongly linked to this is a sense that states belong to an international community, and that each state has a responsibility to work towards the common good of the international system, to work in the 'international' interest rather than purely in what it perceives to be its national interest.

It was the belief in internationalism and an international community that underpinned Labour's support for the establishment of the League of Nations following the First World War and the United Nations after the Second World War. Belief in the international community was even written into the Labour Party's constitution, with the commitment 'for the establishment of suitable machinery for the adjustment and settlement of international disputes by conciliation or judicial arbitration and for such other international legislation as may be practicable'.[19] This commitment to internationalism has continued throughout the twentieth century with Labour's commitment to international agreements and regulation. Anthony Eden's use of force to take back the Suez Canal in 1956, without international support, was bitterly condemned by the Labour leader Hugh Gaitskell as it left Britain isolated and in violation of the UN Charter, and was 'an act of disastrous folly' which had undermined Britain's 'moral authority'.[20] The February 1974 general election manifesto said that Labour's foreign policy would be 'dedicated to the strengthening of international institutions and global co-operation'.[21] By the time that Labour came to power in 1997, it had adopted a strongly internationalist stance, which reflected a new understanding of the post-Cold War, globalised world, where the distinction between domestic and international had to some extent broken down with the rise of transnational problems, which required Britain to work multilaterally. As Robin Cook put it to the 1999 Labour Party annual conference, 'We recognise that globalisation demands a new internationalism, and our internationalism recognises that we cannot deliver our domestic programme working alone in the world'.[22] Blair's 'doctrine of the international community' heralded a liberal internationalist approach which saw Britain as a leading player in an international community that had common interests and values, and which required intervention and engagement. This is because 'Interdependence is the core reality of the modern world'.[23]

The third of Labour's internationalist principles has been that foreign policy should reflect democratic values and universal moral norms. For Labour, domestic and foreign policy were seen as parts of a whole, as inextricably linked, and as impacting on each other. Policies pursued externally should help, or at least not hinder, the kind of society being built domestically. In addition, principles valued domestically, such as democracy and human rights, should be reflected externally and pursued in relations with other states. The key to international peace was social justice at home and abroad. This was strongly emphasised during the Second World War, with Attlee arguing that 'the world that must emerge from this war must be a world attuned to our ideals'.[24] Labour's October 1974 general election manifesto stated that 'A Labour Government, which excluded from its foreign policy the ideals of morality, equality and justice, which are at the heart of our domestic policy, would soon lose such ideals at home'.[25] David Owen, when he was Foreign Secretary made a number of speeches, subsequently published as a book, on human rights and foreign policy.[26] Of course, in more recent years it was associated with Robin Cook's launch of his corporate style 'mission statement' in the Locarno Room of the Foreign and Commonwealth Office (FCO) in May 1997. He declared that he was going to implement a new kind of foreign policy, the aim of which was 'to make Britain once again a force for good in the world';

> The Labour Government does not accept that political values can be left behind when we check in our passports to travel on diplomatic business. Our foreign policy must have an ethical dimension and must support the demands of other peoples for the democratic rights on which we insist for ourselves. The Labour Government will put human rights at the heart of our foreign policy.[27]

The ethical dimension became strongly associated with the issue of human rights, a recurring theme in Labour's foreign policy, from concern over apartheid South Africa to support for liberation movements in Latin America. The defence of human rights became one of Blair's main rationales for the use of military force in Kosovo, Afghanistan and Iraq. Whereas during the Cold War era, defence of human rights was largely associated with the norm of non-intervention, in the post-Cold War era, following Labour's concern over the lack of effective action in Bosnia, defence of human rights became equated with military intervention. Blair, it seemed, had adopted a new convention, that sovereignty was conditional upon the behaviour of the state concerned. Blair argued that 'Non-interference has long been considered an important principle of international order … But the principle of non-interference must be qualified in important respects. Acts of genocide can never be a purely internal matter.'[28]

Linked to the idea of universal moral norms was a belief in a democratic foreign policy. This included, usually, a fairly positive belief in the role of public opinion, for, as Arthur Henderson argued back in 1931, 'the public opinion of nations has always been ahead of what the Governments were prepared to do'.[28] Linked to this was the view that the Foreign Office was the preserve of the upper-class elite. Both secret diplomacy and 'the oligarchical character of foreign services increased the likelihood of armed conflict'.[30] Following both the world wars there were calls for the labour movement to be given a direct voice in foreign policy, as world affairs were seen as too important to be left to the diplomats and politicians. Again, Labour has not always stuck to the principle in practice, and has carried out its own secret negotiations, for example, on the establishment of US bases in Britain, and the development of nuclear weapons. The modern equivalent for the calls for a democratic foreign policy included Cook's desire to reform what he viewed as the stuffy culture of the FCO, and to open up British diplomacy.[31]

A related aspect of the belief in a democratic foreign policy was an underlying assumption that democratic states were more peaceable than authoritarian ones, and that the greater the democratic control over foreign policy-making, the more rationally and peacefully a state would behave. As a consequence, democratic states were far less likely to go to war with each other, and democratic governments would have more to lose from conflict, an early form of the 'democratic peace' theory.[32] Hence, states had much to benefit from good relations with other states, and from encouraging democracy in other states. This was stated in Labour's *Memorandum on War Aims*, written by Ramsay MacDonald, Arthur Henderson and Sidney Webb at the end of the First World War. This declared that the establishment of lasting peace was the principal war aim of British Labour, and 'As a means to this end the British Labour Movement relies very largely upon the complete democratisation of all countries'.[33] This view proved very popular in the years following the 9/11 terrorist attacks, and as a justification for overthrowing the Saddam Hussein regime, with Jack Straw repeatedly referring to the argument that democracies do not go to war with each other. He argued that 'democracy is the best possible guarantee of sustainable, long-term security and prosperity there is', as 'No two full democracies have ever made war on each other – astonishing, but true'.[34] Thus, Labour's approach has tended to include a focus on the internal workings of the state, the idea that different types of states produce different types of foreign policies.

The fourth aspect of Labour's internationalism was the belief in collective security and an avowed rejection of traditional power politics; the belief that the maintenance of the balance of power was ultimately self-defeating; and the rejection of the unilateral use of force. Indeed, the use of force was only really seen as a policy option when used against a fascist regime or dictatorship that had undertaken an act of aggression. Overall, Labour has placed a greater emphasis on multilateral solutions to world problems, and has had less preoccupation with the infringement of British sovereignty, than the Conservative Party. In the interwar period it was hoped that the League of Nations would by-pass the need for balance of power politics, and Labour had envisaged a League that was 'so strong in its representative character and so dignified by its powers and respect that questions of national defence sink into the background of solved problems'.[35] After the Second World War, for some in the Labour Party, collective security should be sought through the UN, whereas for others, collective security was assured through the establishment of the North Atlantic Treaty Organisation (NATO). Indeed, for the Attlee governments, the experience of the Second World War had led to a shift away from international collective security towards support for more traditional balance of power politics, as exemplified by Labour's support for an Anglo-American alliance institutionalised through the establishment of NATO in the face of the threat posed by the Soviet Union within the context of the developing Cold War. However, by the mid-1950s, in part as a result of developing nuclear weapons programmes, Labour again focused on the need for a peace policy based on international diplomacy and agreement, arguing that 'We are faced with the choice between world co-operation and world annihilation'.[36] Part of Labour's support for the UN was because 'the United Nations is the chosen instrument by which the world can move away from the anarchy of power politics towards the creation of a genuine world community and the rule of law'.[37] As will be demonstrated in the following chapter, there has been, in general, a suspicion of power politics, pursuit of which would put international order at risk, and a desire to focus on international peace and security, and not just on national security needs. While the Labour Party never adopted a policy of withdrawing from NATO, and the Labour leadership tended to see the bedrock of British security as the Anglo-American alliance, many in the party had deep misgivings about the role that NATO played and about its nuclear capability. The party supported attempts to alleviate tension between the West and the Soviet Union, such as the Conference on Security and Cooperation in Europe that resulted in the Helsinki Accords of 1975.

Linked to this was the fifth principle of Labour's internationalism, and this has been its belief in 'anti-militarism'. This has been manifested in many different ways. It included a commitment to collective security, arms control and disarmament, regulation of the arms industry, opposition to conscription, support for arbitration, and a suspicion of the use of force as a foreign policy instrument. Annual conference regularly passed resolutions condemning militarism and war, and many in the party believed that war could be avoided through the avowed rejection of armaments and the use of force. The preparation for war was seen as one of the major causes of war, as this destabilised the international system by causing suspicion between states. The Labour Party had been strongly influenced by the pacifist outlook of the Independent Labour Party, who believed that 'War is the result of the preparation for war'.[38] Labour's anti-militarist tendencies manifested themselves in a number of ways, such as attempts to control the arms industry and implement tighter regulations on the sale of arms. The commitment that Labour would not sell weapons to a state where they would be used for internal repression or external aggression was a long-standing one, and appeared in the 1983 and 1992 manifestos as well as the 1997 manifesto. In particular, there was a commitment to controlling the proliferation of weapons, especially weapons of mass destruction, through multilateral negotiations. Labour supported the organisation of disarmament conferences and presented itself as the party able to reach disarmament agreements internationally because of its moral leadership.

One recurring disarmament issue that caused bitter disagreements at various points in the second half of the twentieth century was nuclear disarmament. Nuclear disarmament has always been a long-term goal, but the party has been riven by conflict, especially during the 1980s, over whether this would best be achieved through long-term multilateral disarmament negotiations, or in the short-term through unilateral nuclear disarmament, which, it was hoped, would have the effect of stimulating other nuclear states to give up their weapons. Conflict has also existed over the role of the use of force. For some within the Labour Party, the use of force and military intervention was to be avoided at all costs as it would undermine the pursuit of peace, and where it did occur it should be part of some collective defence measure, whereas for others, the use of military force and intervention was acceptable in the face of aggression, especially against dictators. One of the biggest surprises of the Blair years was that he came to believe in the efficacy of the use of force as a foreign policy instrument, both as the 'right' thing to do for humanitarian reasons as well as being a valuable component of foreign policy in the longer-term pursuit of peace and international security.

In addition to these five principles was one further aspect of Labour's international thought that developed more directly out of its socialist ideology, and this has been a belief in international working-class and socialist solidarity. This was expressed in Labour's early years through a commitment to the international socialist and trade union movements, and through Labour's campaigns for labour movements overseas. Feelings of kinship with workers overseas were engendered not only from a socialist belief in the need for international working-class solidarity, but also from the impact of Nonconformist beliefs in the brotherhood of man. This led to a concern with imperialism and of conditions in the British empire, and at times, support for nationalist movements and for national self-determination, which was often at odds with Labour's belief in Britain's continuing world and imperial role. Indeed, Labour's policy on colonial affairs was usually confused and inconsistent during the first half of the twentieth century.

By the second half of the twentieth century, Labour had come down more clearly on the side of support for national liberation movements and had adopted a fairly pro-active approach to overseas aid and development. Harold Wilson established a new ministry of Overseas Development in 1964, and his first appointment to the post was a left-winger, Barbara Castle, who was given Cabinet rank. By 1970, Labour was publicly condemning the 'white racialist government of South Africa' and offering the full support of the Labour movement to liberation movements in Africa.[39] Labour supported the South West Africa People's Organisation in Namibia, and left-wing and liberation movements throughout Central and Latin America. Unlike the Conservative Party, the Labour Party repeatedly committed itself to working towards the aid expenditure target of 0.7 per cent of gross national product that was adopted by the UN General Assembly in 1970. Labour also linked poverty with stability, arguing that the fact that millions of people were 'condemned to a life of absolute poverty in the Third World is an affront to any version of civilised values, as well as a constant threat to international peace and stability'.[40] Labour condemned the cuts in overseas aid carried out by the Conservatives in the 1980s, and declared 'its support for the poor in the Third World to eradicate hunger, disease and illiteracy'.[41] The view was that 'The objective of a socialist foreign policy is to create the conditions necessary to free the world from poverty, inequality and war and to encourage the liberation of mankind from political and economic oppression'.[42] While by 1990 no mention was being made of a 'socialist' foreign policy, it was still felt that international solidarity demanded that the Labour Party fight to improve the conditions of the poorest in the world. The 1997 general election manifesto said that 'Labour believes that we have a clear moral responsibility to help combat global poverty'.[43] Of course, the extent to which the Labour Party has met such manifesto pledges is debatable, and Britain still spends considerably less than 0.7 per cent of its gross national product on aid and development.

Within the Labour Party there have always been divisions over how these internationalist principles should be interpreted, which of them should be prioritised, and which of them are achievable in the real world, and these divisions are at the heart of this study. The first volume in this study argued that Labour never really came to an ideological agreement over how to be internationalist within an international system dominated by nation-states. Labour did not question the existence of a world of sovereign nation-states, but its internationalist perspective led it to look for ways to control relations between states and ameliorate the inherent conflict in the international system. The tension between national sovereignty and internationalism lay behind many of the battles over Labour's foreign policy, and the party often found itself unable to transcend national barriers in order to meet its commitment to internationalism. In recent years, support for multilateralism appeared to offer a solution. These are themes that are explored throughout the following chapters, and returned to more directly in the conclusion, which will also assess the contribution that Labour's particular worldview and foreign policy doctrine have made to British foreign policy.

Notes

1 This is particularly the case with older accounts such as James Barber, *Who Makes British Foreign Policy?* (Milton Keynes: Open University Press, 1976), pp. 78–9, 87; Joseph Frankel, *British Foreign Policy 1945–1973* (Oxford: Oxford University Press, 1975), p. 32; David Vital, *The Making of British Foreign Policy* (London: Allen & Unwin, 1968), p. 76; William Wallace, *The Foreign Policy Process in Britain* (London: Royal Institute of International Affairs, 1975), p. 93. However, some

more recent accounts also take this line, for example Laurence Martin and John Garnett, *British Foreign Policy: Challenges and Choices for the 21st Century* (London: Royal Institute of International Affairs, 1997), pp. 82–5.

2 Frankel, *British Foreign Policy 1945–1973*, p. 35; Vital, *The Making of British Foreign Policy*, pp. 74–5.

3 Douglas Hurd, speech to the Royal Institute of International Affairs, London, 23 January 1993, quoted in Martin and Garnett, *British Foreign Policy*, p. 61.

4 Peter Katzenstein, ed., *The Culture of National Security. Norms and Identity in World Politics* (New York: Columbia University Press, 1996), p. 2.

5 Martha Finnemore, *National Interests in International Society* (Ithaca, New York: Cornell University Press, 1996), p. ix.

6 Christopher Hill, 'The historical background: past and present in British foreign policy', in Michael Smith, Steve Smith and Brian White, eds, *British Foreign Policy: Tradition, Change and Transformation* (London: Unwin Hyman, 1988), pp. 28–9.

7 See George Shultz, *Turmoil and Triumph* (New York: Macmillan, 1993), p. 336.

8 Frankel, *British Foreign Policy 1945–1973*, pp. 33 and 20.

9 Wallace, *The Foreign Policy Process in Britain*, p. 88.

10 See Steve Smith and Michael Smith, 'The analytical background: approaches to the study of British foreign policy, in Smith, Smith and White, eds, *British Foreign Policy*, pp. 18–9; Roy Jones, *The Changing Structure of British Foreign Policy* (London: Longman, 1974), pp. 130–9.

11 Clement Attlee, *The Labour Party in Perspective* (London: Victor Gollancz, 1937), p. 226.

12 Peter Byrd, ed., *British Foreign Policy Under Thatcher* (Oxford: Philip Allen, 1988), p. 2.

13 See Rhiannon Vickers, *The Labour Party and the World, Volume 1: The Evolution of Labour's Foreign Policy 1900–1951* (Manchester: Manchester University Press, 2004), chs 1, 2 and 3.

14 Michael Gordon, *Conflict and Consensus in Labour's Foreign Policy 1914–1965* (Stanford, CA: Stanford University Press, 1969); Kenneth Miller, *Socialism and Foreign Policy: Theory and Practice in Britain to 1931* (The Hague: Martinus Nijhoff, 1967).

15 Tim Dunne and Nicholas Wheeler, 'Blair's Britain: a force for good in the world?', in Karen Smith and Margo Light, eds, *Ethics and Foreign Policy* (Cambridge: Cambridge University Press, 2001), pp. 167–84; Dunne and Wheeler, 'Moral Britannia: Evaluating the Ethical Dimension in Labour's Foreign Policy', published by The Foreign Policy Centre (April 2004), pp. 1–40; Richard Little and Mark Wickham-Jones, eds, *New Labour's Foreign Policy. A New Moral Crusade?* (Manchester: Manchester University Press, 2000); Nicholas Wheeler and Tim Dunne, 'Good international citizenship: a Third Way for British foreign policy', *International Affairs*, 74:4 (1998), pp. 847–70.

16 Paul Williams, *British Foreign Policy under New Labour, 1997–2005* (Basingstoke: Macmillan, 2005), p. 7.

17 Mark Curtis, *Web of Deceit: Britain's Real Role in the World* (London: Vintage, 2003), p. 5.

18 Leonard Woolf, *Foreign Policy – The Labour Party's Dilemma* (London: Labour Party, 1947), p. 7.

19 *Labour Party Annual Conference Report* (hereafter *LPACR*), 1918, p. 141.

20 *House of Commons Debates*, vol. 558, 31 October 1956, col. 1454, and vol. 560, 13 November 1956, col. 827.

21 Labour manifesto February 1974, in *British General Election Manifestos, 1959–1987*, compiled and edited by F.W.S. Craig (Aldershot: Parliamentary Research Services, 3rd edn, 1990), p. 188.

22 Robin Cook, speech to 1999 Labour Party Annual Conference, *LPACR*, 1999, p. 52.

23 Tony Blair, 'Doctrine of international community', speech to the Economic Club of Chicago, 22 April 1999; Tony Blair, 'At our best when at our boldest', speech to the Labour Party Annual Conference, 1 October 2002.

24 *LPACR*, 1940, p. 125.

25 'Britain Will Win with Labour', Labour manifesto October 1974, in *British General Election Manifestos, 1900–1974*, compiled and edited by F.W.S. Craig (London: Macmillan, revised and enlarged edn, 1975), p. 254.

26 David Owen, *Human Rights* (London: Jonathan Cape, 1978).

27 Robin Cook, Mission statement for the Foreign and Commonwealth Office, FCO, London, 12 May 1997.

28 Tony Blair, 'Doctrine of international community', speech to the Economic Club of Chicago, 22 April 1999.

29 Arthur Henderson, *Consolidating World Peace* (London: Burge Memorial Lecture, 1931), p. 26.

30 Eric Shaw, 'British Socialist Approaches to International Affairs 1945–51', MPhil thesis, University of Leeds, 1974, p. 10.

31 Rhiannon Vickers, 'The new public diplomacy in Britain and Canada', *British Journal of Politics and International Relations*, 6:2 (Spring 2004), pp. 182–94.

32 See Michael Doyle, 'Kant, liberal legacies and foreign affairs', parts 1 and 2, *Philosophy and Public Affairs*, 12:3 (Summer 1983), pp. 205–35; and 12:4 (Autumn 1983), pp. 323–53.

33 Labour Party, *Memorandum on War Aims* (London: Labour Party, 1918).

34 Jack Straw's speech to the Fabian Society, 'Promoting democracy: a progressive foreign policy agenda', 10 March 2005.

35 J. Ramsay MacDonald, *A Policy for the Labour Party* (London: Leonard Parsons, 1920), pp. 131, 161 and 172.

36 'Forward with Labour', Labour manifesto 1955, in Craig, ed., *British General Election Manifestos, 1900–1974*, p. 203.

37 'Let's Go with Labour for the New Britain', Labour manifesto 1964, in Craig, ed., *British General Election Manifestos, 1900–1974*, p. 255.

38 J. Ramsay MacDonald, *Labour and International Relations* (Derby: Derby and District I.L.P. Federation, 1917), p. 5.

39 *LPACR*, 1970, p. 253.
40 Labour Party, 1983 manifesto, *The New Hope for Britain* (London: Labour Party, 1983), p. 37.
41 *LPACR*, 1980, pp. 173–4.
42 Labour Party archive, NEC Minutes 25 February 1981, 'Introduction to Foreign Policy Document', ID/1980-81/97/Feb, agreed at NEC meeting of 25 February 1981.
43 Labour Party, *New Labour: Because Britain Deserves Better* (London: Labour Party, 1997), p. 39.

Chapter 2

The 1950s: new conflicts, rearmament and the bomb

When the Labour Party had assumed power in 1945 there had been high expectations of what it could achieve in international affairs. For the first time in British political history there was a majority Labour government with a clear mandate and programme of reform. Whereas the two minority Labour governments of the interwar period had had to rely on support from the Liberals to pass legislation, this time Labour had power as well as office. However, the Attlee government quickly found that there was a disjunction between what it saw as Britain's leading role in the world and Britain's ability to meet its existing foreign and defence requirements. Despite trying to cling to its role as one of the 'Big Three' of the wartime alliance, it was becoming clear that Britain's power was declining, in particular in relation to the power and reach of the US. The Attlee years saw a period of retrenchment from the empire, which was to be continued, though reluctantly, by successive post-war governments. Britain's hasty withdrawal from Palestine in particular reflected a pragmatic and even unpropitious response to a difficult problem. The central conundrum that had to be faced was how to cut back expenditure while continuing to have as powerful a role in the world as possible. Somewhat surprisingly given the focus of sections of the party on the interlinking of economic and political issues, Labour was often just as reluctant as their opponents to admit to Britain's decline, or to be open about its inability to afford a worldwide role in security issues. Its response to its problems was to turn to the US for support, as Britain could no longer afford to maintain its world role unaided. Bevin in particular predicated his foreign policy on a close relationship with the US, as America's involvement in Europe became institutionalised through the Marshall Plan and NATO.

Labour won the election of 23 February 1950, but with a much-reduced majority of only five seats. After struggling on for a year and a half, Attlee called an election for 25 October 1951. Despite Labour gaining a majority of the votes, the Conservatives won the majority of the seats.[1] Winston Churchill became Prime Minister and appointed Anthony Eden as his Foreign Secretary. While the loss of power was a severe blow to the Labour Party, it at least provided it with a chance to recuperate following the tiring years of power which had seen many of its chief politicians suffer ill health. As George Brown noted,

> By 1951 Bevin had gone, Cripps had gone, Attlee and Morrison were both ageing. Moreover, Morrison had had a disastrous period at the Foreign Office when he succeeded Bevin. In-fighting by the Bevanites hampered the political development of the younger men who succeeded these great figures of the past.[2]

Labour had also run out of new ideas. Their 1950 and 1951 election manifestos had offered consolidation of the successes of the 1945 government and the continuation of its reforms through state planning and nationalisation, rather than new proposals. The Labour Party was confident that unemployment would rise under the Conservatives as they reverted to pre-war economic policies, and so it thought that it would win office again soon enough. Labour had in fact failed to realise the extent to which the Conservative Party had spent the 1945–50 period renewing and modernising itself and its policies, implementing reforms recommended by the Maxwell Fyfe committee on party recruitment, finance, and policy. Subsequently, Labour lost further elections in 1955 and 1959, failing to gain power again until 1964, spending thirteen long years in opposition.

The Labour Party became increasingly divided during the 1950s. The left-wing of the party, the 'idealists', looked to Bevan for leadership. They wanted to go further than the Attlee governments and to implement a fully socialist programme, in contrast to the 'revisionists', led by Hugh Gaitskell, who wanted to focus on the effective management of the mixed economy.[3] The divisions over foreign and defence policy that had been masked during Bevin's period as Foreign Secretary, partly as a result of his force of personality and his standing in the labour movement, and partly as a result of the developing Cold War, reasserted themselves once Labour was in opposition. They were compounded by a shift in the leadership of the trade unions, with the bloc vote being used against the party leadership on the issue of foreign and defence policy for the first time in the late 1950s.

Both the Bevanite left and the centre-right 'revisionists' had their own deeply held values, which actually were very similar when it came to foreign policy. The Labour Party was largely united on the basic principles of a Labour foreign policy based on internationalism, a commitment to the UN and the international rule of law. A 1952 publication, *Problems of Foreign Policy*, said that the aim was to replace the system of international anarchy by a world order that could create the framework of a world society.[4] This theme continued sporadically throughout the decade. The party was united in its perception of the continuing importance of Britain's world role, and of its potential for leadership within the Western alliance and the Commonwealth. This affected the party's views on Europe, with Labour rejecting joining the Common Market because of its special role in the Commonwealth. It also affected the party's reaction to the events in Suez. Gaitskell condemned Eden's actions, arguing that they 'will have done irreparable harm to the prestige and reputation of our country', as Britain's world role rested on its good standing within the world.[5] However, while the party was united in its commitment to internationalism, and in its perception of Britain's continuing world role, there were increasingly different implications for the left and the centre-right when it came to defence strategy, rearmament and the production and testing of nuclear weapons.

For the left, its internationalism grew into the desire for the party to commit a future Labour government to taking an ethical stance in the world by renouncing its nuclear weapons. They felt that unilateral disarmament would be a way for Britain to exert it moral leadership in the world, with the hope that other countries would follow Britain's example. For the centre-right of the party, internationalism meant a continuing commitment to collective defence through the Atlantic alliance and NATO in the fight against Communism, and Britain's possession of nuclear weapons meant that it could take a leadership role in the world as a mediator between the US and the Soviet Union. While the fundamental goal of negotiations for 'an effective system of general disarmament' were affirmed by Labour's governing body, the National Executive Committee (NEC) in March 1955, unilateral British nuclear disarmament was rejected as 'folly', as 'Until world disarmament can be achieved weapons of mass destruction in the hands of Britain and her allies in N.A.T.O. form the most effective deterrent against aggression by a potential disturber of the peace'.[6] However, the divisions on defence and the bomb were not resolved, and proved problematic for the rest of the decade.

Rearmament and Britain's defence strategy

The Labour government had declared its support for American action in Korea on 28 June 1950, following the invasion of South Korea by North Korean troops, and the call for a ceasefire by an emergency session of the UN Security Council. Britain, along with the other NATO pact countries, had received a request from the US administration for support. It is doubtful whether there was any choice but to comply with Washington's request. Gordon argues that the Labour Cabinet 'realized that to hesitate, to appear indecisive in the face of the requested sacrifices, would be to jeopardize the entire system of Atlantic security that it itself had worked unflaggingly to construct'.[7] This lead to a massive crash rearmament programme. Defence estimates had originally been set at £780 million for 1950–51. Following the outbreak of the Korean War, the government then proposed an increase in defence expenditure to £3.4 billion over the next three years, which then increased to £3.6 billion.[8] On 29 January 1951, Attlee announced in the House of Commons that the rearmament programme was to expand from £3.6 billion to a possible total of £4.7 billion over the next three years.[9] This meant that defence spending rose from 8 per cent of Gross National Product (GNP) before the crisis to 14 per cent after it.[10] By the spring of 1951, Britain was contributing 12,000 troops to the UN forces in South Korea. National Service was increased to two years.

Following Labour's election defeat in 1951, the Conservative government continued with this policy of sending troops to Korea. However, the Conservatives cut back on the increasing defence expenditure and agreed to phase the rearmament programme over four years instead of three. The rearmament programme was unpopular with Labour Party activists, and while nearly all MPs had supported it when in government, once Labour was in opposition, criticism of rearmament became a major rallying point for the left of the party. There was a fierce debate over it at the 1952 annual conference, and fifty-seven Labour MPs, mostly Bevanites, defied the party whip to abstain from the vote on the 1952 Defence White Paper in protest at the rearmament programme.

It was not only British rearmament that provoked conflict within the party: the issue of German rearmament also became extremely contentious, especially amongst the Bevanites. The Attlee governments had been adamant that they wanted to prevent the errors of the peace settlement after the First World War and so had been keen to integrate

Germany into the heart of Europe, and for Germany to join NATO. This would mean the rearmament of Western Germany. However, many in the party were against the rearmament of Germany on any terms, and once in opposition, lobbied against German membership of NATO.

The Conservative government was due to bring the treaties on rearming Germany within NATO, as part of its overall NATO policy, to the House of Commons in November 1954. In preparation for this, at the September 1954 annual conference, Attlee moved an emergency resolution for the NEC supporting a German contribution to collective security – in effect limited rearmament – and opened the debate by saying that emotional hostility to a rearmed Germany was natural, but that conference must not be swayed by emotion.[11] The policy of German rearmament was narrowly supported following an extensive and heated debate by 3,270,000 votes to 3,022,000 votes.[12] There was a rebellion in the Parliamentary Labour Party (PLP), where Attlee only narrowly won the vote on whether to support German rearmament.[13] When the treaties were brought before the House of Commons, Attlee only managed to secure the support of his party by arguing that opposition to German rearmament would mean opposition to NATO itself. Denis Healey spoke in favour of ratification and support for NATO, for 'the necessity of the age meant that we must all try to have interdependent foreign policies and interdependent armed forces'.[14] Gaitskell made his first major foreign policy speech arguing in favour of ratification, giving his full support to NATO, as 'I do not think there can be the slightest doubt that the establishment of NATO, together with the defence programmes, has stopped the danger – and it was a very real danger – of Soviet expansion in Europe'.[15] In the end, only four Labour MPs rebelled and voted against the government.

Overall, the Conservative's defence policy was similar to that intended by Labour, based on support for NATO, containment of the Soviet Union, and a defence rearmament programme of £4.7 billion. Indeed, Churchill rather provokingly congratulated Attlee on having agreed in July 1948 to the establishment of an American air base in East Anglia, which 'places us in the front line should there be a third World War'.[16] This decision had been made without consulting the full Cabinet, and was subsequently very unpopular within the Labour Party. It was understood by both Labour and the Conservatives that Britain could not maintain the same sort of defence expenditure as that of the US, but also that its defence role was more important than that of its European allies. Britain still saw itself as a great power. The demands on defence – how to maintain a strong world position while cutting back on expenditure – lay behind the Conservative policy put forward in the 1954 Defence White Paper, that of massive retaliation through the hydrogen bomb while reducing conventional forces. While many Cabinet ministers questioned the expense of Britain's nuclear programme, and it was asked in Cabinet whether it was 'morally right that we should manufacture weapons with this vast destructive power?', Churchill argued that 'we could not expect to maintain our influence as a world power unless we posses the most up-to-date weapons'.[17] Indeed, as William Wallace pointed out, 'The prospect which the hydrogen bomb offered to the British Government was appealing. Its overwhelming power appeared to bring back equality of status for Britain with America and the Soviet Union, despite her much smaller resources.'[18]

By the end of 1954, German rearmament had seemingly been dealt with, and it was now this issue of the hydrogen bomb that proved the most contentious issue in foreign and defence policy for Labour. The next rebellion, led by Nye Bevan, was over the 1955 Defence White Paper, which said that Britain would retaliate with nuclear weapons against an attack *even* by conventional forces. During the debate on the 1955 Defence White Paper, Bevan not only condemned this policy, but also the amendment to it put forward by Attlee. This had referred to the reliance on the threat of using nuclear weapons as a deterrent against aggression. Bevan noted with anger that if the leaders of the Labour Party meant that 'nuclear weapons will be used with the support of the British Labour movement against any sort of aggression' then he would not vote for the Labour amendment.[19] Dismayed by Nye's behaviour, Crossman and some of the other rebels then decided to vote with Attlee.[20] Even so, sixty Labour MPs defied the party whip and abstained from voting for the Labour amendment on the government's Defence White Paper. Crossman complained that as a result of the party in-fighting, 'it is now the dispute itself and not the issues that people are worrying about'.[21] Bevan was almost expelled from the party, but Attlee prevaricated and then accepted his assurances of adhering to the party line in future.[22] The party, however, remained divided on many issues, and even the prospect of the looming election, announced on 15 April for 26 May, did not produce the hoped for unity. Indeed, 'The impression was created that for many on both wings of the party a General Election would be a mere interlude in their principal business of fighting each other'.[23] Hugh Dalton noted in his diary that 'This is my 10th general election … And it was the most tedious, apathetic, uninteresting and, I think, worst organised of them all'.[24]

Labour fought the 1955 general election from a somewhat ambivalent position on the hydrogen bomb. Its manifesto, *Forward with Labour*, started by talking of the menace of the hydrogen bomb looming over all mankind: 'We are faced with the choice between world co-operation and world annihilation. The time is short.' Labour's answer was its call for talks and a 'positive peace policy'. This was to be based on, first, the aim of world disarmament, with Britain ceasing its hydrogen-bomb tests as a first step. Second, the need to reduce world tension in general, for instance by admitting Communist China to the UN and the reunification of Germany. Thirdly, the need to tackle 'the most profound challenge of our time – the gap between the highly developed industrial nations of the West and the peasant millions of Asia and Africa'. The Labour government, it said, had 'earned the confidence of the colonial peoples' before, and 'no one is better fitted to represent Britain at high-level talks than Clement Attlee – the man who freed India'. However, the manifesto also pointed out that 'We believe that in the absence of all-round disarmament, the democratic powers must be strong and united, and their defensive power sufficient to deter aggression'.[25]

Labour not only failed to recapture power at the May 1955 election but also lost eighteen seats. This led to a rethink about its policies and political principles. For those on the left, it demonstrated that Labour had alienated its core supporters by not being socialist enough. They felt that the power of the state should be extended with further nationalisation, and that there should be greater redistribution of wealth and income. They were mistrustful of the Atlantic alliance, favoured a 'third way' between the Soviet Union and the United States, and tended to argue that Britain should demonstrate moral leadership through unilateral nuclear disarmament. For the centre-right revisionists, such as Hugh Gaitskell and Tony Crosland, the 1955 election defeat demonstrated the need to modernise the party and to offer something more than the consolidation of the gains of the 1945–51 Attlee governments. They felt that the party should make more of a national than a class appeal, and favoured regulation rather than nationalisation of industry, seeing nationalisation as a means to an end, and not an end in itself. They saw Britain's foreign and defence policy as based on a strong Atlantic alliance, with Britain demonstrating moral leadership through campaigns for *multilateral* nuclear disarmament.

Attlee, who was by this time seventy-two, secretly told the Shadow Cabinet in June 1955 that he would resign as party leader in October. The leadership contest, the first since Attlee's unexpected leadership victory in 1935, took place on 14 December 1955. Gaitskell won the contest with the votes of 157 MPs, Bevan gaining seventy votes, and Herbert Morrison forty votes.[26] To some extent, the leadership election put a temporary stop to the revisionist/idealist schism in the party, with Gaitskell reaching an 'accommodation' with Bevan during 1955–56, which culminated in Bevan becoming Shadow Spokesman for Foreign Affairs in 1957. While divisions over foreign policy continued, to some extent the party was united in its condemnation of events in Suez and Hungary, and its dismay that the antagonists involved largely ignored the UN and international law.

Labour's response to Suez and Hungary

Churchill's health had deteriorated during the 1950s and on 5 April 1955 he stood down as Prime Minister. The following day he was replaced by Anthony Eden, who had been waiting – increasingly impatiently – for his chance to succeed Churchill. Eden felt that he would make a first-class Prime Minister. He had had a very distinguished political career, had been involved in foreign policy for thirty years, and had been second-in-command in the Conservative Party since 1940. However, by this time he was himself unwell, having suffered from internal pains for some time, and he had had two unsuccessful operations in April 1953 that had left his bile duct severely damaged.[27] He never fully recovered from this, and it has been suggested that his ill health affected his judgement, in particular over the Suez affair when on 26 July 1956 President Nasser of Egypt announced that he had nationalised the Suez Canal. Eden's response was to use military force to take back the canal. Faced by mounting international hostility and a lack of support from the US, Britain had to back down and withdraw its troops. This was a humiliation for Britain and very publicly confirmed that Britain was neither a superpower that could do just as it wished, nor could it act without American backing. Eden had failed to understand that Britain was not the global power that it had been when he had first come to office. He resigned on 9 January 1957.

The position that Gaitskell and the Labour Party took over Suez was that the government should refer Nasser's actions to the UN Security Council; that Britain should not take independent action as other countries – including the United States – had interests in the Suez Canal; and that Britain should not use force to retake the canal as this would mean acting outside of the UN Charter and international law. However, Gaitskell did initially approve of Eden's plan to take 'military precautions', which he thought would be for defensive purposes only. Eden spoke privately to Gaitskell on the morning of the first Parliamentary debate on Suez on 2 August 1956, and Gaitskell was led to believe that force was only to be used if Nasser took some further action. He did not know that the Conservative Cabinet had already agreed to use force *unless* a negotiated solution was quickly found.[28] In the debate in the House of Commons, Gaitskell warned against the use of force, except 'in self-defence or as part of some collective defence measures'. He pointed out that British policy had for many years avoided any international action which would be 'in breach of international law or, indeed, contrary to the public opinion of the world', and so Britain must not get into a position where it might be denounced as an aggressor. Instead the issue should be referred to the UN.[29] At a meeting of Labour's Shadow Cabinet on 13 August, Gaitskell's speech in the House of Commons was unanimously endorsed, even by Nye Bevan. Indeed, Gaitskell wrote in his diary that at the meeting, 'To my particular astonishment Nye Bevan himself was very much in agreement with me … He was in no doubt about Nasser being a thug … [or] about the need for international control' of the canal. Bevan also said to Gaitskell that 'You will be surprised to hear this from me but I think it would be a great mistake to say anything at the moment which would embarrass the Americans'.[30]

In September, following the Parliamentary recess during which there had been a number of unsuccessful conferences held to resolve the Suez crisis, Gaitskell reiterated in the House of Commons the case against the use of force. He again urged the government to take the dispute to the UN for it would be 'disastrous' if Britain were to use force against Nasser, for it would have no international support. He said that such action would be against the UN Charter, and it would mean that in future Britain would not be able to object to other states using force. This would put the whole post-war international order at risk and mean 'reverting to international anarchy' where 'only power counts'.[31] Gaitskell was supported by the party in his statements, but faced something of a test over Suez at this first annual conference as party leader in October when Labour passed an emergency resolution. This stated that the conference 'condemns the Government's lamentable handling of the Suez crisis and compliments the Parliamentary

Labour Party on the stand it has taken and in particular on the part it has played in committing the Government to refer the dispute to the [UN] Security Council'.[32] The debate was a little more revealing than the resolution, with speeches that were heated and strongly pro- and anti-Nasser. Gaitskell brought the debate to an end with his speech in which he condemned Nasser's behaviour, but said that it did not justify the use of force against Egypt, and that Labour's view all along was that 'we must abide only by the [UN] Charter in making our decisions in this matter'.[33] Gaitskell was seen to have regained control over unruly delegates. Crossman noted that 'It's a real test, for a new, untried, suspect Leader to have to start by rebuking and educating the Party'. He thought that Gaitskell 'did extraordinarily well'.[34]

In the meantime, Eden had developed a secret tripartite plan with France and Israel. In order to provide a pretext for military action, Israel had agreed to invade Egypt. France and Britain would then issue an ultimatum for the fighting to cease, and when that failed, they would enter the fray to separate the combatants by seizing control of the Suez Canal. On 29 October Israel duly mobilised its troops and invaded the Sinai peninsular. The following day Eden issued the Anglo-French ultimatum, which, as expected, Nasser rejected. On 31 October, Britain and France vetoed an American resolution in the UN Security Council. Gaitskell condemned Eden, proclaiming that the government had 'committed an act of disastrous folly whose tragic consequences we shall regret for years … because it will have done irreparable harm to the prestige and reputation of our country'.[35] On the night of 5–6 November, British and French troops invaded Port Said and took control of the Suez Canal, ostensibly to ensure the safety of the canal's traffic. The UN, the Soviet Union and, perhaps more importantly, the United States all condemned this action. The lack of American supported resulted in a plunge in the value of sterling. President Eisenhower, furious with Britain's adventurism and concerned about the impact on wider Arab relations, refused to shore up the value of sterling unless Britain agreed to withdraw its troops. Britain and France then quickly agreed to a ceasefire and to withdraw their troops.

Gaitskell was so appalled that the Conservative government was acting in this way that during a broadcast to the nation on 4 November he called on Eden to resign in order to 'save the reputation and the honour of our country'.[36] Denis Healey felt that 'In conception Suez was a demonstration of moral and intellectual bankruptcy. In execution it was a political, diplomatic and operational disgrace.'[37] At the time he said that the government's use of force had 'sacrificed and shattered all the pillars of our foreign policy without achieving the aims which the Government had in mind at the very beginning of this operation.'[38] With hindsight, this was indeed the case. British actions in Suez were seen by many as the desperate act of a declining imperial power. Suez had a long-term impact on Britain's foreign policy, undermining confidence in Britain's world role and in its ability to act independently in a major crisis, while revealing how reliant Britain was on the US, economically, politically and militarily.

To make matters worse, at the same time as the Suez crisis had peaked, Russia had sent its tanks into Budapest to destroy the Hungarian uprising. Following Khrushchev's 'secret speech' of January 1956 in which he had denounced Stalin, the people of Eastern Europe had expected liberalisation and a relaxation of Soviet rule, but this had not been implemented. In October there was a dramatic eruption of popular protests demanding change in Hungary. On October 23, martial law was declared in Hungary and Soviet troops were 'invited' to enter Budapest to restore order. On 28 October a ceasefire was established, and agreement was reached between Moscow and a new nationalist-communist Hungarian government, headed by Imre Nagy, over the withdrawal of Soviet troops. This agreement was overturned when on 1 November Soviet troops invaded Hungary. Nagy declared Hungary's neutrality, and appealed to the UN for support, but with the world's attention focused on events in Egypt, Russia was able to act with relative impunity. On the dawn of 4 November the Russians began attacking Budapest. Many Hungarian civilians were killed, thousands sought refuge abroad by escaping to Austria, and Nagy was executed.

For the British Labour Party, events in Suez and Hungary reflected each other, and were symptomatic of the need for a new approach to international relations. Part of the anger over Suez was due to the fear that Britain's use of military force there had helped facilitate the Soviet Union's invasion of Hungary. Gaitskell declared that 'Our moral authority has gone because of what we did in Egypt', and that 'if, by that in intervention in Egypt and all that it implied, in any way whatever we tilted the balance or influenced the Russians to suppress the Hungarian national revolt, nothing can excuse it'.[39] Arthur Henderson pointed out that,

> [M]any people in this and other countries will believe that the action of Her Majesty's Government in using force against the people and Government of Egypt offered a direct encouragement to the Government

of Russia to employ the brutal force that they did yesterday, in Budapest, to suppress the struggles of the Hungarian people for freedom and independence.[40]

In fact, the Soviet use of force in Hungary received very little attention in the House of Commons and was not debated until 19 December. This angered many in the Labour Party, who saw the brutal suppression of the Hungarian uprising as dashing the hope of democratisation in Eastern Europe. On 9 November the National Council of Labour sent a delegation to see the Soviet Ambassador in London, which called upon the Soviet Union instantly to 'abandon its policy of aggression and bloodshed in Hungary and to allow the Hungarian people the elementary right to decide their own future.' In reply the Ambassador said that 'events in Hungary had been misinterpreted and that the uprising was of a fascist and revolutionary character'. Gaitskell said that the Ambassador's statement was 'unacceptable'.[41] During the debate on Hungary in the House of Commons on 19 December 1956, Foreign Secretary Selwyn Lloyd outlined Britain's main response to the situation, which was to relax the rules on accepting refugees by admitting 11,500 Hungarian refugees into the country directly, and to support resolutions at the UN calling upon the Soviet Union to end its intervention and withdraw its troops.[42] Gaitskell urged further action, including support for the International Red Cross programme in Hungary, and declared that 'There is a new situation in Central and Eastern Europe', and now was the time to re-examine proposals for a neutral buffer zone between East and West. He argued that including Hungary in this neutral zone might provide a face-saving dilemma for the Soviet Union in that it could remove its troops from Hungary while maintaining adequate national security.[43] His proposal was not taken up by the government.

The controversy over Britain's reactions to Suez and Hungary had largely united the party on foreign and defence policy during the second half of 1956. Suez had demonstrated that Britain was not the global power that it had been and further had demonstrated Britain's reliance on its alliance with the United States. Both the Conservatives and Labour continued to believe that Britain should play a leading world role, but it was clear that a method needed to be found by which Britain could 'punch above her weight' without the continued commitment to defences east of Suez. The Conservative's 1957 Defence White Paper proposed a solution to this problem, namely reliance on nuclear weapons and Britain's independent nuclear deterrent. This reignited the fires of contention over foreign and defence policy within the Labour Party, undermining the party leadership in its attacks on Eden's policies as it sought to wrest control over its own defence policy as a looming gulf opened up within the party over attitudes towards nuclear weapons.

The hydrogen bomb and the 1957 Defence White Paper

The Labour Party did not have a clear-cut position on nuclear weapons and the hydrogen bomb at a time when the issue was becoming increasingly important in British politics. The policy agreed by the party in 1955 was that Labour supported the manufacture of a British hydrogen bomb, because 'Labour believes it is undesirable that Britain should be dependent on another country for this vital weapon'. However, Labour did not support the *testing* of the hydrogen bomb.[44] As a response to this, the party's NEC decided in December 1956 to set up an Ad Hoc Committee on Disarmament, which included Barbara Castle, Arthur Henderson and Philip Noel-Baker.[45] An immediate concern, as expressed by the party's Defence Sub-Committee in advance of the 1957 annual conference, was that 'It can be assumed with certainty that there will be a substantial number of resolutions on defence and disarmament submitted to Annual Conference this year'. It was very probable that the question of nuclear tests would be 'the most prominent by far', and 'It is however not certain that any resolution or probable composite will contain a coherent line of policy which would be acceptable to the National Executive Committee'. Thus the NEC should carefully consider those issues to be presented to conference and the recommended party policy on defence and disarmament. The Defence Sub-Committee itself even admitted it was not altogether clear as to the existing policy of the party.[46] However, while the Ad Hoc Disarmament Sub-Committee met during 1957 to prepare a party paper on defence and disarmament, it was unable to reach a consensus. The resulting paper was not presented to the party at the annual conference as there was extensive disagreement over its contents between Hugh Gaitskell, George Brown and others on the right of the party, and Crossman, Noel-Baker and others with a stronger disarmament position.[47] This was especially problematic as the issue was increasing in saliency within the party following the Conservative government's 1957 Defence White Paper, making agreement even harder.

Harold Macmillan had replaced Eden in January 1957, and one of his first actions as Prime Minister was to ask his new Defence Secretary, Duncan Sandys, to initiate a review of defence costs and commitments. Macmillan wanted a drastic overhaul of British defence policy, with substantial savings in defence expenditure, to be met by major reductions in conventional forces, and an increased emphasis on the nuclear deterrent.[48] This was to be done through the 1957 White Paper on Defence, which was published in April, two months later than usual.

The 1957 Defence White Paper was the most drastic attempt to rethink British defence policy and expenditure since the Second World War, and it proposed a solution to the dilemma of how Britain could retain its role as a leading power while cutting back expenditure on defence. Britain was to meet its increasingly costly defence requirements through the application of modern technology, in particular through the use of nuclear weapons. These, it was argued, had made conventional war obsolete by deterring any potential aggressor, and so conventional forces would only be needed for small-scale local conflicts. Thus, the primary aim for British defence policy was not to be defence, but deterrence through the threat of nuclear retaliation. Whereas the 1954 Defence White Paper had upgraded the role of nuclear weapons vis-à-vis conventional forces, the 1957 Defence White Paper saw nuclear weapons as *replacing* the need for extensive conventional forces. This meant that Britain would require fewer overseas bases, and fewer service men, and so compulsory National Service could be ended. This last point was difficult for Labour to oppose as it was now firmly behind the abolition of National Service.

Labour's existing policy, based on the compromise to produce but not to test hydrogen bombs, became moot when it became known in March 1957 that in May Britain was to test its first hydrogen bomb at Christmas Island. This ignited the flames of debate over nuclear weapons, especially as health hazards associated with testing were then becoming known. However, some in the party leadership thought it made no sense for Britain to produce a bomb that could not then be tested, and foolish for the party to support such a policy. Certainly some of the defence experts in the party felt that 'the ending of H-bomb tests would not, or itself, reduce the danger to humanity'.[49] On 1 April the House of Commons debated Macmillan's discussions with President Eisenhower in Bermuda, which included discussion of nuclear weapons. Macmillan set out to provoke Labour, and challenged Gaitskell to say whether in office Labour would cancel the tests, which would mean abandoning the bomb, and accept as consequences both permanent conscription and permanent military inferiority.

Gaitskell, attempting to avoid exacerbating the divisions within the Labour Party, said that as Leader of the Opposition, he did not have enough information to make such a decision, either in terms of the military significance of the tests, or in terms of the potential health hazards of increased radiation in the atmosphere caused by such tests, and said that 'I would not commit myself to going ahead with these tests in all circumstances'.[50]

The issue was discussed by a special meeting of the Parliamentary Labour Party on 3 April. Christopher Mayhew proposed a compromise, which the Shadow Cabinet recommended. This was to call for a temporary suspension of the British tests while appealing to the superpowers to cancel theirs.[51] When the Defence White Paper was debated in the House of Commons on 16 and 17 April, the Labour Party tabled an amendment, stating that the House 'regrets the undue dependence on the ultimate deterrent on which the policy set out in the White Paper appears to be based', that 'international disarmament is the only real solution to the problem of defence', and called on the government to postpone its tests and propose the abolition of hydrogen-bomb tests through international agreement.[52] Thus the party's policy was to work towards multilateral disarmament, while supporting Britain's independent nuclear deterrent, but opposing the testing of its weapons, for the time being. This compromise position was to dog the party for the next few years.

While many on the left agitated for the Labour Party to take a firmer stance on disarmament, the Labour leadership continued to support Britain's attainment of status as a nuclear power. Indeed, there were few on the left who actually questioned Britain's world status, just its method of attainment. While the party membership pressed for disarmament, the leadership argued that 'controlled international disarmament was the only solution', and urged against the weakening of NATO and the Anglo-American alliance.[53] Bevan was to play an important part within the continuing conflict over nuclear weapons and defence, but somewhat surprisingly worked to support Gaitskell's leadership on this contentious issue.

Aneurin Bevan had been appointed to the post of Opposition Spokesman on Foreign Affairs in 1957. Bevan, a leading left-winger who had been periodically critical of NATO and rearmament in the early 1950s, turned out to be far less radical in this post then expected, defending the party's official position on defence policy. At the 1957 annual conference, Bevan was jeered by those on the left who had previously seen him as their leader, when he gave a passionate speech against a resolution on unilateral disarmament that pledged that 'the next Labour Government will take the lead by itself refusing to continue to test, manufacture or use nuclear weapons'.[54] The Labour leadership could not afford such a resolution to be passed, he said, without opening it up to attack from the Conservative government, for it not only negated its existing defence policy but would also undermine Labour's position on Britain's defence alliances, in particular NATO. Nye Bevan, in what became one of the most famous Labour Party conference speeches, argued that while 'There is no member of the Executive in favour of the hydrogen bomb', to pass a resolution calling for the abandonment of it would be to 'send a British Foreign Secretary ... naked into the conference chamber'. He stressed that such a resolution could not be passed without thinking about the consequences, for if a British Foreign Secretary were to stand up in the UN and, without any consultation, were to announce that 'the British Labour movement decides unilaterally that this country contracts out of all its commitments and obligations entered into with other countries and members of the Commonwealth', this would not be statesmanship, it would be an 'emotional spasm'. Britain should keep its nuclear weapons, as 'We want to have the opportunity of interposing between those two giants', the US and the USSR, and to have on them 'modifying, moderating, and mitigating influences'.[55]

Bevan's speech was at times incoherent, but was magnificent none the less, and Bevan won the support of the annual conference in a way in which someone with less respect from the left would not have been able to. What was remarkable about this speech was that it represented a reversal of the position that Bevan had taken only a few days before. At the first of two pre-conference NEC meetings, Bevan had proposed, along with Sydney Silverman and Barbara Castle, a motion explicitly advocating the unilateral cessation of the manufacture of nuclear weapons in Britain.[56] According to Richard Taylor, Ian Mikardo had recalled that Bevan's reversal of opinion had come after he had talked with Sam Watson, the miners' leader, who had said to him that 'only through Nye's becoming Foreign Secretary could détente be brought about, and there was no way he could become Foreign Secretary if he stuck to the unilateralist line. And that's what I think caused the change.'[57] Whatever the reason, his sudden conversion to nuclear weapons left his friends and supporters baffled and disappointed.

The *volte-face* in Bevan's position did not go unnoticed by the Conservatives, and Harold Macmillan later mocked him in a debate on foreign policy by saying that Bevan had been 'thoroughly tamed and chastened. I feel sorry for him as he gropes about, abandoned by his old friends and colleagues – a shorn Samson surrounded on the Front Bench by a bevy of prim and ageing Delilahs.'[58] However, according to Peggy Duff, who was later to become the Secretary of CND, Bevan was never a unilateralist, nor he did oppose the manufacture of the H-bomb, but 'He objected to its *first use* by Britain against an attack with conventional arms'. Thus, Bevan's speech at the Brighton conference opposing the resolution calling for unilateral disarmament, did not involve a renunciation of his principles.[59] The party's policy when put to the vote won a huge endorsement, while the resolution on unilateral disarmament was heavily defeated. However, the Labour Party leadership's success in reining in the desire for unilateral disarmament at the 1957 annual conference did not end the conflict over the issue, which flared up again by the end of the year.

Labour, CND and disarmament

The successful launch of the Russian Sputnik, the first Earth-orbiting artificial satellite, in October 1957 added to the general climate of concern over the Cold War arms race, technological developments and nuclear weapons. When J. B. Priestly published an article in the *New Statesman* calling on Britain to disarm, he got more than one thousand spontaneous letters of support. The Campaign for Nuclear Disarmament (CND) was established at a meeting in January 1958, and by March 1959 over 270 local groups and twelve regional committees had been formed around the country.[60] CND had support from many in the Labour Party, attracting the kind of radical liberals, pacifists and Christian socialists that had tended to be most critical of British foreign policy early in the twentieth century. Indeed, the CND leadership regarded the Labour Party as the instrument through which it could implement its policy. Kingsley Martin argued that 'I know of no way of obtaining a non-nuclear Britain except by converting the Labour Party'. Thus, 'one of our first aims should be to win a majority for CND policy within the Labour Party', so that it can then 'put the case for British nuclear disarmament to the British public as a whole'. The plan was that once Labour had won a general election it could then implement CND policy.[61] Of course, in the 1980s the first of these aims – converting the Labour Party – was met, while the second became impossible because of Labour's disastrous electoral performance.

Not everybody in the Labour Party had sympathy for CND. Hugh Dalton denounced its campaign for unilateral disarmament as 'national egoism gone mad'.[62] Certainly there was concern that CND was adding further confusion to the existing complexities of Labour's defence policy. During the debate on the 1958 Defence White Paper, which degenerated into an argument amongst Labour MPs over the nature of Labour's defence policy, Emanuel Shinwell referred to leading CND member Bertrand Russell as a 'superannuated philosopher', and J. B. Priestly as 'about as woolly as any person I have known since the days of Ramsay MacDonald'. He also noted scathingly that 'However competent an orator I may regard myself, I have not yet reached the stage of being able to interpret with clarity what is called the unofficial defence policy of the Labour Party'.[63] There was also concern that CND was using the Labour Party to further its agenda, and that 'What started as a "moral crusade," now looks suspiciously like another faction in the Labour Party'.[64]

CND was able to appeal to traditional, internationalist and pacifist sentiments within the party, and offered an opportunity for left-wingers to express their frustration with the party leadership's defence policy. CND was unusual in that it mobilised young people who felt alienated from the mainstream political parties and felt that their beliefs and values were not met by them. It was profoundly middle class, attracting left-wing and liberal intellectuals, clergy, writers and actors. CND was less successful in attracting working-class Labour members; some of them worried that CND was drawing attention away from economic issues, and workers in the defence industry felt threatened by its stance on unilateral disarmament. However, in the mid-1950s there had been a shift of power within the trade unions, with many key leadership positions going to those on the left of the movement. Whereas the largest unions had used their bloc votes to support the Attlee government in the 1940s, the unions could no longer be relied upon in this way. In particular, Frank Cousins had become head of the massive Transport and General Workers Union (TGWU) in 1955, and he supported unilateral nuclear disarmament. John Horner, the left-wing leader of the Fire Brigades Union, became head of the Labour Advisory Committee within CND, and some of the other major unions – the engineers, the mineworkers, the railwaymen, the shop-workers and the General and Municipal Workers – came out in support of unilateral disarmament.[65]

The trade unions became increasingly involved in the disarmament debate. At the Trades Union Congress (TUC) 1957 annual conference a resolution was passed calling for the manufacture and testing of atomic and hydrogen bombs to be ceased immediately, and for the TUC's General Council to press this policy with the government.[66] The TUC and the Labour Party then held a series of meetings during February 1958 to develop a joint declaration on *Disarmament and Nuclear War*, and it was agreed that they would organise an educational campaign about this, to include regional conferences within the labour movement. Reprinted in the 1958 Labour Party Annual Conference Report, *Disarmament and Nuclear War* urged the government to give a lead to other nations by suspending British nuclear tests, called for a general agreement to suspend all nuclear tests, a declaration banning the use of all nuclear weapons, the discontinuation of patrols by aircraft based in Britain carrying hydrogen bombs and said that no steps should be taken to set up missile bases in Britain before a fresh attempt had been made to negotiate with Russia.[67]

CND's initial success added momentum to the calls for unilateral disarmament within the Labour Party. In the run-up to the 1958 annual conference, the Labour Party's Ad Hoc Disarmament Sub-Committee met to discuss resolutions received on disarmament. These included thirty-eight resolutions supporting the general renunciation of production of nuclear weapons; thirty-two resolutions against nuclear missile bases in the UK; and eighty-six resolutions for unilateral British renunciation of nuclear weapons (and/or renunciation of use and/or elimination of stocks).[68] At the 1958 Labour Party conference, resolutions proposed for unilateral disarmament, total disarmament and rejecting the establishment of missile bases in Britain, were defeated when put to a card vote, and the NEC/TUC statement on *Disarmament and Nuclear War* accepted, but only after an extensive and heated debate had taken place.[69]

What CND and the unilateralists did not do was to call for Britain to withdraw from NATO. However, if Britain were to adopt a policy of unilateral nuclear disarmament then this would have repudiated its role within the alliance, which based its strategy largely on nuclear deterrence. Thus, the likely consequences of unilateral disarmament were that Britain would have to withdraw from NATO and adopt a neutralist stance. The labour leadership were well aware of this issue and how embarrassing it could prove. Gaitskell argued that Britain's possession of nuclear weapons allowed it to pursue an independent foreign policy, and that to withdraw from NATO would be 'disastrously dangerous to the peace of the world', as 'either in disgust

America would adopt an isolationist policy', or America would continue in NATO, but Britain would be unable to exert any influence on America.[70]

The defeat of the unilateralists was short-lived, and the issue again flared up during discussions of the Parliamentary Labour Party over the defence estimates in February 1960. The party's International Department decided that a new statement of policy on defence and disarmament was required. This was partly because the government's abandonment of the American Blue Streak missile, which was intended as the successor delivery system to the V-bombers for British nuclear weapons, led to uncertainty over Britain's independent nuclear deterrent, and partly due to concern that 'a unilateralist victory at Party Conference would be open to serious misunderstanding'.[71] This led to another round of talks between the TUC and the Labour Party, and they produced a joint statement on *Foreign Policy and Defence* in July. In a concession to the unilateralists, this announced the abandonment of the *independent* British nuclear deterrent, but not the use of nuclear weapons as such:

> If our strategy is to be based on military, not on prestige considerations, we must accept the truth that a country of our size cannot remain in any real sense of the word as 'independent nuclear power'. We believe that in future our British contribution to the Western armoury will be in conventional terms, leaving to the Americans the provision for Western strategic deterrent.

Britain would remain within NATO, which would be able to use tactical nuclear weapons being developed by the US.[72] Thus, nuclear weapons would still form part of Britain's defence policy.

However, the party and the trades unions were still divided on the issue of nuclear weapons and disarmament. The July statement was passed at the 1960 TUC after a very long debate on defence, but so too was a motion on world peace proposed by Frank Cousins of the TGWU that appeared to run counter to the statement. It included the 'complete rejection of any defence policy based on the threat of the use of strategic or tactical nuclear weapons' by a future Labour government.[73] This would mean that Britain could not remain within a nuclear-armed NATO. Even worse, at the 1960 Labour Party annual conference, Frank Cousins' resolution was again passed, while the carefully worded joint statement on *Foreign Policy and Defence* was defeated. The trade union bloc vote had been effectively turned against the Labour Party leadership, with the result that the Labour Party's international policy continued to be overwhelmed by the issue of defence and disarmament, which at this point appeared to be more radical and left-leaning than at any point since the pacifism of the early 1930s. CND thought that it had achieved its goal of getting the Labour Party to commit to unilateral disarmament. For CND, however, it was to be a hollow victory, for it was 'torn by internal dissensions at a moment of triumph that might have been turned into victory'.[74] This disarray was over the launching of the Committee of 100, which favoured the use of direct action and had divided the peace movement over the kind of tactics that were appropriate to use in their campaigns.

The failure to produce a coherent defence policy had political significance for the Labour Party on several levels. First of all, the party had to demonstrate to its members that it could produce a policy that, even if not popular, was at least intelligible and could command enough support to be workable as a policy proposal. Second, the continuing debacle over defence undermined Gaitskell's leadership, and soured the relationship between the party and the unions as the battle between Frank Cousins and Gaitskell became increasingly personal. Third, the party, if it were to govern, needed to demonstrate to Britain's allies that they would be able to work with a Labour government on defence issues. If Labour were to accept unilateralism as a matter of principle, then it could not accept remaining within a nuclear NATO. To withdraw from NATO would jeopardise what both Labour and the Conservative Party leaderships saw as the special relationship with the United States and the bedrock of Britain's security, and would leave Britain vulnerable. Fourth, the party had to produce a policy that was acceptable to the general public if it were to be electable at the next general election. Unilateralism was not popular amongst the wider population, though opinion was divided on what policy Britain should follow on nuclear weapons.[75] Gallup opinion polls at the time of the 1959 election had shown that 48 per cent of interviewees approved of Labour's position on defence and armaments and 54 per cent approved of the Conservatives' policy. One month after the 1960 annual conference, only 27 per cent of interviewees approved of Labour's position on defence and armaments, and 48 per cent disapproved, while 61 per cent approved of the Conservative government's position on defence.[76] However, Gallup had found that for every one person who said their opinion of Labour had gone down because of the party's actual defence policy, twelve attributed their disappointment to the party's inability to preserve unity while at the same time tolerating debate. It was the fighting within the party rather than the actual details of the defence policy that were causing the problem. Gallup concluded that 'Labour, it seems, would be better off with unity and no defence policy, than with a defence policy and no unity'.[77]

Lastly, the conference defeat also raised questions about the internal workings of the Labour Party. The Labour Party prided itself on its internal democracy and conference decisions tended to be seen as binding. On 27 July 1960 the NEC had adopted a statement prepared by General Secretary Morgan Philips, which aimed at clarifying the relationship between the annual conference, the NEC and the PLP. This pointed out that 'the one thing to which, under the [Labour Party] constitution, the Parliamentary party is bound' was the election manifesto. Resolutions passed at the annual conference should be taken as the 'opinions' of the conference, and not necessarily as binding on the MPs' action in the House of Commons.[78] However, adding to the confusion, on the eve of the 1960 annual conference the Labour Party's NEC voted by twelve votes to eleven, against the wishes of Gaitskell, that party policy on 'major questions of principle' should be determined by the annual conference.[79] This meant it was unclear to the Labour Party as to whether the PLP should say that party policy was unilateralism and a complete rejection of nuclear policy as voted for at the 1960 conference, or gradual multilateral disarmament as espoused by the NEC and Gaitskell.

The fighting over defence policy continued, with unilateral disarmament proving an ideological fault-line within the labour movement. Drafting meetings for a new joint statement on defence took place in February 1961, involving Richard Crossman, Sam Watson, Tom Driberg, Hugh Gaitskell, George Brown, Denis Healey, and Sir Alfred Roberts and Frank Cousins from the TUC. Frank Cousins was not present at the meeting at which the final draft was approved, being in bed with influenza.[80] This statement, *Policy for Peace*, declared that the first essential step to lasting peace was to 'halt the arms race and bring the Cold War to an end'. This would involve 'Multilateral and comprehensive disarmament under international control'. With regards to nuclear weapons,

> We seek the banning of all nuclear weapons everywhere. But the West cannot renounce nuclear weapons so long as the Communist bloc possesses them. Britain, however, should cease the attempt to remain an independent nuclear power, since this neither strengthens the alliance nor is it now a sensible use of our limited resources.

In addition, 'The West must never be the first to use the H-bomb'.[81] Thus, Britain would give up its independent nuclear deterrent, but it would not renounce nuclear policy as such, and so Britain would remain within NATO. There was an alternative draft prepared by Frank Cousins, which was rejected by the drafting committee.[82]

The statement was not so very different from that of the previous year. This time, however, the joint statement devised by the Labour Party and the TUC was passed at both their annual conferences. Frank Cousins proposed a version of his alternative draft of *Policy for Peace* as a resolution at both the conferences, which was very similar to his resolution of the previous year. This committed a future Labour government to the 'complete rejection of any defence policy based on the threat of the use of strategic or tactical nuclear weapons', and 'the permanent cessation of the manufacture or testing of nuclear and thermo-nuclear weapons'. This policy would mean that Britain would have to leave NATO. Cousins' resolution was rejected by a large majority by both the TUC annual conference and the Labour Party's annual conference. Thus, at this point, the Labour Party leadership had regained control over the labour movement on the issue of defence and disarmament. As Groom points out, it had been helped in its battle by the realisation amongst trade unions that the resolution supporting the unilateralist position was itself just the 'tip of an iceberg without the submerged part', just the acceptance of a vague principle, but one which had great implications for both foreign and defence policy.[83] To reject the nuclear deterrent completely would mean withdrawing from the collective defence of NATO and reconsidering the whole basis of British defence and foreign policy. The Guardian noted that 'open opposition to NATO would cut no ice with the vast majority of trade unionists, for whom collective security is not an abstraction but a regular practice'.[84] Gaitskell was also helped by the recently established pro-revisionist Campaign for Democratic Socialism, led by Bill Rodgers, in the grassroots of the local parties and trade unions, which pushed for a return to multilateralism.[85]

However, the debate over defence did not focus only on nuclear weapons. The appropriate role of NATO in Europe, and the strategy that NATO should follow, were also questions of concern. One suggestion was that there could be a neutral belt in Europe. Foreign troops were to be removed from East and West Germany, Poland, Czechoslovakia and Hungary, to be replaced by national conventional troops. These states would then withdraw from NATO and the Warsaw Pact.[86] Denis Healey had been urging this proposal, contained in a

Fabian lecture in October 1957 which was subsequently published as a Fabian pamphlet entitled *A Neutral Belt in Europe*? It appeared to him that 'the strategy of NATO, which relied wholly on the threat of nuclear retaliation to prevent war in Europe, was both irrelevant and dangerous in the situations most likely to arise' there.[87] This was similar to the Rapacki Plan, proposed by the Polish Foreign Minister, which the Labour Party supported.[88] Another viewpoint, pressed by George Brown, who had become Shadow Spokesman on Defence following the 1951 election defeat, was that European defence could be strengthened through European integration. Indeed, he eventually came to the conclusion that Britain's role was inside Europe, providing political stability and leadership. 'It may be that Britain is destined to become *the* leader of Europe'.[89]

Labour and the Common Market

The issue of Britain's role in Europe flared up in the early 1960s, with Harold Macmillan negotiating from 1961 to 1963 for Britain to join the six members of the European Economic Community, namely France, Germany, Italy, the Netherlands, Belgium and Luxembourg. In 1960 the Labour Party Research Department published an information pamphlet on *Britain and the Common Market*. This recognised that while 'It is argued by some that Britain should join the Common Market' the Labour Party 'cannot accept this'. 'If Britain was to join the Common Market certain special interests will have to be satisfied, notably the Commonwealth and British agriculture, and certain safeguards laid down. Unconditional membership of the European Economic Community is out of the question.'[90] The issue was debated several times at annual conference in the early in 1960s. In 1961, a resolution was passed that declared,

> This Conference does not approve Britain's entry into the Common Market, unless guarantees protecting the position of British agriculture and horticulture, the EFTA countries and the Commonwealth, are obtained, and Britain retains the power of using public ownership and economic planning as measures to ensure social progress within the United Kingdom.[91]

However, the National Executive made it clear that Labour would support Britain's entry if those terms were met. Then in a 1962 broadcast, Gaitskell went further, saying

To go in on good terms would, I believe, be the best solution to this difficult problem ... Not to go in would be a pity, but it would not be a catas-
trophe. To go in on bad terms, which really meant the end of the
Commonwealth, would be a step which I think we would regret all our
lives, and for which history would not forgive us.[92]

At the annual conference Gaitskell argued that Britain needed to ask
about the political implications of joining the Common Market, given
that 'all who framed it saw it as a stepping stone towards political integration' and a federal Europe. He delighted the anti-Europeans, and
horrified the pro-Marketeers, when he made a passionate declaration
that joining the Common Market would mean the end of Britain as
independent nation state, and 'It means the end of a thousand years of
history'.[93] This was as he introduced the National Executive policy
statement which set out five conditions which would 'constitute
reasonable terms of entry' to the Common Market. These were first,
the safeguarding of trade between Britain and the rest of the
Commonwealth; second, freedom for Britain to pursue an independent foreign policy; third, fulfilment of Britain's pledge to maintain
trade agreements with the European Free Trade Area countries, which
should be granted the trade benefits of associate membership of the
Common Market; fourth, the retention of the right for Britain to plan
its own economy and not be subject to the limits on state intervention
enshrined in the Treaty of Rome; and fifth, guarantees to safeguard the
position of British agriculture.[94]

The debate over Britain's relationship with Europe took place
within the context of Britain's post-imperial world role. For Gaitskell,
as for many in the party, a closer relationship with Europe implied less
emphasis on Britain's Commonwealth ties. It would mean the abandonment of free entry of Commonwealth goods to Britain, with the
imposition of tariffs on imports from non-Common Market countries,
which they felt would be an abjuration of Britain's responsibilities to
the Commonwealth. However, for many younger members of the
party, in particular those involved in the Campaign for Democratic
Socialism, closer relations with Europe were vital given the realities of
Britain's relative international decline. They were desperately disappointed with Gaitskell's position on Europe at the 1962 conference.[95]
Labour's policy remained unresolved to some extent, but the issue was
shelved temporarily when General de Gaulle vetoed Britain's entry in
1963.

To conclude, it could be argued that in early 1950s the Labour Party did maintain to some extent a position of bipartisanship on foreign affairs and defence. However, by the mid-1950s, partly due to internal divisions in the party, and partly due to developments in weapons and the perception of the intensification of the nuclear threat, bipartisanship had clearly broken down. The Labour Party was largely united in its repudiation of the Conservative government's handling of the Suez crisis, and in its condemnation of events in Hungary, arguing that the use of military force should only be used when a country was faced with a direct military threat, or as part of an international defence commitment. The party was united in its support for the UN and the rule of law, which it felt had been undermined by the Conservative government. The party was also united in its opposition to the government's plans to test the British nuclear deterrent. However it was strongly split over whether Britain should continue to develop nuclear weapons, and this division gave the party a reputation for in-fighting that damaged it in the eyes of the general public. Possibly because the fight over unilateral disarmament consumed so much attention within the party, there was greater consensus over domestic policy than might have been the case given the continuing differences of opinion over how to further the socialist agenda within Britain. The ability of the divisions to stymie the leadership was a product of the party's structure and constitution, with the annual conference being used first by the Bevanites and then by the unilateralists as a platform to overturn existing party policy. Harold Davies, a left-wing MP, proclaimed at the 1954 conference that 'The purpose of a Conference is to clarify its position and tie this Executive down to socialist principles in foreign policy'.[96] However, as far as Gaitskell was concerned, the Labour Party conference could not dictate foreign or defence policy to a future Labour government. Remarkably, the party recovered from the bitter conflict over disarmament in time for the 1964 election, and entered the election campaign with a manifesto largely based on its late 1950s policies. Gaitskell's most memorable and impassioned speeches were on foreign policy and defence, but his unexpected death on 18 January 1963 meant that he never had the opportunity to implement the policies that he had fought for.

Notes

1   Labour won 48.8% of the votes, the Conservatives 48.0%. Labour won 295 seats, the Conservatives 321, David Butler and Gareth Butler, *British Political Facts 1900–1985*, 6th edn (London: Macmillan, 1986), p. 226.

2 George Brown, *In My Way: The Political Memoirs of Lord George-Brown* (London: Victor Gollancz, 1971), p. 57.
3 See Brian Brivati, *Hugh Gaitskell* (London: Richard Cohen Books, 1996), pp. 287 and 295.
4 Labour Party, *Problems of Foreign Policy* (London: Labour Party, 1952), p. 2.
5 *House of Commons Debates* (hereafter *H.C. Deb.*), vol. 558, 30 October 1956, col. 1454.
6 *Labour Party Annual Conference Report* (hereafter *LPACR*), 1955, NEC statement, p. 25.
7 Michael Gordon, *Conflict and Consensus in Labour's Foreign Policy 1914–1965* (Stanford, CA: Stanford University Press, 1969), p. 223.
8 *H.C. Deb.*, vol. 478, 12 September 1950, col. 959.
9 *H.C. Deb.*, vol. 483, 29 January 1951, col. 584.
10 Philip Williams, *Hugh Gaitskell* (London: Jonathan Cape, 1979), p. 246.
11 *LPACR*, 1954, p. 92.
12 *Ibid.*, p. 108.
13 See Williams, *Hugh Gaitskell*, p. 331; Bernard Donoughue and George Jones, *Herbert Morrison. Portrait of a Politician* (London: Weidenfeld & Nicolson, 1973) p. 530.
14 *H.C. Deb.*, vol. 533, 18 November 1954, cols 609–10.
15 *Ibid.*, col. 583.
16 *H.C. Deb*, vol. 494, 6 December 1951, cols 2596–7.
17 The National Archives, London (hereafter TNA), CAB 128/27, CC (54) 48, Cabinet conclusions, 8 July 1954.
18 William Wallace, 'World status without tears', in Vernon Bogdanor and Robert Skidelsky, eds, *The Age of Affluence 1951–1964* (London: Macmillan, 1970), p. 199.
19 *H.C. Deb.*, vol. 537, 2 March 1955, col. 2118.
20 Janet Morgan, ed., *The Backbench Diaries of Richard Crossman* (London: Hamish Hamilton and Jonathan Cape, 1981), p. 394.
21 *Ibid.*, p. 397.
22 See *ibid.*, pp. 393–414; Williams, *Hugh Gaitskell*, pp. 336–45.
23 David Carlton, *Anthony Eden: A Biography* (London: Allen Lane, 1981), p. 371.
24 Ben Pimlott, ed., *The Political Diary of Hugh Dalton, 1918–40, 1945–60* (London: Jonathan Cape, 1986), p. 671.
25 'Forward with Labour', Labour manifesto 1955, in *British General Election Manifestos, 1900–1974*, compiled and edited by F.W.S. Craig (London: Macmillan, revised and enlarged edn, 1975), p. 203.
26 Butler and Butler, *British Political Facts*, p. 142.
27 Carlton, *Anthony Eden*, p. 3278.
28 Williams, *Hugh Gaitskell*, pp. 422–4. Gaitskell himself refers to the discussion in *H.C. Deb.*, vol. 558, col. 18, 12 September 1956.
29 *H.C. Deb.*, vol. 557, 2 August 1956, cols 1613–17.
30 Philip Williams, ed., *The Diary of Hugh Gaitskell, 1945–1956* (London: Jonathan Cape, 1983), p. 581.
31 *H.C. Deb.*, vol. 558, 12 September 1956, cols 22–32.
32 *LPACR*, 1956, p. 70.

33 *Ibid.*, p. 77.
34 Morgan, ed., *Backbench Diaries of Richard Crossman*, 26 October 1956, p. 523.
35 *H.C. Deb.*, vol. 558, 31 October 1956, col. 1454.
36 Hugh Gaitskell's broadcast on behalf of the Labour Party, 4 November 1956, in Williams, ed., *Diary of Hugh Gaitskell*, p. 622.
37 Dennis Healey, *The Time of My Life* (London: Penguin, 1990), p. 169.
38 *H.C. Deb.*, vol. 560, 13 November 1956, cols 827–8.
39 *H.C. Deb.*, vol. 560, 6 November 1956, cols 36–9.
40 *H.C. Deb.*, vol. 558, 5 November 1956, col. 1948.
41 *LPACR*, 1957, pp. 10–11.
42 *H.C. Deb.*, vol. 562, 19 December 1956, cols 1318–22.
43 *Ibid.*, cols 1332–4.
44 Labour Party archive, Museum of Labour History, Manchester, Defence Sub-Committee and Disarmament Sub-Committee, Minutes and Documents, 'Labour Party Policy on the Hydrogen Bomb', February 1957.
45 Labour Party archive, Ad Hoc Disarmament Sub-Committee, 1957, correspondence, letter from Morgan Phillips to Frank Beswick, MP, 20 December 1956.
46 Labour Party archive, Defence Sub-Committee and Disarmament Sub-Committee, 1956/57, 'Defence and Disarmament', June 1957.
47 Labour Party archive, Ad Hoc Disarmament Sub-Committee, 1956–59, various minutes and correspondence; and Ad Hoc Disarmament Sub-Committee, Minutes and Documents 1957.
48 Alistair Horne, *Macmillan, 1957–1986: Volume II of the Official Biography* (London: Macmillan, 1989), pp. 45–8.
49 Labour Party archive, Defence Sub-Committee and Disarmament Sub-Committee, 1956/57, 'Defence and Disarmament', June 1957, item 10.
50 *H.C. Deb.*, vol. 568, 1 April 1957, in particular cols 45, 55, 68 for Macmillan and cols 71–3 for Gaitskell. See also Healey's comments, cols 129–33.
51 Williams, *Hugh Gaitskell*, p. 453.
52 *H.C. Deb.*, vol. 568, 17 April 1957, col. 1929.
53 *LPACR*, 1956, p. 60, referring to foreign policy debate in the House of Commons, 23–24 July 1956.
54 *LPACR*, 1957, p. 165.
55 *Ibid.*, pp. 179–83.
56 Richard Taylor, 'The Labour Party and CND: 1957 to 1984', in Richard Taylor and Nigel Young, eds, *Campaigns for Peace: British Peace Movements in the Twentieth Century* (Manchester: Manchester University Press, 1987), p. 103.
57 *Ibid.*, citing a conversation with Ian Mikardo.
58 *H.C. Deb.*, vol. 602, 16 March 1959, col. 155.
59 Peggy Duff, *Left, Left, Left: A Personal Account of Six Protest Campaigns, 1945–65* (London: Allison & Busby, 1971), pp. 70–1. Italics in original.
60 Robert Taylor, 'The Campaign for Nuclear Disarmament', in Bogdanor and Skidelsky, eds, *Age of Affluence*, p. 226.

61 Canon L. John Collins, *Faith Under Fire* (London: Leslie Frewin, 1966), pp. 326–7.
62 Quoted by David Marquand in his article 'Bombs and scapegoats', *Encounter*, 16:1 (January 1961), p. 45.
63 *H.C. Deb.*, vol. 583, 27 February 1958, col. 576.
64 Marquand, 'Bombs and scapegoats', p. 43.
65 Healey, *The Time of My Life*, p. 241; Taylor, 'The Campaign for Nuclear Disarmament', p. 233.
66 *Trades Union Congress Annual Report* (hereafter *TUCAR*), 1957, p. 471.
67 'Disarmament and Nuclear War', *LPACR*, 1958, pp. 5–7.
68 Labour Party archive, Ad Hoc Disarmament Sub-Committee, 1956/59, annual conference 1958, 'Brief Survey of Disarmament Resolutions', July 1958.
69 *LPACR*, 1958, pp. 191–224.
70 *Ibid.*, p. 221.
71 Labour Party archive, International Department, INT/1959-60/21, 'Defence and Disarmament: Some Points for Consideration', David Ennals, May 1960.
72 *TUCAR*, 1960, p. 218.
73 *Ibid.*, p. 396.
74 Collins, *Faith Under Fire*, p. 325.
75 A Gallup poll in September 1960 found that 36% of interviewees agreed with the statement that Britain should 'continue to make our own nuclear weapons'; 31% said that Britain should 'pool all nuclear weapons with other NATO countries and rely mainly on American production'; 21% said Britain should 'Give up nuclear weapons entirely'; with 12% on 'don't know'. *Gallup Political Index*, No. 9 (September 1960), p. 10.
76 Gallup Political Index, no. 9 (September 1960), tables 3 and 4, pp. 6–7; and *Gallup Political Index*, no. 11, tables 3 and 4, pp. 12–13.
77 *Gallup Political Index*, no. 11 (November 1960), p. 9.
78 *Keesing's Contemporary Archives*, vol. 12, 1959–60, p. 17744.
79 *Ibid.*, p. 17745.
80 Labour Party archive, drafting committee 1961 for joint statement on Foreign Policy and Defence, NEC 22.2.61, Sec. 129, Joint Labour Party/TUC Statement on Foreign Policy and Defence.
81 *TUCAR*, 1961, p. 219; *LPACR*, 1961, pp. 7-8.
82 Labour Party archive, drafting committee 1961 for joint statement on Foreign Policy and Defence, from International Department to R. H. S. Crossman, 15 February 1961; Draft Statement by Frank Cousins, February 1961.
83 A.J.R. Groom, *British Thinking about Nuclear Weapons* (London: Pinter, 1974), p. 439.
84 *Guardian*, 15 Dec. 1960.
85 Brivati, *Hugh Gaitskell*, pp. 381–2; Groom, *British Thinking About Nuclear Weapons*, pp. 448–9.
86 *LPACR*, 1958, pp. 7–8.
87 Healey, *The Time of My Life*, p. 178; Dennis Healey, *A Neutral Belt in Europe?* (London: Labour Party, 1957).

88 *LPACR*, 1958, p. 8.
89 Brown, *In My Way*, pp. 207 and 209.
90 Labour Party, *Britain and the Common Market*, Information Series No. 14 (London: Labour Party, 1960).
91 *LPACR*, 1961, p. 211.
92 Cited in Brown, *In My Way*, p. 216.
93 *LPACR*, 1962, pp. 158–9.
94 Ibid., NEC statement on 'Labour and the Common Market', p. 246.
95 See Brivati, *Hugh Gaitskell*, pp. 414–17.
96 *LPACR*, 1954, p. 76.

Chapter 3

The Wilson governments, 1964–1970

The Labour Party in the early 1960s was far more united on foreign and defence policy than it had been during the second half of the 1950s. Exhausted from the in-fighting over nuclear disarmament, and having reached the position at the 1961 annual conference of broad agreement in this area, the party turned to focus on domestic issues. Following Gaitskell's unexpected early death at the age of fifty-six, Harold Wilson was elected leader of the party in February 1963, and this created a sense of renewal for Labour. Wilson, the Labour Party's Shadow Foreign Affairs Spokesman since November 1961, had failed in previous bids at both the party leadership and deputy leadership, but this time beat both George Brown and James Callaghan in the leadership contest. Both of these men became his closest colleagues and his closest rivals. Wilson had automatically got the vote of the left and Brown scored heavily with the right, while Callaghan got the votes of those who preferred neither candidate, coming bottom of the poll. According to Callaghan, 'This was the right result, for although George Brown exceeded us all in his darting imagination, his demonic energy and his persuasive power, Harold Wilson had the stability and unifying influence that the Party needed'.[1] Wilson noted in his memoirs that 'After all the in-fighting the Party rallied round' when he became leader.[2] Wilson was only forty-seven years old, full of energy and ideas.

In contrast, the Conservative government appeared worn out. It was being held responsible for the sluggish economy, with a much-publicised slow rate of growth blamed on amateurism and low productivity. The government was also still suffering from the shock of the Profumo affair of summer 1963, when Minister of War John Profumo was found to have lied to the House of Commons over his affair with

Christine Keeler, a call-girl who was simultaneously having an affair with Yevgeny Ivanov, an assistant naval attaché at the Soviet embassy in London. Harold Macmillan had been replaced by Lord Douglas Hume as party leader and Prime Minister, and he was seen as out of touch and old fashioned. This aided Wilson in his chosen campaign platform of modernisation through the application of a scientific revolution. His first major speech to the party at its annual conference in September 1963 was seen as a *tour de force*, when he argued that 'The Britain that is going to be forged in the white heat of this revolution will be no place for restrictive practices or for outdated methods on either side of industry'. Instead, 'we must use all the resources of democratic planning, all the latent and underdeveloped energies and skills of our people, to ensure Britain's standing in the world'.[3] Wilson continued his modernisation and regeneration theme with a series of speeches in run-up to the 1964 election.

The much-anticipated election was eventually held on 15 October 1964. After thirteen years of opposition, Labour was returned to power promising 'A New Britain' with 'fresh and virile leadership' under Harold Wilson. The Labour Party rank-and-file had very high expectations of what could be achieved by a government headed by Wilson, who had traditionally been seen as a left-winger. As in 1945, there were expectations that Labour would implement a foreign policy that was radically different from the traditional foreign policy pursued by the Conservatives, which would be a 'socialist' foreign policy, especially in terms of being anti-imperialist, internationalist and based on universal moral norms. Labour's 1964 election manifesto had promised an end to colonialism; that a Labour government would work towards relaxing Cold War tensions; the introduction of new initiatives on disarmament; and leadership at the UN, as 'the United Nations is the chosen instrument by which the world can move away from the anarchy of power politics towards the creation of a genuine world community and the rule of law'.[4] However, despite having lead in the opinion polls since mid-1961, Labour actually polled slightly fewer votes than it did in 1959. The Labour Party won 317 seats, the Conservatives 304 and Liberals nine seats.[5] This only gave the Labour government a tiny majority of four seats. While the Labour Party had high hopes of a new, radical political dawn, this small majority constrained Wilson both in party political and policy issues. Conversely, this situation also provided Wilson with an excuse for not undertaking radical initiatives in foreign affairs.

Despite being from the centre-left of the party, Wilson appointed many colleagues from the right to his Cabinet. Patrick Gordon Walker, a 'quiet, acquiescent' man,[6] whom nevertheless was very knowledgeable about foreign and Commonwealth affairs, became Foreign Secretary, even though he had lost his seat at the election. Following his unsuccessful attempt to regain a seat at the Leyton by-election on 22 January 1965, he had to resign from his Cabinet position, and was replaced by another right-winger, Michael Stewart. Denis Healey became Defence Secretary, a position that he held throughout the two Labour governments. Wilson established a new Ministry of Overseas Development, and his first appointment to the post was a left-winger, Barbara Castle, who was given Cabinet rank.

Labour had regained power at a time of considerable change when questions were being asked about the role that Britain could, or should, play in the world. Britain still had a vast military commitment across the globe, with troops in Europe, the Middle East and Far East, including Germany, the Mediterranean, Aden and the Persian Gulf. Britain was providing military support for the Federation of Malaysia, which had been formed in September 1963, and which was under attack from the authoritarian leader of Indonesia, General Sukarno, in a campaign of what he called 'confrontation'. However, it was becoming increasingly apparent that Britain's relative economic decline compared with other industrialised countries meant that it could no longer project itself as a major force in the world in the way that it had during the first half of the twentieth century. It was also clear that Britain had become increasingly dependent upon the United States in terms of security policy. Wilson described on how his first day in office he found himself facing a 'stormy welcome':

> The Chinese had, the previous day, exploded their first nuclear weapon …
> There was a telegram appraising the situation in the Soviet Union following the overthrow, less than twenty-four hours earlier, of Mr Khrushchev
> … There was a telephone call from President Johnson … And, grimmest of all, there was the economic news.[7]

The economic news was that there was a £800 million balance of payments deficit, knowledge of which the Conservatives had not made public.

While Wilson had known in advance that there was a balance of payments problem, he had no idea about the extent of the deficit. He and Callaghan, his new Chancellor of the Exchequer, were also concerned at the prospect of speculative attacks on sterling in the event of a Labour victory. This meant that the option of devaluing sterling in order to deal with the deficit was seen as completely unacceptable. Wilson had repeatedly said during the election campaign that devaluation would be seen as a defeat for Britain. Moreover, it would be seen as a repeat of the 1947 devaluation and as evidence that Labour could not be trusted economically. As Callaghan put it, 'The Conservatives would have crucified us'.[8] Added to this was the concern that devaluation would provoke a self-fulfilling prophesy of panic on the financial markets and cause concern internationally. Wilson's solution to this was to shore up sterling by turning to the US for financial support, while introducing a series of severe financial restraints domestically. Both these measures alienated the government from the Labour Party. This chapter will argue that the economic problems were to greatly influence, but not determine, Wilson's foreign policy – and it was Wilson's foreign policy, rather than that of any of his rather short-lived Foreign Secretaries. Despite all this, the first Wilson government was generally seen as a success, and the party remained unusually supportive of its leader, a situation that was rather ironically reversed during the 1966–70 government, when Wilson governed with a larger majority.

Anglo-American relations

Wilson had undertaken two trips to the US before the 1964 general election, the first to meet President Kennedy, the second to meet his successor, President Lyndon Johnson. As a result of these trips, and of the favourable news coverage that accompanied them, Wilson felt that he had a special rapport with the Americans in general, and a personal special relationship with Johnson in particular. However, during 1963 and 1964 the US administration had undertaken a reassessment of Anglo-American relations. Britain's continued economic weakness, combined with the failure of its bid to enter the European Economic Community at a time when the US was hoping for an increased European role for Britain, resulted in a decline in its importance to the US. The stormy debates over foreign and defence policy within the Labour Party during the late 1950s, with the left of the party supporting unilateral nuclear disarmament, also meant that a Labour victory was viewed with some trepidation by an American administration more used to dealing with a Conservative government.

Less than two months after gaining power, Wilson visited Washington with Denis Healey and Gordon Walker. A great deal of advance work was undertaken before the visit, with the Prime Minister being warned that he 'should not bank on everything going his way when he got face to face with the President'. It was even pointed out that the President was not looking forward to the talks with anything approaching the same eagerness as the Prime Minister, as he had many other problems on his mind and saw the visit 'as more of a chore than a major act of policy'.[9] Yet despite such warnings, this visit did pass off fairly successfully. The main topics of discussion were first, the issue of nuclear weapons within NATO and the idea of a multilateral force (MLF), which the US had proposed under Kennedy but which Britain was largely opposed to, and second, the situation in Vietnam.

The US Congress had authorised Johnson to undertake direct military action in Vietnam in August 1964 following the Gulf of Tonkin incident and hostilities, and the US commitment to Vietnam, were set to escalate rapidly. During the talks, Dean Rusk, the US Secretary of State, asked for a British military commitment regarding Vietnam, stressing that 'it was important to have a significant number of people in the country in order to create the necessary international effect, both in Saigon and Hanoi, and on public opinion in the United States'. Gordon Walker replied that the UK already had 54,000 troops in Malaysia, a former British colony under attack from Indonesia, which were comparable in number with the United States' presence in Vietnam, and 'he was emphatic that the United Kingdom could not have troops on the ground in Vietnam'. However, the UK would be prepared to help in other ways which could be made public and which would amount to an increased commitment. These were by training more men in jungle warfare; by having more policy advisors in Saigon; and by co-operating more in the medical field.[10] Wilson sent a message to his colleagues at home to reassure them that 'We have not accepted any new commitment as regards South Viet Nam'.[11]

Wilson made much of his personal relationship with Lyndon Johnson, in particular to his Cabinet colleagues. Following his next visit to Washington in 1965, which had been described in the press as his most successful to date, he could not help telling them that Johnson had asked him to help turn the Christmas tree lights on in the White House, the first time a British Prime Minister had been given this honour since Churchill in 1943. Barbara Castle noted that 'Obviously the two get on like a house on fire'.[12] While Johnson did appear to find his first few meetings with Wilson as something of 'a chore', he also made an effort to demonstrate the strength of the Anglo-American relationship, as it was felt that America's problems would be 'increased by the political or economic demise of the only other Western country which exercises genuine worldwide responsibility'.[13]

Indeed, the US administration did need Britain's support. An American review of Anglo-American policy relations noted that 'The simple, hardly debatable answer' to questions of the future of the special relationship 'is that we need the support and sympathy of the British. If they are unable to go it alone, in their relative weakness, neither can we everywhere. We touch one another at too many points and are still affected by what the other does in too many situations to be able to dispense with mutual support of some kind.'[14] There were four particular issues. First, the United States still needed Britain's influence within Europe. Second, in economic terms, the US administration needed Britain to keep sterling at $2.80, and not to devalue, in order to protect the dollar at a time when the America was suffering its own balance of payments problems. It was feared in the United States that it might be forced to devalue the dollar if the pound devalued, which would cause instability in the international financial system. Third, in terms of defence, the US wanted Britain to continue to provide military support both in Germany and across the globe, and in particular to retain its bases in the Persian Gulf, Aden and Singapore and the Indian Ocean. It was feared that if Britain reduced its defence commitments east of Suez, then the region might fall prey to Soviet influence, at a time when the US was devoting increasing defence resources to Vietnam. Fourth, the US administration wanted British support over Vietnam, preferably by providing troops, but if not troops, then at least strong public diplomatic backing, in order for the US to present its actions in Vietnam as having the support of the international community.

To a large extent, Wilson agreed with the first three of these four US objectives. Wilson and most members of his Cabinet were also opposed to devaluation as a policy solution to Britain's huge balance of payments deficit, as it would mean revealing the full extent of Britain's economic problems. It would also mean playing into the hands of Labour's opponents who argued that Labour governments were disastrous for the British economy, and that a devaluation took place whenever Labour were voted into power. James Callaghan had been concerned before the election that a Labour victory would be followed by an attack on sterling, and so had made regular visits to America to get to know people at the US Treasury and the Federal Reserve Bank, and had managed to get an assurance that if such a situation did arise, then he could turn to the US for help.[15] When a sterling crisis followed the budget of 11 November 1964, the Labour government received large-scale support for sterling from the US Federal Reserve Bank. Then, in the summer of 1965, when the pound came under increasing pressure at a time of dwindling exchange reserves, Wilson agreed to a rescue package from the US to support sterling and prevent devaluation. This, according to Clive Ponting, came at a price: in return for the rescue package, Wilson had to agree to maintain British worldwide defence commitments, and a statutory wages and prices policy.[16] Those involved in making this controversial deal were Wilson, Callaghan and George Brown, but the details of the deal was not made known to Wilson's other Cabinet colleagues, let alone the public.

Yet debate has raged over whether such an agreement was reached, and, if it was, the degree to which the United States was able to use its financial aid as leverage over Wilson.[17] To a large extent, Wilson's goals coincided with those of the Americans, namely to avoid devaluation at any price, to maintain defence commitments east of Suez, and to prevent wage and price increases. Wilson, while aware of the need to cut defence expenditure, did not want a dramatic decline in Britain's international defence commitments. While paying lip service to the need to rationalise Britain's commitments to reflect the loss of its imperial role, Wilson simultaneously emphasised Britain's continuing world role. Roy Jenkins, a Cabinet minister from December 1965, argued that 'if they [Wilson and Callaghan] could get American support for what they wanted to do anyway this could be regarded as serving a British interest and, from the point of view of the 1966 election, even a Labour Party interest'.[18] What Wilson had managed to do with this agreement was to avoid any commitment to Vietnam. Wilson 'repeated time after time that the Americans had never made any connection between the financial support they gave us and our support for them in Vietnam'. However, at the same time he also urged his Cabinet members to remember that American financial support 'is not unrelated to the way we behave in the Far East; any direct announcement of our withdrawal, for example, could not fail to have a profound effect on my personal relations with LBJ and the way the American's treat us'.[19] This could, of course, have been Wilson's way of forestalling criticism from within his Cabinet. Wilson was, like many successful politicians, an opportunist, and US financial support provided him with the opportunity to rein in recalcitrant colleagues.

Britain and the Vietnam War

Michael Stewart, Harold Wilson's Foreign Secretary for nearly four years in the 1960s, said that Vietnam 'was to prove the most difficult and the most agonizing of all the problems I had to face'.[20] While the party leadership saw Vietnam within the context of the Cold War contest against the spread of Communism, the party membership saw Vietnam largely as a war of national liberation. Vietnam galvanised left-wing opposition to Wilson's pro-American stance, causing anger and disillusionment amongst Labour Party members and activists, who were never at ease with the government's stance of providing moral, but not military, support for the US. As a result, at the 1966 and 1967 annual conferences, the Labour Party rejected the government's policy towards the Vietnam War. This was the first time in the party's history that it had rejected government policy at an annual conference, which not only highlighted the problems of internal party democracy, but also conspicuously demonstrated the deep divisions within the party over Vietnam. This then meant that Wilson was facing enormous and conflicting pressure from within his own domestic support base and from the US.[21]

President Johnson's demands were for public support from Britain, and the deployment of British troops fighting alongside the US military in Vietnam. British support would provide US action with international credibility and legitimacy. This issue, according to the British Ambassador to Washington, 'acquired an almost dramatic importance when the President began to reflect seriously upon the potential consequences of Britain drifting seriously out of line'. In particular, 'it is extremely important from the point of view of American standing with world opinion that the leading socialist-governed country in the world should support their objectives in South East Asia'. This was true for domestic public opinion as well as international, 'since American public opinion still has a latent sense of guilt which it is much easier to allay when the Administration can point to the moral and physical support of other countries for what the U.S. is trying to do in Vietnam'.[22] Johnson was 'outraged by Wilson's stead-fast refusal' to send troops, telling his advisors that he had made it clear to Wilson at their meeting in December 1964 that 'the only effective contribution Britain could make to the war effort would be soldiers on the ground'.[23] Wilson was willing to say publicly that he was in support of American actions in Vietnam, but he continued to refuse to send British troops to Vietnam.

Wilson did not appear to be opposed to sending troops on purely ethical grounds. He confided to Jack Jones, the leader of the TGWU, that 'he would have much more influence with President Johnson on Vietnam if we could send in a token force'.[24] Rather, Wilson was confined by opposition from within his party. Sending British troops to fight in Vietnam would have caused outrage within the Labour Party and the Labour government. It could have resulted in resignations from certain government ministers, and in some cases Labour MPs might have withdrawn from the Labour Party whip in protest, in effect refusing to co-operate with the government. Thus, given that Wilson only had a governing majority of four MPs, sending British troops would have meant risking his premiership for Johnson, which he was not prepared to do. Instead, Wilson was prepared to give the US very public moral support, thus providing the semblance of international agreement and legitimacy over the American decision to intervene in Vietnam.

Wilson's position of stating publicly that he was in support of America's military intervention in Vietnam became a major focus of revolt amongst backbench MPs from early 1965. Following the introduction of heavy bombing raids on North Vietnam in February by the US, the Tribune Group of left-wing MPs started pressing for a debate on Wilson's policy in the House of Commons.[25] Significantly, resolutions raising concerns over the government's position and over American actions in Vietnam suddenly started flooding in to the Labour Party headquarters. The Overseas Department had received only three resolutions concerning Vietnam between October 1964, when Labour came into office, and early February 1965.[26] By the time of its 9 March 1965 meeting, it had received twelve resolutions from Constituency Labour Parties expressing concern over Vietnam, condemning US bombing of the North, and urging the government to bring about peace by reconvening the Geneva Conference.[27] At the Labour Party's NEC meeting of 28 April 1965, the Overseas Sub-Committee pointed out that it had received another thirty-one resolutions.[28] In May it received twenty-eight more resolutions, and by July it had received another forty from constituency Labour parties and two from trade unions. This was an unprecedented number of resolutions for the party headquarters to receive on any one topic. In May, the PLP noted that 'Many Party workers felt the Government should show greater independence from the USA in its foreign policy'.[50] As a result, on 27 September 1965, just in time for the annual conference, the NEC released a statement on the government's foreign policy saying that 'We endorse the successive attempts by the Government to secure a just and peaceful solution' to the problem of Vietnam, and listing the recent attempts by the government to promote a diplomatic solution.[31]

Meanwhile, on 22 March 1965 the US Defense Department had announced that they were using napalm and CS gas in Vietnam, and that there was no limit to the potential increase of the war. As a result there was a 'storm' in the PLP and six senior backbenchers, including Philip Noel-Baker, chairman of the Labour Foreign Affairs Group, sent a telegram to Foreign Secretary Michael Stewart, then visiting Washington, demanding that he express the 'horror and indignation' felt in Britain at this action.[32] The telegram appealed to Wilson to dissociate Britain from the US position, and said the party could not understand the government's apparent determination to support the Americans in actions that were 'in conflict with accepted morality'. They feared that disillusionment with the Labour Party's ideas and ideals might be quite disastrous 'to the Party's future and to the Government now'.[33] Certainly Wilson was very concerned that the use of gas and napalm 'has greatly aggravated the concern felt here in Parliament and indeed more widely', and that it made it harder for him to counter the jibe that the British government 'is the tail-end Charlie in an American bomber'.[34] In his conversation with Dean Rusk, Michael Stewart 'emphasised the extremely strong feelings that had been aroused by the use of gas and napalm bombs which inflicted undue suffering and were of limited military value' Rusk reminded Stewart that Britain had used such weapons before and informed him that 'This Viet-Namese war was not a Sunday-school party. It was a rough business.'[35] At his speech to the National Press Club that day in Washington, Stewart said that 'In the choice of measures everyone responsible should consider not only what is militarily appropriate for the job in hand but the effect on people around the world'. He further asked the US to display a 'decent respect for the opinions of mankind'. Wilson wrote that Stewart's 'uncompromising approach won the approval of Labour MPs'.[36] In the Commons on 23 March, Wilson managed to avoid directly criticising US policy by saying that Stewart was at that moment discussing the situation with the US Secretary of State, and promising that Britain would 'take the initiative' to bring about peace negotiations.[37]

A further intensification of the conflict occurred in May 1966 with the bombing of Hanoi. Under pressure from the PLP, Wilson had repeatedly told the Commons that 'we could not support any extension of the bombing against North Vietnam by stages to Hanoi and

Haiphong',[38] and so was left with little choice but to condemn the US. Wilson, while urging Johnson 'to reconsider whether this action, whatever its results in terms of immediate military advantage, is worth the candle', hoped that Johnson would understand that he had been left with no choice but to condemn the bombing as a result of ongoing pressure from his party in the Commons, and reassured him that 'this will not affect my general support of American policy in Vietnam'.[39] On 29 June 1966 Wilson announced that the government had decided to 'dissociate itself from the bombing of oil installations in the Hanoi and Haiphong areas', and made a statement in the House of Commons to this effect following repeated requests from his own backbenches on 7 July.[40] This was a polite way of criticising the US. David Bruce, reporting back to Washington, said that 'My estimate is that Prime Minister will weather storm in Commons by reiterating doubtful distinction between disassociation Haiphong Hanoi action, and support for basic US policy Vietnam'.[41] This distinction between the specific targeting of North Vietnam and US policy in general 'has for long been his stock in trade for fending off left wing attacks'.[42]

From 1965, concern over the war in Vietnam had become a central rallying point for the left of the party at the annual conferences, and provided an issue that could be used to garner support from across the party. At the 1965 annual conference, two resolutions condemning American intervention in Vietnam were defeated, but the debate over them was lengthy and heated.[43] At the 1966 Labour Party annual conference, a resolution from the Fire Brigades Union was passed which called upon the government 'to bring all pressures on the United States of America to end the war in Vietnam', for a peace settlement based on the 1954 Geneva Agreement, and called 'for the cessation of the bombing by the United States of North Vietnam'.[44] This went slightly further than the position of the NEC in that it called for an *unconditional* cessation of the bombing of the North, and was taken by conference at the time to imply the rejection of the NEC position, and thus a rejection of the government's position.[45] This was partly a matter of semantics, and came down to a discussion of the placing of a semi-colon in the NEC statement, which called for 'the cessation of bombing operations against North Vietnam; the cessation of the movement of North Vietnamese military forces or material to South Vietnam'.[46] At the 1967 Labour Party annual conference a resolution was narrowly passed which called upon the government to 'dissociate itself completely' from US policy in Vietnam, to persuade the US to end its bombing of North Vietnam 'immediately, permanently and unconditionally', and for a peace settlement based on the 1954 Geneva Agreement. The proposer, from the Cambridge Constituency Labour Party, continued that it was high time that Britain stopped supporting Johnson in 'his ill-begotten, misdirected and wholly criminal policy'. He pointed out the dilemma the government's policy had placed Labour Party members in, having to defend British policy while out campaigning:

> I find myself, in answer to questions about Vietnam, having to hold my tongue, cross my fingers and drag my feet, and I am wondering personally how long I can remain in this uncomfortable posture and at the same time have a hand still willing to hold a Labour Party card.

He went on that 'Our support for the American policy hampers our efforts to find peace. It is quite intolerable and it is anomalous. We press for peace, yet we send our soldiers and police to train the South Vietnamese.'[47] George Brown, the Foreign Secretary, pleaded with the conference not to support the resolution, but the resolution was passed nevertheless by 2,752,000 votes to 2,633,000.[48] This was a clear rejection of government policy by the Labour Party membership.

This was the first time in the party's history that it had rejected its own government's policy at an annual conference, which not only again highlighted the problems of internal party democracy, but also conspicuously demonstrated the deep divisions within the party over Vietnam. This then meant that Wilson was facing enormous and conflicting pressure from within his own domestic support base and from the US. It was not impossible for the Labour Party and the Labour government to hold different policies on the same issue, and Wilson's foreign and defence policy was rejected at the annual party conference on several occasions between 1966 and 1968.[49] Wilson publicly treated the situation as an inconvenience rather than an intractable problem for the party, telling the 1968 conference that 'Every resolution carried against the platform [i.e. the NEC] this week – and you have not been unproductive in this regard – we accept as a warning to the Government. A warning, not an instruction.' He said that the government was responsible to Parliament, not conference, and that this had been the case since the first Labour government.[50] Indeed, he had warned his own MPs in June 1966 that there while there were those among them 'who do not see the Labour Party as a Party of power, who see it more as a Party of protest who are much happier in Opposition, who find it hard to face up to what power means, and what is involved in using that power to realise our international ideals', this was not an acceptable attitude for a government to take.[51]

However, the situation was more problematic than this. According to Tom McNally, the Labour Party's International Secretary during this period, Wilson and the party leadership went to great lengths to avoid being defeated at the party's annual conference.[52] As far as most Labour Party activists were concerned, conference decisions were binding upon a Labour government, and for the annual conference to reject a policy being pursued by a Labour government was a terrible situation. In addition, party left-wingers erroneously thought that given Wilson's left-wing past, he would take the view that Conference decisions would be binding upon a Labour government.[53] Certainly the last Labour Prime Minister, Clement Attlee, had treated conference decisions as a form of a vote of confidence, and went to great efforts to prevent government policy being rejected at conference because of this.[54] Thus, it was a terrible shock to the party's activists to find that Wilson in fact ignored the annual conference, and this added to the growing sense of betrayal amongst the left of the party. This sense of betrayal was not only over the Vietnam policy, but also over the relationship between the Labour Party and the Labour government, and the way that Wilson appeared to be ignoring the wishes of the party. Indeed, such was the concern over the issue of conference sovereignty that in 1970, following Labour's defeat in the general election, a resolution was passed at the annual conference that stated that MPs should reflect the views of the Labour movement and that conference 'deplores the Parliamentary Labour Party's refusal to act on Conference decisions'.[55]

While Wilson carried on regardless, there was concern at the damage that the issue of Vietnam could do to the party. Wilson's Chief Whip, Edward Short, repeatedly said in his memoir that Vietnam 'caused me more trouble and embarrassment' and 'problems' in the PLP than any other issue.[56] Dissent over Vietnam and over Labour's defence review prompted the PLP's Liaison Committee in November 1966 to propose two motions concerning party organisation, one condemning personal attacks made by MPs against their colleagues, the other reminding MPs that they could not belong to groups not officially recognised by the PLP. This was aimed at controlling concerted actions by groups of dissidents in the party, as 'A civil war in the Party must be avoided. The situation today was more dangerous than in 1945–51' and a 'higher degree of discipline was needed' within the PLP.[57] A review in 1970 said that Vietnam had been 'the issue which caused most disillusionment within the Party', and urged that 'Leaving foreign policy to the foreign policy pundits' was dangerous, 'especially since the Labour Party has always had among its rank a higher percentage of people deeply concerned about foreign policy issues than can be found among the electorate as a whole'.

> The lesson to be learnt from this is that a wrong foreign policy decision may lose us only a minute percentage of votes; but it can lose us a much higher percentage of party activists. Foreign policy has, for this reason, a much greater importance for the Labour Party than crude statistics of voting motivations would suggest. For many thousands of our activists their socialism only has meaning if a socialist domestic policy is also reflected in our foreign policy.[58]

As disillusionment with the Labour government increased, left-leaning students and intellectuals sought avenues of protest outside of the party system. From April 1965 onwards CND's monthly newsletter, *Sanity*, regularly had articles about Vietnam on the front page criticising Wilson as a hypocrite over his support for the US. CND also published pamphlets on the topic.[59] The International Confederation for Disarmament and Peace, which was an international version of CND consisting of over fifty peace organisations, was formally established in 1964. This in turn set up a Vietnam emergency liaison committee in London, which published *Vietnam International*, and was involved in organising the Stockholm World Conference on Vietnam. This was first held in July 1967, and brought together representatives of peace organisations from all over the world to lobby for peace in Vietnam and to increase pressure on their own governments to dissociate them from the Vietnam policy of the US.[60] The Communist Party set up the British Council for Peace in Vietnam. The Bertrand Russell Peace Foundation and the War Crimes Tribunal, along with the Trotskyite International Marxist Group, set up the Vietnam Solidarity Campaign in June 1966.

The Vietnam Solidarity Campaign circulated the whole of the Labour Party and trade union movement with appeals to give money for medical aid to Vietnam, and 'as a result dozens of contacts with sections of the Labour movement were made which were extremely useful'.[61] The Vietnam Solidarity Campaign also had a great deal of support from the student population, and organised two mass demonstrations in London in March and in October 1968, with marchers converging on the US embassy in Grosvenor Square. While these demonstrations did include people from across the political spectrum, by far the biggest contingent was the student movement. According to Ellis, 'Vietnam played a crucial part in politicising British youth', and while they were not directly involved in the war, 'Vietnam was mainly of humanitarian and symbolic importance'.[62] Morgan notes that Vietnam brought 'a kind of passionate political violence to the London streets unknown since the anti-fascist battle of Cable Street in 1936'.[63] Tariq Ali, a key founding member of the Vietnam Solidarity Campaign, felt that 'Revolutionary socialism was reborn in 1968'.[64] Certainly violence was thought a possibility: in the run-up to the October 1968 demonstration, articles appeared in the press outlining supposed plots to use home-made bombs and commit violence at the coming demonstration. These stories had apparently been planted by Special Branch.[65] James Callaghan, who was Home Secretary at the time, said that he came under great pressure in Parliament to ban the march, and that there was 'an agitated atmosphere built up based on very little reliable information, with newspaper reports making the ordinary citizen's blood curdle about the horrors to expect'.[66] Estimates of the number of demonstrators were between 10,000 and 25,000 at the 17 March, and possibly as many as 100,000 at the 27 October event.[67]

However, it was not only the far left that was critical of the Wilson government's stance; the Fabian Society said that 'Mr Wilson's Vietnam policy is not wrong because it is unpopular, it is wrong because it is wrong'. Indeed, it argued that the escalation of the Vietnam War was threatening seriously to undermine the Western Alliance itself, for 'The bleak anger of the French at American policy, and the sheer contempt in which they hold the British for their pusillanimous attitude, suggest the days of Atlantic co-operation are numbered'.[68] Individual Labour Party MPs also got involved in campaigning for Vietnam. Hugh Jenkins, for instance, set up the Vietnam Fund in his Putney constituency to raise money to help victims of the war, sending one hundred pounds to the Ambassador to Vietnam for the 'aid of people in the village recently bombed by accident by the Americans'.[69]

While Wilson did not bend to this pressure to condemn US military action in Vietnam, one way that he did seek to reassure public opinion and to deal with the massive pressure coming from within the Labour Party was through his peace diplomacy. Acting as a go-between for the US and the Soviet Union in an attempt to broker a deal on the cessation of hostilities had the potential to be an important role, for the North Vietnamese were refusing to have face-to-face talks with the US administration, and it was thought that the Soviet Union had a great deal of influence in Hanoi and could act as an intermediary for the North Vietnamese. Wilson believed himself to have a special relationship not only with the US but also with the Soviet Union, which he had visited several times over the past two decades. His most recent visits had been in May 1963 and April 1964, when he had discussed East/West tensions with Khrushchev. If Wilson had managed to broker a peace deal, this would have legitimised his stance on Vietnam and pleased the party, as well as raising his profile as a world statesman who could succeed where so many others had failed. However, these attempts were not always welcomed by the US; the Soviet Union did not necessarily have authority to negotiate a deal on behalf of the Vietnamese; and none of Wilson's diplomatic efforts resulted in an agreement, which possibly undermined Wilson's international standing while distracting him from other foreign policy issues.[70] The Labour Party continued to complain vociferously over Vietnam and Wilson's refusal to condemn the US undoubtedly hurt the party in terms of alienating many liberals as well as those on the left. Wilson was seen by many not only as a pragmatist, but also as having sacrificed his socialist principals for the sake of keeping in with the Americans. As soon as Labour lost the 1970 election, the party line changed to one of outright condemnation of the US intervention in Vietnam.

Defence and Britain's role in the world

There were a number of security issues facing the incoming Labour government in 1964, but the two most immediate and far-reaching were the future of Britain's independent nuclear deterrent, and the future of Britain's overall defence commitments in the context both of mounting financial problems and of the over-stretch of Britain's conventional forces. In each of these, close defence relations with the US were maintained and even strengthened, for instance over defence procurement. Labour's 1964 manifesto had pledged a review of weapons expenditure and a greater emphasis on conventional forces, and promised to end the 'Tory nuclear pretence' of an independent British deterrent by renegotiating the Nassau agreement to buy Polaris from the US. Buying the American Polaris missile system, Labour argued, would mean that the United States would in effect have a veto over Britain's use of its nuclear capability, which undermined the whole point of Britain trying to retain an independent nuclear deterrent. Therefore, it was a waste of money. According to the manifesto, a

Labour government would either cancel the purchase of Polaris or the Polaris submarines would be handed over to NATO, as

> We are against the development of national nuclear deterrents ... and will put forward constructive proposals for integrating all NATO's nuclear weapons under effective political control so that all the partners in the Alliance have a proper share in their deployment and control.[71]

However, once in power Wilson, Defence Minister Denis Healey and Foreign Secretary Gordon Walker decided not to cancel the purchase of the Polaris missile system on the grounds that it was too far advanced to be cancelled except at an inordinate cost, and accepted the terms of the Nassau agreement negotiated between Kennedy and Macmillan for the purchase of Polaris.[72] This effectively meant the rejection of unilateral disarmament, which the left of the party had been advocating since the late 1950s. As Dean Rusk noted, while other defence commitments were being cut,

> The British nuclear deterrent has so far escaped the economy axe. The reason is simple. The nuclear deterrent is the most important of the great power symbols still in British possession. Although Wilson is committed to give it up, he has so far shown no disposition to do so.[73]

Britain's independent nuclear forces not only gave Britain the appearance of power and diplomatic leverage, but also remained the cornerstone of Britain's deterrence against Soviet aggression during the Wilson governments.

Wilson remained opposed to the American proposal for Britain to incorporate its nuclear capability into a combined West European MLF. Instead, he proposed that Britain would put its four Polaris submarines and its V-bomber force, which could potentially launch short-range nuclear bombs on Soviet territory, into NATO as part of an Atlantic nuclear force (ANF), on the basis that the US would contribute at least an equal number of Polaris submarines to the ANF. As far as Britain was concerned, 'This could be represented as taking the British out of the possession of a national nuclear deterrent and would be a real break through toward non-proliferation'.[74] The nuclear weapons would then be subject to collective NATO authority, but, Wilson explained to the Commons, the contributors of the weapons would enjoy a privileged position in the management of the ANF, would have a veto over its use, and dissemination of nuclear technology would be prevented.[75] Part of the rationale for both these plans was concern that West Germany might attempt to develop its own independent nuclear deterrent, which was a prospect that appalled both the British and the US administrations. However, the Americans rejected Wilson's plan, and in the end neither the plan for the MLF nor the ANF were developed. Denis Healey, the Defence Minister, also announced the cancellation of the production of the British TSR2 military aircraft, which could launch short-range nuclear bombs on Soviet territory, but unlike the V-bomber could fly under the Russian radar system. Instead, Britain would purchase fifty American F1-11 aircraft. This decision provoked grumbling from the left of the Labour Party over job losses. It also increased British reliance on the US for defence procurement and its nuclear deterrent.

The other main security issue that the 1964–70 Labour governments faced concerned the future of Britain's overall defence commitments, given the twin problems of over-stretch of existing defence resources, in particular troops, combined with the need to cut defence spending in light of Britain's increasing economic problems. When Labour came to power in 1964, Britain still retained the bulk of its global network of military bases that had been assembled during the heyday of the empire to protect Britain's colonies and its trade and supply routes. However, by the mid-1960s, Britain's financial problems, especially the massive balance of payments deficit, were such that it was clear that existing defence commitments could not be maintained. Indeed, it was estimated that three-eighths of the 1964 balance of payments deficit was accounted for by defence expenditure.[76] Nor was it clear why certain bases had been retained for so long, given that Britain no longer had to protect the trade routes to India, and that 'the political problems caused by large fixed bases in developing countries would increase as fast as their military utility, in the nuclear age, would diminish'.[77]

On 16 December 1964, Wilson informed the House of Commons that he would initiate a comprehensive review of Britain's defence needs and commitments. The 1964 defence estimate was for £2 billion, representing 7.1 per cent of GNP, and which was expected to increase to £2.4 billion during the next five years. Wilson therefore insisted that 'we have to relate our decisions in the field of defence to the broader objectives of our foreign policy and we have to relate both to the realities of the economic position which Britain faces'. Indeed, 'the plain fact is that we have been trying to do too much. The result has been gravely to weaken our economic strength and independence without producing viable defences.'[78] Consequently, Labour would develop a new defence policy, based on its comprehensive defence review, which would have a £2 billion budget ceiling. However, Wilson, like all of his predecessors, did not want to appear to be down-grading Britain's status as a world power. He therefore continued that 'we cannot afford to relinquish our world role – our role which, for shorthand purposes, is sometimes called our "east of Suez" role'. Britain's world role is 'one which no one in this House or indeed in the country, will wish us to give up or call in question'. In particular, Britain had much to contribute to international peacekeeping, either as part of a UN force, or on its own, and what impressed 'our Americans allies' in terms of Britain's claim to be a world power, was not its nuclear weapons, but 'our ability to mount peacekeeping operations that no one else can mount'.[79] Denis Healey also emphasised Britain's need to maintain a military capacity of mobile conventional forces outside Europe in order to undertake peacekeeping operations when needed in Africa, or the Middle East or Asia, and to perform a world role that no other country was capable of.[80]

Denis Healey presented the long-awaited defence review on 22 February 1966, calling it 'essentially an exercise in political and military realism'. He outlined how Labour would cut the previous Conservative government's planned expenditure by 16 per cent through savings gained by getting better value for money, by reducing substantially the deployment of British forces in the Mediterranean, and by cutting the level of forces in the Far East once the confrontation with Indonesia was over. Also, from 1968 Britain would give up its Aden base.[81] Overall, deployment of troops outside of Europe would be cut by 30 per cent, but responsibilities east of Suez would continue 'for many years'.[82] This plan was condemned by many within the Labour Party who had hoped for a more far-reaching review that abandoned Britain's residual imperial role and withdrew from the Far and Middle East, and which subsequently focused on Britain's defence role within Europe. As Kenneth Waltz remarked, the Labour government's new defence policy amounted to 'keeping the roles, reducing the means, and changing the rationalizations', of Britain's defence commitments.[83] Christopher Mayhew, Healey's junior Minister for the Navy, resigned in protest, arguing that 'the proposed cuts in resources are not matched by the proposed cuts in commitments and that the result will be strain on the Armed Forces, or dependence on the United States beyond what this House should accept'.[84]

Shortly after the defence review, Wilson called a general election for 31 March. The 1966 election manifesto argued that the defence review had achieved its objectives, and that under Labour there was a new realism in Britain's defence policy.[85] This time Labour was returned with a larger majority of ninety-seven seats. Somewhat ironically the improved majority signalled deterioration in Wilson's fortunes. People's expectations of what the government could achieve increased with the increased Commons majority, but Wilson's ability to deliver solutions to the multitude of problems that Britain faced appeared to decrease. At the same time his colleagues and the electorate were no longer willing to give him the benefit of the doubt.

The balance of payments crisis continued, which impacted on all areas of policy, including foreign policy and defence. While Wilson had been concerned to maintain Britain's east of Suez role, it rapidly became clear that this was no longer sustainable. The tide of opinion shifted during the economic crisis of 1966, which coincided with the cessation of the Indonesian policy of confrontation towards Malaysia in August 1966, and the issue became not whether Britain should withdraw, but when. As Darby points out, 'For all Harold Wilson's romantic conception of Britain's world role and his determination to preserve it, economic and political pressures forced his hand'.[86] In addition to Britain's economic constraints, the British army was suffering from over-stretch, with 54,000 men stationed in the Far East and 27,000 in the Middle East.[87] There was also increasing nationalist discontent to deal with as British bases in Aden, Cyprus and the Suez Canal became targets of nationalist agitation and symbols of continued British imperial repression, and thus increasingly expensive to maintain in return for a decreasing amount of security. On 27 July 1967 Dennis Healey outlined the Supplementary White Paper on Defence in the House of Commons, which marked the culmination of the Wilson government's defence review, and laid out Britain's defence strategy for a projected ten years ahead. This included major cuts in the armed forces in the Far East and Southeast Asia, with the removal of forces from Borneo and a reduction in the forces in Malaysia and Singapore, with the intention of withdrawing British forces altogether from Malaysia and Singapore by the mid-1970s – that is, the withdrawal of troops from east of Suez.[88]

The US administration did not approve of Wilson's plans and continued to urge most strongly that Britain keep its military presence in the Far East, but to no avail. The reasons for the ensuing withdrawal of troops were financial, military and political; financially, Britain could not afford to maintain its defence commitments; militarily, British forces were over-stretched and could not meet their commitments; and politically, Wilson wanted an announcement to appease the left of the Labour Party, which was growing increasingly restless over defence issues. Wilson then further annoyed the US in November 1967 by announcing that sterling would be devalued. In January 1968 it was announced that Britain's withdrawal from east of Suez would be accelerated, and would take place by the end of 1971. Thus, the three main issues on which the United States had sought British co-operation, and which Wilson had agreed to in the first few years of his premiership – no to devaluation, retention of military commitments east of Suez, and public support over Vietnam – had been rejected by the end of 1967.

There were a number of other defence and security issues that concerned the 1964–70 Wilson governments and which warrant a brief mention here. Diplomatic relations with the Soviet Union improved following the confrontation over the Cuban Missile Crisis, and Cold War tensions eased somewhat with the period of détente. Wilson also prided himself on his good personal relationships with Soviet politicians, having made a number of trips to the Soviet Union both before and after gaining office. However, the Soviet invasion of Czechoslovakia on 20 August 1968 caused consternation and shock within the government. Wilson issued a statement that called the Soviet intervention 'a flagrant violation of the United Nations Charter and of all accepted standards of international behaviour', and recalled Parliament to discuss the situation.[89] He felt that the invasion of Czechoslovakia highlighted the need for vigilance within the Western alliance, and for greater unity within Europe so that it could respond more strongly to any threat to its freedom.[90] The Arab-Israeli Six Day war of June 1967 also caused alarm, not least because about 70 per cent of British oil imports came from Arab sources at that time.[91]

Other security issues developed nearer to home. Tension, civil unrest and intimidation between Catholic and Protestant communities in Northern Ireland had increased to such an extent that following a riot on 12 August 1969 during an Orange Day parade, the Unionist government of Northern Ireland requested that Wilson provide troops to police the situation. Wilson agreed, on condition that the cause of the disturbances would be investigated. The subsequent Hunt and Cameron Reports were critical of civil rights abuses of the Catholic minority and of security operations in Northern Ireland. In particular, the Hunt Report of October 1970 recommended that the B-Special auxiliary police, who were seen by the Catholics as a discriminatory Protestant force, should be abolished.[92] The British army moved onto the streets of Belfast and Londonderry and took over responsibility for maintaining law and order. While some saw the mobilisation of the British army in Northern Ireland as a temporary measure which would be required for a few months only, Wilson apparently said in private the British troops would have to remain in the Province for at least seven years.[93] Another problematic issue that the Wilson governments had to deal with was Southern Rhodesia, where the white minority government announced a Unilateral Declaration of Independence (UDI) in response to Britain's plans to introduce universal suffrage to the colony.

Southern Rhodesia

Southern Rhodesia was a self-governing British dependency, which was governed on the basis of apartheid and white minority rule. Britain had been urging Rhodesia to widen the franchise to include the black population, while the Rhodesian regime wanted to continue its existing system of white rule. The Rhodesian Front had been elected to power at the end of 1963 and had asked Britain for independence, which the Conservative government had refused. In April 1964, Ian Smith ousted the existing Prime Minister, Winston Field, and immediately threatened to make a UDI. This would undermine Britain's credibility both in the international arena and more specifically in the Commonwealth, where the Rhodesian Front regime was seen as completely unacceptable. Wilson refused to grant independence unless the Smith government promised unimpeded progress to majority rule and progress towards ending racial discrimination.

However, Smith was not prepared to offer any concessions, and embarked on a clampdown of opposition groups. The black Zimbabwe African National Union (ZANU) and Zimbabwe African People's Union (ZAPU) were banned, their leaders imprisoned without trial, and the press tightly controlled. Wilson attempted to negotiate privately with Smith in order to find a solution, meeting with him at the occasion of Winston Churchill's funeral on 30 January 1965. No progress was made, and a visit by Smith in October 1965 also ended in deadlock. If anything, Smith returned to Rhodesia with a heightened determination to declare independence, as he had been told that Britain would not retaliate with the use of force. Smith's advisor was convinced that if Britain had threatened to use force, Smith would have backed down, as Rhodesia did not have the capability to resist attack.[94] However, given Labour's tiny Commons majority, Wilson would have needed support from both Labour and Conservative MPs to invade or attack Rhodesia, which would not have been forthcoming. Furthermore, Britain did not have troops in the region that could be mobilised for such an assault, and the cost of military action would have problematic given that the government was planning large-scale cuts to the defence budget. Thus, while some Commonwealth members proposed that Britain consider taking military action to overthrow the Smith regime, it was never a serious option within British political circles. Instead, Wilson went to Rhodesia in a last-ditch attempt to persuade Smith to a compromise, to the consternation of his advisors. As Pimlott puts it, Wilson 'believed – as highly intelligent people sometimes do when confronted by an opponent who is behaving illogically – that Smith could still be talked round'. The visit was a disaster, serving to demonstrate Britain's weakness and inability to control events, as 'the ultra-reactionary Rhodesian Cabinet regarded the British premier with macho scorn, while he treated them with headmasterly distaste'.[95]

On 11 November 1965, Ian Smith issued the threatened UDI. Britain refused to acknowledge the legal independence of Southern Rhodesia before satisfactory constitutional arrangements could be established for African majority rule, and so declared the Smith government to be illegal. However, while Wilson said that it was the duty of the people of Rhodesia to refrain from doing anything which would assist the Smith regime in its rebellion against the British Crown, he also maintained that it was the duty of public servants in Rhodesia to carry on with their jobs in order to help to maintain law and order.[96] Ultimately, 'The practical effect was to "legitimize" the action of public servants, who decided to continue to function just as they always had before November 11, 1965'.[97] Smith also acted in defiance of Britain by proclaiming a new constitution.

Southern Rhodesia was an unwelcome remnant of a colonial era. Decolonisation had accelerated in the early 1960s under Prime Minister Harold Macmillan following his declaration to the South African Parliament in 1960 that the days of colonialism were over and that the 'winds of change' were blowing through Africa. Labour was committed to continuing this process of decolonisation, granting independence to Gambia in 1965, Botswana, Guyana and Lesotho in 1966 and Swaziland in 1968. Northern Rhodesia had been granted independence as the Republic of Zambia on 24 October 1964. For Labour though, the issue of what do to do about Southern Rhodesia was more problematic than it had been for the Conservatives, given the party's anti-colonial and anti-racist stance. To fail to take some kind of retaliatory action would have been seen as a sell-out by Commonwealth members and would have appalled Labour Party members. Simply turning the matter over to the UN would have made Britain look weak at best, and would itself have achieved little. The Labour government's response to the announcement of the UDI was to impose sanctions on imports from Southern Rhodesia and an embargo against oil exports to Rhodesia, and to freeze financial assets in London. Wilson thought such sanctions would be enough to force the Smith regime to back down, a calculation which led him to reassure the special Commonwealth Prime Ministers' Conference in Lagos in January 1966 – which Nigeria had insisted be called to discuss Rhodesia – that the collapse of the Rhodesian economy would occur in 'a matter of weeks rather than months'. In this he was mistaken, for Wilson had overestimated the effect of sanctions – which were ignored by Rhodesia's main trading partner, South Africa – and underestimated the amount of time it would take for the Smith regime to fall. Subsequently, 'The survival of the Smith regime became a testament to British impotence, and fallen status'.[98] However, this was not apparent when Britain went to the polls in March 1966.

The Rhodesia problem continued to haunt the re-elected Labour government throughout its second term. In November 1966 Wilson was still trying to find ways of keeping the dialogue going, believing that his ministerial colleagues were being defeatist for feeling that there was no point in further negotiations. Richard Crossman noted that 'The trouble is that for Harold this is his Dunkirk or his Cuba', and he was determined not to admit that Britain had failed over Rhodesia.[99] Wilson also wanted to bring to an end the criticism he was facing from within the Labour Party, the Commonwealth and the international community. Talks between Wilson and Smith were held on HMS *Tiger* in December 1966 and on HMS *Fearless* in October 1968, but the Smith regime refused to accept the formula adopted by Wilson of 'no independence before majority rule'. The ongoing situation revealed Britain's weakness in dealing with the Commonwealth and its impotence to act alone. Institutionally, the Commonwealth Relations Office was seen to have failed in its purpose. It was renamed the Department of Commonwealth Affairs in August 1966 when it was merged with the Colonial Office (which was abolished in January 1967), and was then merged with the Foreign Office on 17 October 1968. As Arthur Bottomley, the Commonwealth Relations Minister pointed out, 'The way in which the Rhodesian rebellion is brought to an end will determine the future of the modern Commonwealth'.[100] The Rhodesian 'rebellion' did not end until the late 1970s.

One of the consequences of the impasse over Southern Rhodesia was that it demonstrated the weakness of Britain's political leadership of the Commonwealth and led Wilson to rethink the future of Britain's Commonwealth role. Wilson had previously ruled out a closer relationship with Europe as this implied placing less emphasis on Britain's Commonwealth ties, especially as it would mean the abandonment of free entry of Commonwealth goods to Britain. Indeed, one of Labour's five conditions that would constitute 'reasonable terms of entry' to the Common Market outlined in 1962 had been the safeguarding of trade between Britain and the rest of the Commonwealth. However, by 1966, Commonwealth countries were decreasing their trade with Britain and were seeking to increase their trade with the EC. On returning from the Commonwealth Prime Ministers Conference in January 1966, Wilson endorsed secret studies of the implications of Britain's membership of the EC.[101]

Wilson's bid to join the European Community

The Labour Party had not supported the terms of the Macmillan government's bid for entry to the European Community (EC) in 1963, which the French President Charles de Gaulle had vetoed. Wilson was not known to be in favour of British membership, and so another bid to enter seemed very unlikely. However, by the summer of 1966, Wilson had undergone a change of heart, and a second bid for membership of the EC was firmly on the political agenda. In response to the sterling crisis of July 1966, Wilson had pushed through Cabinet an austerity programme that meant cuts in many areas, including a six-month standstill on all wages and salaries, to be followed by six months of severe restraint. Many in the Labour government felt by this time that Wilson should have taken the opportunity to devalue, but Wilson was not even allowing devaluation to be discussed in Cabinet meetings for fear of leaks precipitating the event that he was trying to avoid. These cuts meant that it was impossible for Labour to implement its domestic programme outlined in its 1966 election manifesto. As a result of the worsening economic situation, the attraction of joining the European Community increased. The economies of the EC members were growing while Britain's was in decline, and many business leaders, economists and even Labour politicians had come to the conclusion that entry to the EC could provide the basis for a revived British economy.

However, the Labour Party remained deeply divided over membership of the EC. Labour's commitment to internationalism was seen in terms of its role in the UN, its relationship with the Commonwealth countries and the Anglo-American relationship, rather than in terms of Britain's role in Europe. Many in the party felt that joining the EC would actually hamper Britain's world role, in particular by undermining ties to the Commonwealth, and that it could hamper the development of socialism at home. Indeed, 'In the sixties, the left saw the Common Market as a capitalist conspiracy to frustrate socialism'.[103] Within the Cabinet, George Brown, Roy Jenkins and Michael Stewart were firmly in favour of joining the EC, and several other members, such as Barbara Castle on the left and Douglas Jay on the right, were firmly opposed. Callaghan, who previously been firmly against joining the EC, came out in favour of joining in October 1966 as he felt it was the only way to end the crisis of confidence in industry and the pressure on sterling. Denis Healey was fairly agnostic, but was against Britain making another bid for membership in 1966 'not least because I was certain that Wilson would be no more successful than Macmillan, so long as de Gaulle was alive'.[104] Wilson had not previously been in favour of joining as he had felt that this would look like Britain was deserting the Commonwealth, and because he staked so much on the Anglo-American relationship, though by this point the US was very keen for Britain to enter the EC. The State Department's view was that the 'UK's long-term economic problems are most likely to be solved if UK industry is subjected to the pervasive effect of a large and competitive market; and that the common US and UK interest in an outward looking Europe will only be assured if the UK plays a leading role in the European Community'.[105] It was 'basically unhealthy to encourage the United Kingdom to continue as America's poor relation, living beyond her means by periodic American bailouts. We must, in other words, redefine the so-called "special relationship"', and 'Britain should join the Common Market, and offer to sign the Rome Treaty as now written'.[106]

On 10 November Wilson told the House of Commons that the government had conducted 'a deep and searching review of the whole problem of Britain's relationship with the E.E.C.' and 'Every aspect of the Treaty of Rome … and all the implications and consequences which might be expected to flow from British entry, have been examined in depth'. Wilson and the Foreign Secretary, George Brown, would engage in a series of discussions with the member states, and the government was approaching these discussions 'with the clear intention and determination to enter the E.E.C. if, as we hope, our essential British and Commonwealth interests can be safeguarded. We mean business.'[107] Richard Crossman noted that there was no cheer from the somewhat flabbergasted Labour MPs who did not know whether to praise the statement or not. 'Altogether it was a disappointing great occasion. There was no sense of history partly because the Statement may have been difficult to assess at first hearing, especially when people know that Mr Wilson is a crafty little man, and partly because it sounded so curiously *ad hoc*.'[108]

Wilson and Brown embarked on their trip round the capitals of the EC member countries to hold their exploratory talks on British membership in January 1967. Brown notes that 'Gradually our line got firmer and firmer, and by the time we had finished we had virtually decided to make our application'.[109] At the end of their tour, Brown and Wilson submitted to Cabinet a report proposing a bid to enter Europe before the next election. This was passed at a Cabinet meeting at Chequers on 30 April, where ministers voted by thirteen to eight for an unconditional bid. This marked a shift from the previous Labour Party position of being in favour of joining eventually, but only after certain conditions, such as the safeguarding of trade between Britain and the rest of the Commonwealth and guarantees to safeguard the position of British agriculture, had been met. By removing these conditions, Wilson hoped to minimise the opportunity for de Gaulle to veto Britain's entry to the EC. The proposal was presented to the House of Commons as a White Paper in early May, where it received support from the Conservative Party. Both Wilson and Heath refused to allow their parties a free vote on the proposal to enter the EC, which was carried by 488 votes to sixty-two. Despite a three-line whip, thirty-six Labour MPs voted against entry, with fifty-one abstaining. Britain's formal application to join the EEC was made on 11 May 1967.

On 16 May de Gaulle gave a press conference at which he argued that Britain was not economically ready for entry, while insisting that he was not actually vetoing British entry. Despite this rebuff, Wilson pressed on with his bid to enter Europe. He again visited de Gaulle on 19 June, where de Gaulle expressed his concerns over Anglo-American relations, and his doubts that Britain was ready to follow a policy distinct from that of America. His concern was that if Britain joined the European Community, 'Britain would introduce an element that inclined towards an Atlantic type of Community'. This was why he was cautious about British entry.[110] Wilson was still optimistic that agreement could be met with de Gaulle, but France formally vetoed the British application on 27 November 1967. This was shortly after Wilson had finally taken the step of devaluing sterling from $2.80 to $2.40, an action which the government had thought would demonstrate to the EC members that Britain was determined to tackle its economic problems, and which had been viewed as a pre-requisite for membership. The French veto was a disappointment and an embarrassment for the government at the time. However, recent accounts have argued that this second application to the EC 'represented a "successful failure" for the Prime Minister and, indeed, for British European policy. This was because it 'satisfied a number of personal, domestic and party ends and, by demonstrating Britain's commitment to a European future, prepared the foundations for Britain's entry' to the EC in 1973.[111] According to Helen Parr, 'Wilson's strategic priority in 1967 was to ensure British accession to the European Community whether or not the initiative failed in the short term'.[112]

Wilson managed to maintain party unity during the run-up to the 1970 general election by avoiding discussion of Labour's position on the EC, even though discussions for entry had been due to begin again shortly after the date of the election. Once the party was in opposition, this fragile unity did not hold, and many in the party shifted away from support of membership of the EC, and it quickly became clear that the issue was becoming deeply divisive for Labour.

The foreign policy of the Wilson governments was marked by the ongoing debate about Britain's role in the world. Despite the disappointment over Europe, the withdrawal from east of Suez, the failure to reach an agreement on Southern Rhodesia, and the ongoing realisation that Britain's relative economic decline meant that it could not return to the days when Britain really was a great power, Wilson continued to present himself as a major player on the world stage. Indeed, his attachment to Britain's world role and its imperial legacy prevented him from accepting sooner what many in his party argued, namely that Britain should retreat from its old imperial commitments east of Suez, not merely for economic reasons, but for ideological ones as well. Indeed, in terms of foreign policy, there appeared to be little retained of Wilson the left-wing opposition MP. Edward Heath complained shortly after the 1970 general election that Wilson's foreign policy decisions were influenced by 'considerations of party unity', or due to 'emotional pressures', and were based on short-term factors, and did not reflect the national interest.[113] However, there is little evidence of this, and whereas the Labour Party in the early 1960s had been fairly united on foreign and defence policy, by the end of the decade there were enormous divisions over foreign policy.

Despite the optimism and expectations of change when Wilson came to power in 1964, Wilson's foreign policy decisions were largely pragmatic, and actually caused a great deal of moral anguish to Labour Party members. He asked his Cabinet in the Autumn of 1967 to reconsider whether to sell weapons to South Africa, even though the UN Security Council had passed three resolutions in 1963 and 1964 that banned the sale of arms, military vehicles and equipment for the manufacture and maintenance of arms and ammunition to South Africa.[114] Wilson also continued to sell arms to the Nigerian government following the outbreak of civil war in 1967 when the eastern region of the country declared itself the independent state of Biafra. While publicly the British government said it was taking a 'neutral' position on the conflict, by supplying arms to the federal government it was clearly supporting the cause of a united Nigeria. Britain had extensive trade and investment links with Nigeria, and received around one-tenth of its oil imports from the eastern region of the country, and it was felt that these would be at risk if Britain shifted its support away from the federal government.[115] Wilson's view was that as Britain was the traditional supplier of arms to the Nigerian government, to stop selling weapons would be a hostile act against a Commonwealth country. As Nigeria would then turn to the Soviet Union for weapons, it would increase Soviet influence and diminish British influence in Nigeria.[116] This was despite growing public concern and discontent within the Labour Party at all levels over the plight of the Biafrans, with estimates of between 500,000 and one million civilians dying of malnutrition during the civil war. As we have seen, Wilson was not opposed to sending troops to Vietnam for moral purposes, and Wilson's refusal to condemn the US undoubtedly hurt the party in terms of alienating many on the left, and resulting in an upsurge of New Left groups. Wilson was seen as a pragmatist and as having sacrificed his socialist principals for the sake of keeping in with the Americans. However, despite this, Wilson was successful in resisting demands from the US administration for British troops to be sent to Vietnam. Indeed, while the Vietnam War became part of the lexicon of the left that the party had been betrayed by Wilson, with hindsight it can be argued that Wilson did actually manage the issue of British policy on the Vietnam

War fairly successfully, in that he managed to keep Britain out of the Vietnam War and yet retain the 'special relationship' with the US.

Notes

1 James Callaghan, *Time and Chance* (London: Collins, 1987), p. 150.
2 Harold Wilson, *Memoirs: The Making of a Prime Minister 1916–64* (London: Weidenfeld & Nicolson and Michael Joseph, 1986), p. 192.
3 *Labour Party Annual Conference Report* (hereafter LPACR), 1963, p. 140.
4 'Let's Go with Labour for the New Britain', Labour manifesto 1964, in *British General Election Manifestos, 1900–1974*, compiled and edited by F.W.S. Craig (London: Macmillan, revised and enlarged edn, 1975), p. 255.
5 David Butler and Gareth Butler, *British Political Facts 1900–1985* (London: Macmillan, 6th edn, 1986), p. 227.
6 Edward Short, *Whip to Wilson: The Crucial Years of the Labour Government* (London: Macdonald, 1989), p. 21.
7 Harold Wilson, *The Labour Government 1964–1970: A Personal Record* (London: Weidenfeld & Nicolson, 1971), pp. 2–3.
8 Callaghan, *Time and Chance*, p. 159.
9 The National Archives, London (hereafter TNA), PREM 13/103, Derek Mitchell to Lord Harlech, 30 November 1964, with note of conversation with Richard Neustadt on 29 November.
10 TNA, PREM 13/104, 'The Prime Minister's Visit to the United States and Canada', 6-10 December 1964, p. 31.
11 TNA, PREM 13/104, telegram from Prime Minister to First Secretary of State, No. 4046, 9 December 1964.
12 Barbara Castle, *The Castle Diaries 1964–1970* (London: Weidenfeld & Nicolson, 1984), p. 78.
13 TNA, PREM 13/1262 letter from Sir Patrick Dean, British Ambassador to Washington, to C.M. MacLehose, Foreign Office, 6 August 1966.
14 US National Archives II, RG59 1964-66, POL 1 UK-US, Box 2786, airgram A-2843 from US Embassy in London to State Department, Washington, 'A View of US-UK Policy Relations', 23 May 1966.
15 Callaghan, *Time and Chance*, p. 159.
16 Clive Ponting, *Breach of Promise: Labour in Power 1964–1970* (London: Hamish Hamilton, 1989), pp. 52–3.
17 See C.J. Bartlett, *"The Special Relationship": A Political History of Anglo-American Relations Since 1945* (London: Longman, 1992), pp. 110–11; Alan Dobson, *The Politics of the Anglo-American Economic Special Relationship 1940–1987* (Brighton: Wheatsheaf, 1988), pp. 213–14; Ponting, *Breach of Promise*, pp. 53–4.
18 Roy Jenkins, review of Ponting's *Breach of Promise*, *Observer*, 5 March 1989.
19 Richard Crossman, *The Diaries of a Cabinet Minister, Volume 1: Minister of Housing, 1964–66* (London: Hamish Hamilton and Jonathan Cape, 1975), 14 February 1966, p. 456.

20 Michael Stewart, *Life and Labour: An Autobiography* (London: Sidgwick and Jackson, 1980), p. 151.

21 For a more detailed account, see Rhiannon Vickers, 'Harold Wilson, the British Labour Party and the war in Vietnam', *Journal of Cold War Studies*, 10:2 (Spring 2008), pp. 43–72.

22 TNA, PREM 13/1262, Letter from Sir Patrick Dean, British Ambassador to Washington, to C.M. MacLehose, Foreign Office, 6 August 1966.

23 Fredrik Logevall, *Choosing War: The Lost Chance of Peace and the Escalation of War in Vietnam* (Berkeley, LA: University of California Press, 1999), p. 373.

24 Jack Jones, *Union Man: The Autobiography of Jack Jones* (London: Collins, 1986), p. 176.

25 Labour Party archive, Museum of Labour History, Manchester, Jo Richardson papers, RICH/3/1/3, Tribune Group Meeting of 15 March 1965. See also N.H. Twitchell, *The Tribune Group: Factional Conflict in the Labour Party 1964–1970* (London: Rabbit Publications, 1998), p. 28.

26 These were discussed at the NEC meeting of 27 January, 1965. Resolutions from constituency parties, January 1965, in Labour Party archive, Overseas Department, OV/1963-4/32.

27 Labour Party archive, Overseas Department, OV/1965/7, Resolutions from constituency parties, 9 March 1965.

28 Labour Party archive, NEC/5/1964-5, NEC minutes of meeting 28 April 1965, referring to resolutions in constituency parties, Overseas Department, OV/1965/9.

29 Labour Party archive, Overseas Department, OV/1965/11, Resolutions from constituency parties, 11 May 1965; OV/1965/14, Resolutions from constituency parties, 13 July 1965.

30 Labour Party archive, PLP minutes, 12 May 1965.

31 *LPACR*, 1965, Appendix III, p. 278. This was a slightly toned-down version of the draft proposed by the Overseas Department, in Labour Party archive, NEC mins 25 September 1965, OV/6, 7 September 1965.

32 Wilson, *Labour Government*, p. 85; TNA, PREM 13/693, telegram from Philip Noel-Baker to Michael Stewart, 22 March 1965.

33 TNA, PREM 13/693, Sydney Silverman to Harold Wilson, 22 March 1965.

34 TNA, PREM/13/693, Harold Wilson to Michael Stewart, tel. no. 2328, 23 March 1965.

35 TNA, PREM 13/693 DV 103145/60, Record of a Conversation between the Foreign Secretary and Dean Rusk, 23 March 1965.

36 Wilson, *Labour Government*, pp. 85–6.

37 *House of Commons Debates* (hereafter *H.C. Deb.*), vol. 709, 23 March 1965, cols 324–8.

38 For example, *H.C. Deb.*, vol. 722, 21 December 1965, col. 1909; H.C. Deb., vol. 724, 8 February 1966, col. 259.

39 US National Archives II, RG59 1964–66, POL 1 UK-US, Box 2786,

telegram from Department of State to US Embassy in London, 28 May 1966, referring to message from Wilson to Johnson, 24 May 1966.

40 *H.C. Deb.*, vol. 731, 7 July 1966, col. 682.

41 US National Archives II, RG59 1964–66, POL 1 UK-US, Box 2786, telegram from David Bruce, London, to Acting Secretary of State, Washington, 3 July 1966.

42 US National Archives II, RG59 1964–66, POL 1 UK-US, Box 2786, telegram from David Bruce, London, to Secretary of State, Washington, 2 June 1966.

43 *LPACR*, 1965, pp. 182–200.

44 *LPACR*, 1966, p. 255. For the resolution 3,851,000; against 2,644,000, p. 273.

45 *Ibid.*, pp. 256 and 302.

46 *Ibid.*, p. 302. Lewis Minkin, *The Labour Party Conference: A Study in the Politics of Intra-Party Democracy* (Manchester: Manchester University Press, 1980), p. 291, takes the decision to mean a rejection of the government's policy on Vietnam.

47 *LPACR*, 1967, pp. 223–5.

48 *Ibid.*, pp. 235–6.

49 Minkin says this occurred six times, but this number includes the debatable example of the 1966 resolution. Minkin, *The Labour Party Conference*, p. 291.

50 *LPACR*, 1968, p. 299.

51 Speech by Harold Wilson to the meeting of the PLP on 15 June 1966, in LPA, PLP mins 1964–66.

52 Author's interview with Lord Tom McNally, 25 July 2006, House of Lords.

53 Minkin, *The Labour Party Conference*, p. 290.

54 See Rhiannon Vickers, *The Labour Party and the World, Volume 1: The Evolution of Labour's Foreign Policy, 1900–51* (Manchester: Manchester University Press, 2004), pp. 168–71.

55 *LPACR*, 1970, p. 180.

56 Short, *Whip to Wilson*, pp. 97, 117 and 160.

57 Labour Party archive, NEC mins, 2 November 1966.

58 Labour Party archive, International Department, ID/1970–71/65, held in NEC mins, box LI, 23 June 1971, Foreign Policy Formation, written by Tom McNally, June 1970.

59 John McDermott, *Vietnam Profile: A History of the Vietnam Conflict and its Origins* (London: CND, 1965); Peggy Duff, *Vietnam: The Credibility Gap* (London: CND, no date); *Vietnam Briefing* (London: CND, no date). All available in Labour Party archive, 328.68 Vietnam Pamphlets.

60 Campaign for Nuclear Disarmament archive, Modern Record Centre, University of Warwick, MSS 181/6 Box 90.29, Letter from Stockholm World Conference on Vietnam editorial committee to W. H. Ferry, 22 February 1967.

61 John Callaghan, *British Trotskyism: Theory and Practice* (Oxford: Basil Blackwell, 1984), p. 128.

62 Sylvia Ellis, "'A demonstration of British good sense?" British student

protest during the Vietnam War', in Gerard DeGroot (ed.), *Student Protest: The Sixties and After* (London: Longman 1998), pp. 54 and 56.

63 Kenneth O. Morgan, *The People's Peace: British History 1945–1990* (Oxford: Oxford University Press, 1992 edn), p. 294.

64 Tariq Ali, *1968 and After: Inside the Revolution* (London: Blond and Briggs, 1978), p. vii.

65 See Stephen Dorril and Robin Ramsay, *Smear! Wilson and the Secret State* (London: Grafton, 1992 edn.), pp. 185–6.

66 James Callaghan, *A House Divided: The Dilemma of Northern Ireland* (London: Collins, 1973), p. 8; Callaghan, *Time and Chance*, p. 258.

67 See Ellis, 'British student protest during the Vietnam War,' pp. 63–4.

68 Peter Shore Papers, British Library of Political and Economic Science, London, 527 Vietnam, *Venture*, 17:4 (April 1965), published by the Fabian Society.

69 Hugh Jenkins Papers, British Library of Political and Economic Science, London, 1/2 Vietnam Fund, letter from Hugh Jenkins to the Ambassador for Vietnam in London, 3 November 1965.

70 See, for example, John Dumbrell and Sylvia Ellis, 'British involvement in Vietnam peace initiatives, 1966–1967: marigolds, sunflowers and "Kosygin Week"', *Diplomatic History*, 27:1 (2003), pp. 113–49.

71 Craig, *British General Election Manifestos, 1900–1974*, pp. 271–2.

72 Wilson, *Labour Government*, p. 40.

73 US National Archives II. RG59 1964–66, POL 7 Box 2779, memo from Dean Rusk to the President, visit of Prime Minister Wilson July 19, 1966, 27 July 1966.

74 US National Archives II, RG59 1964–66, POL 7 Box 2779, memo from Dean Rusk to the President, visit of Prime Minister Wilson, 19 December 1965.

75 *H.C. Deb.*, vol. 704, 16 December 1964, cols. 434–8.

76 Hugh Hanning, 'Britain east of Suez – facts and figures', *Review of International Studies*, 42:2 (April 1966), p. 225.

77 Michael Howard, 'Britain's strategic problem east of Suez', *Review of International Studies*, 42:2 (April 1966), p. 181.

78 *H.C. Deb.*, vol. 704, 16 December 1965, cols 418–21.

79 *Ibid.*, cols 419, 423–6.

80 *Ibid.*, col. 612.

81 *H.C. Deb.*, vol. 725, 22 February 1966, col. 240.

82 *Ibid.*, 7 March 1966, cols. 1778–9.

83 Kenneth Waltz, *Foreign Policy and Democratic Politics: The American and British Experience* (London: Longmans, 1968), p. 156.

84 *H.C. Deb.*, vol. 725, 22 February 1966, col. 255.

85 Craig, *British General Election Manifestos, 1900–1974*, pp. 308–9.

86 Phillip Darby, *British Defence Policy East of Suez 1947–1968* (London: Oxford University Press for the RIIA, 1973), p. 283.

87 Hanning, 'Britain east of Suez', p. 253.

88 *H.C. Deb.*, vol. 751, 27 July 1967, cols 989–94; Wilson, *Labour Government*, p. 422.

89 See *H.C. Deb.*, vol. 769, 26 August 1968, cols 1273–420.

90 Wilson, *Labour Government*, pp. 552–4.

91 Crossman files, Modern Records Centre, MSS 154/3/DH/4/68-99, Joint Intelligence Committee report, 'British Economic Interests in Israel and the Arab World', JIC (B) (69) 33 Final, 30 September 1969.

92 See, for example, Caroline Kennedy-Pipe, *The Origins of the Present Troubles in Northern Ireland* (London: Longman, 1997), pp. 49–51.

93 Ben Pimlott, *Harold Wilson* (London: HarperCollins, 1993 edn), p. 549.

94 Ken Flower, *Serving Secretly: An Intelligence Chief on Record. Rhodesia into Zimbabwe 1964 to 1981* (London: John Murray, 1987), p. 51.

95 Pimlott, *Harold Wilson*, p. 369.

96 *H.C. Deb.*, vol. 720, 11 November 1965, cols 349–62.

97 Robert Blake, *A History of Rhodesia* (New York: Alfred Knopf, 1978), p. 389.

98 Pimlott, *Harold Wilson*, p. 381.

99 *Richard Crossman, The Diaries of a Cabinet Minister, vol. 2, Lord President of the Council and Leader of the House of Commons, 1966–68* (London: Hamish Hamilton and Jonathan Cape, 1976), 8 November 1966, p. 114.

100 Bottomley Papers, British Library of Political and Economic Science, Box 10, notes for speech 8 March 1966.

101 Helen Parr and Melissa Pine, 'Policy towards the European Economic Community', in Peter Dorey, ed., *The Labour Governments 1964–1970* (London: Routledge, 2006), p. 112.

102 The EEC became the EC on 1 July 1967.

103 Author's interview with Lord McNally, 25 July 2006.

104 Healey, *The Time of My Life*, p. 330.

105 US National Archives II, RG59 1964–66, POL 7 Box 2779, memo by Dean Rusk to the President re 'Wilson Visit', 24 July 1966.

106 US National Archives II, RG59 1964–66, POL 7 Box 2779, memo by George Ball to the President re 'Harold Wilson's Visit – The Opportunity for an Act of Statesmanship', 21 July 1966.

107 *H.C. Deb.*, vol. 735, 10 November 1966, cols 1539–40.

108 Crossman, *Diaries, Vol. 2*, 10 November 1966, pp. 118–19.

109 Brown, *In My Way*, p. 206.

110 Wilson, *Labour Government*, p. 409.

111 Oliver Daddow, ed., *Harold Wilson and European Integration: Britain's Second Application to Join the EEC* (London: Frank Cass, 2003), p. 2.

112 Helen Parr, *Britain's Policy Towards the European Community: Harold Wilson and Britain's World Role, 1965–1967* (London: Routledge, 2006), p. 10.

113 *H.C. Deb.*, vol. 803, col. 82, 2 July 1970.

114 See Tim Bale, '"A deplorable episode"? South African arms and the statecraft of British social democracy', *Labour History Review*, 62:1 (Spring 1997), pp. 22–40.

115 TNA, PREM 13/2261, memo 'Why we support the Federal Government', December 1968.

116 Wilson, *Labour Government*, pp. 555–7.

Chapter 4

Defence and foreign policy in the 1970s

At the general election of 18 June 1970, the Conservatives won with 330 seats and 46 per cent of the vote, while Labour achieved 287 seats and 43 per cent of the vote.[1] At the time, Labour's loss of power came as a shock to the party. Subsequently, however, left-wing critics have tended to see the 1970 result as 'somehow fitting – a disastrous end for a disastrous government'.[2] According to one Labour insider, there 'was somehow this idea that the government had betrayed the party and betrayed the manifesto', although he believes that the 1964–70 government 'will stand as one of the great social reforming governments of the century'.[3] With Wilson keen to keep control of the manifesto, the writing of it had been delayed until the eve of the campaign, and the manifesto had largely promised a continuation of existing policies.

For Wilson, losing in 1970 was both a 'shock and humiliation', and left him determined not to be 'bundled out again' from 10 Downing Street.[4] It was the first time that he had suffered 'unequivocal and calamitous defeat', and losing to Heath was a particularly bitter blow as Wilson both 'disliked and despised' him.[5] Wilson began writing *The Labour Government 1964–1970: A Personal Record* in July 1970, and the 850-page book was published in July 1971. Despite the election defeat, Wilson had no direct challenger for the party leadership at that time, and no leadership contest was held. An election was held for the deputy leadership of the party, which was won by Roy Jenkins.

During the early 1970s the Labour Party moved to the left in its political programme. This was partly as a reaction against six years in government, partly in an attempt to recuperate its base inside the trade unions and reconnect with the constituency parties and, according to Callaghan, partly because 'changes in the organisation of the Labour

Party had resulted in the influx of a number of extreme left-wing very active Militants'.[6] As a consequence, foreign policy positions also moved leftwards. Party divisions over whether Britain should join the EC re-emerged, but the biggest shift was over defence policy and nuclear weapons. Whereas the party had been fairly acquiescent over Britain's nuclear policy during the 1964–70 Wilson governments, once Labour lost power, its attitude changed. Resolutions passed at the 1972 and 1973 annual conferences advocated the dissolution of NATO, the closure of nuclear bases, and the rejection of a British defence policy based on the threat of the use of nuclear weapons. Over Vietnam – the issue that had caused so much division in the 1960s – the party was pretty much united. The Conservative manifesto made no mention of Vietnam, whereas Labour's merely stated that 'A lasting settlement in Indo-China must be based on the Geneva agreement and the withdrawal of all foreign troops', and that 'Labour believes that no purely military solution is possible'.[7] Now in opposition, the Labour Party was more supportive of resolutions sent in from constituency parties condemning the Vietnam War.[8] In May 1972 the International Committee of the Labour Party issued a statement condemning the decision of President Nixon to escalate the war by mining and blockading North Vietnamese ports, urging the immediate recall of the Geneva Conference, and expressing its strong support for those in the US who were urging the withdrawal of American forces from Vietnam and an end to the war.[9] In December 1972 the party's NEC issued a statement condemning the American resumption of bombing in Vietnam, saying 'This continued slaughter of the Vietnamese people is a complete contradiction of the statements made by both Mr. Nixon and Dr. Kissinger in the days leading up to the recent Presidential elections'.[10] On 27 January 1973 the US and North Vietnam signed the Paris Peace Accords, and the US withdrew its ground forces from Vietnam, though the conflict between South and North Vietnam continued. In February 1973 a delegation of three MPs, including the shadow Foreign Secretary James Callaghan, went on a three-week visit of the area, and held meetings with the President of South Vietnam, and the Prime Ministers of North Vietnam and Laos respectively.[11] At the end of their mission the delegation concluded that Labour Party policy should urge that all participants implement the ceasefire 'fully and genuinely', and press for the release of all political prisoners and for the recognition of North Vietnam.[12] The Labour Party, till the last, was being a little over-optimistic about the immediate prospect of peace for Vietnam.

The Heath government

Neither Labour nor the Conservatives, who had come to see Heath as something of a liability, had anticipated Labour's loss of the 1970 general election. Because of this, Heath saw the election success as his own personal victory and entered 10 Downing Street with 'the swagger of the conquering hero whose victory was such a surprise'.[13] Lord Carrington succeeded Denis Healey as Defence Minister; Sir Alec Douglas-Home, the former Conservative Prime Minister, became Foreign Secretary; and Reginald Maudling became Home Secretary. Domestically, Heath had promised to overhaul economic policy, cut inflation and tackle industrial relations. To do this, he was determined to resist large pay demands in the public sector, overhaul industrial relations legislation and disengage the government from inefficient nationalised industries in particular, and Keynesian interventionism in general. The 1970 manifesto promised free-market solutions to Britain's economic problems. According to Norman Tebbit, 'no one should doubt that at the time of the election in 1970 Ted Heath was committed to the end of [the] corporate consensus and to the new liberal economics'. Heath's programme was the Conservative Party's 'first repudiation of the post-war Butskellite consensus'.[14]

Internationally, Heath's overall aim was to produce 'an efficient Britain in the van of a West European superpower able to confront the Americans and the Russians as an equal'.[15] Heath had discussed his view of foreign policy in an article published in the influential American journal *Foreign Affairs* in 1969. This largely focused on why Britain needed to join the European Community, arguing that this would be good for Britain and that in the long run a united Europe 'can grow to match the achievements of the United States and the Soviet Union'. However, it was also interesting in terms of how luke-warm he was about the Anglo-American relationship, saying that there had been 'a realization that a special relationship does not mean special privileges'.[16] Heath was the only post-war Prime Minister who did not see the Anglo-American relationship as the bedrock of British foreign and security policy. The *Foreign Affairs* article also raised an issue he returned to at length in 1970, namely that British foreign policy was being made on the basis of short-term considerations, and lacked a coherent theme; he proposed that British foreign policy should be 'based on a realistic assessment of British interests'.[17] He reiterated this during the 1970 general election, arguing that the Wilson government was pursuing a policy based on short-term pressures, ideology and party politics, and not on Britain's national interest.

In the debate on the Queen's speech laying out Heath's policies for the next Parliament, Heath said 'I believe that the main aim of our foreign policy must be to make a modern and broadly based assessment of where British interests lie. Then, our task is to sustain those interests.' He complained that in the case of the withdrawal of troops from the Far East and the Gulf, policy 'was influenced by considerations of party unity, without regard to considerations of foreign policy'.[18] The 1970 Conservative manifesto had criticised Labour for deciding to withdraw British forces from east of Suez by the end of 1971. However, Heath faced the same problem that Wilson had, namely that the total strength of the armed forces was below that required to meet all Britain's defence commitments. The Heath government issued a Supplementary Statement on Defence in October 1970 that outlined a continuation of Labour's plans, but did announce that the further rundown of major army units planned by the Labour government would be halted to the extent permitted given manpower shortages.[19] However, by 1974 all three services were actually smaller than they had been when Labour left office in 1970.[20] Denis Healey noted in his autobiography that 'Every important decision that I had made' to remedy the situation of Britain's forces being 'over-stretched, underequipped, and underpaid' had been 'bitterly opposed by the Conservatives in Opposition. None of them was reversed when they finally took office themselves.'[21]

One issue on which Heath did diverge from the policy of the Wilson governments was over the sale of military equipment to South Africa. Heath had announced in the debate on the Queen's speech that Britain has 'vital defence interests' in South Africa 'which we cannot ignore'.[22] This included his plan to restart selling frigates and helicopters to the South Africans. This was an issue upon which the PLP could unite in condemning. The UN Security Council had passed three resolutions in 1963 and 1964 that had called for a comprehensive ban on the sale of arms, military vehicles, and equipment and materials used for the manufacture and maintenance of arms and ammunition to South Africa.[23] In 1964 the incoming Wilson government had declared an embargo on the sale of arms and military equipment to South Africa, though it had allowed existing sales of Buccaneer aircraft to go through, and in autumn 1967 had reconsidered whether to sell arms in the light of economic problems following devaluation. However, Wilson had not resumed arms sales, and to do so in contravention of the UN resolutions was extremely controversial. Heath proposed to sell arms 'which could be used for external defence, but not those which could be used internally against the civil population. This formula was not perfect, of course, and we immediately became embroiled in controversy over which grouping helicopters should be placed into.'[24] The UN had clearly stated that all military equipment was included in the ban, and did not follow an internal/external distinction. The UN Security Council even passed a new resolution on 23 July 1970 (resolution 282) reaffirming the arms ban and condemning the violations of the arms embargo, and calling for states to withhold the sale of vehicles and equipment for use by the armed services in South Africa, ceasing the supply of spare parts and training. Heath's decision provoked outrage amongst many Commonwealth members and as a result the Commonwealth conference in Singapore in 1971 was particularly difficult, with some African countries threatening to the leave the organisation altogether in protest.

As far as Labour was concerned, Heath's policies were giving succour to the South African regime. At the 1970 Labour Party annual conference, two resolutions deploring the Conservative government's decision to resume the supply of arms to 'the white racialist government of South Africa' were passed unopposed, as was a resolution stating that 'Conference fears that the policies of the Conservative Government may lead to direct British involvement in a guerrilla war in South Africa'. It also offered the full support of the Labour movement to liberation movements in Africa.[25] Similar resolutions were passed at the 1971 conference, and at the 1972 annual conference a resolution was passed which went further in that it said that a Labour government would 'curb further investment and bring to an end all investment in South Africa'.[26] Anger at the apartheid regime in South Africa, its continuing occupation of neighbouring Namibia, and its support of the Smith regime in Rhodesia, was something the whole of the Labour Party could agree on.

The Cold War and détente

Diplomatic relations between London and Moscow had been strained since the invasion of Czechoslovakia in 1968. In September 1971, Heath expelled 105 Soviet diplomats and trade representatives, whom he said had been identified as intelligence officers. Many had been exposed by Oleg Lyalin, a Soviet intelligence officer who had defected to Britain. Labour accused the government of over-reacting. Rather oddly, Heath subsequently said in his memoir that 'The expulsion of 105 spies was the most important security action ever taken by any Western government'.[27] It was certainly the largest expulsion of Soviet diplomatic personnel ever taken by any Western government. In retaliation, the Soviet Union expelled eighteen British embassy staff from Moscow.

Despite this action, the 1970s actually saw a decline in the tensions between the West and the Soviet Union, with a period of détente seeming to herald a new approach to the Cold War, and Heath went on to develop a more cordial relationship with the Soviet Union. A major development at this time was the proposal for a Conference on Security and Cooperation in Europe (CSCE) as a forum for talks between the West and the Soviet bloc. The aim of the CSCE was to reduce Cold War tension, secure stability in Europe, regularise military activity, increase economic co-operation, and, as far as the West was concerned, improve human rights for the populations of the Communist bloc. The CSCE opened in Helsinki on 3 July 1973 with representatives from thirty-five countries. Heath says in his memoir that he was keen to influence the CSCE, and that Foreign Secretary Alec Douglas-Home played a large role in these preparatory Helsinki talks. However, Nixon notes in his memoirs that 'Heath's views paralleled ours. He shared our scepticism about the European Security Conference.'[28] According to Jim Callaghan's political advisor, Heath had seen the CSCE as part of a Soviet plot, and had not taken the talks seriously. It was only when Labour had been elected in 1974 that the Foreign Office, under Jim Callaghan, geared up for them and took them seriously.[29] The CSCE did not actually reach its final agreement until 1975, when the Helsinki Accords were signed.

For Labour, the priority was to reduce Cold War tensions. The party placed a great deal of hope in the CSCE, arguing that it could 'provide a permanent machinery within which the countries of Europe with differing political systems may demonstrate how to replace confrontation by co-operation and so create a zone of peace'.[30] At this time, the Labour Party's attitude towards defence, NATO and nuclear weapons was shifting away from that of the 1960s governments and towards those supported by the peace movement. At the 1972 annual conference a resolution was passed that reiterated support for the proposed CSCE, and said that its main objectives should be the 'dissolution of NATO and the Warsaw Pact, the creation of a nuclear free zone in Central Europe, and a substantial measure of nuclear and

general disarmament'.[31] Another resolution was passed that said that
conference was 'opposed to any British defence policy which is based
on the use or threatened use of nuclear weapons either by this country
or its allies and demands the removal of all nuclear bases in this
country'.[32] At the 1973 annual conference a resolution was passed that
called for cuts in military spending, reaffirmed Labour's opposition to
a defence policy based 'on the use of threatened use of nuclear
weapons either by this country or its allies', and demanded the closure
of all nuclear bases on British soil or in British waters, whether British
or American, also demanding that this be included in Labour's general
election manifesto.[33] What Labour wanted was an end to the Cold War,
and it would no longer to take the bi-polar system as an article of faith.
For the Labour Party, détente demonstrated that there were possibilities for disarmament, dialogue and an end to hostility between East
and West.

One of Heath's other actions was to develop relations with China.
Britain had not had full diplomatic relations with China since the
establishment of the People's Republic in 1949, maintaining only a
counsellor at the head of a diplomatic office in Beijing. There had been
no mention of China in the Conservatives' 1970 general election
manifesto, and it had always been Labour who had taken a more co-
operative stance towards the People's Republic of China; they had
actually said in their 1970 manifesto that 'Labour still believes that
China should be a member of the United Nations'.[34] In 1972, Britain
acknowledged for the first time the Chinese position that Taiwan was
part of the mainland of China, and established an ambassador and full
staff in Beijing, while leaving in Taiwan a commercial representative
only.[35] Of course, this was happening at the same time as Nixon's
rapprochement with China, resulting in his momentous visit in
February 1972.

Joining the European Community

Heath's major triumph as Prime Minister was seen as his successful bid
for Britain to join the EC, which happened on 1 January 1973.
However, this success was not down to just Heath, for as he pointed
out in his memoir, Nixon 'wanted the British to join the European
Community, and certainly did everything possible, particularly behind
the scenes, both to encourage us and to drum up support for us among
the existing members'.[36] In addition, Harold Wilson's unsuccessful bid

in 1967 had softened up public opinion in support of British member-ship of the EC.[37] And Heath's legislation for joining the EC was only passed with the votes of sixty-nine Labour MPs, with thirty-nine Conservative MPs voting against the legislation.

By 1970 there was a growing realisation that Britain had more to lose by remaining outside the EC than by joining it. Whereas in the early years of the EC, Britain could point to its higher standard of living and higher economic output and growth as reasons why it did not need the EC, by 1970 Britain was beset by economic problems and was sliding down the rankings as an economic world power. Europe was growing in spending power and Britain needed unrestricted access to the European market; businesses in particular were supportive of Britain joining so that they did not have to pay tariffs. In addition, whereas it had previously been argued that Britain did not need the EC because so much of its trade was with the Commonwealth, by 1970 the Commonwealth was declining as a trade bloc and Commonwealth countries were increasingly looking to have trade links with the EC rather than the UK. And of course, the US under Johnson and then Nixon were pushing for Britain to join the EC, and there was concern that if Britain remained outside the EC, then the US would switch its so-called 'special relationship' from Britain to the EC.

The terms of Britain's entry have subsequently been seen as 'not good enough', and Holmes argues that 'Heath was desperate to join the EC at any price'.[38] Europe was Heath's lifelong passion and he felt that the EC promised 'a voice for Europe in world affairs which indi-vidual European countries cannot hope to achieve by themselves.' He thought that a united Europe would grow to match the economic power and achievements of the United States and the Soviet Union.[39] Of course, Heath never envisaged Britain being just another EC member. Britain would, once inside the EC, be able to exert its lead-ership. The assumption was that as Britain had so much diplomatic experience, its government and civil servants would consequently be able to dominate EC political activity. If the EC were to be an increas-ingly important international political actor, then by being at the head of it, Britain would gain, rather than lose, power. As Chris Lord points out, 'Entry was seen as a calculus as how best to manipulate multilat-eral and bilateral contacts to achieve maximal influence and manoeuvre for the British state'.[40]

Given Labour's ongoing commitment to internationalism and multilateralism, having a positive attitude towards the EC might have been seen as more natural to the Labour Party than the Conservative

Party. However, as discussed in the previous chapter, Labour's internationalism was often seen more in terms of having ties and commitments to the Commonwealth than to Europe, and Labour's internationalism tended to view Britain as a world leader, not as one of many European countries Both the Conservative and Labour parties had an enduring resistance to giving up – or being seen to be giving up – British sovereignty in any way; and both wished to prevent the EC from being influenced down the path of federalism and supranationalism advocated by France and Germany. Labour's 1970 general election manifesto had said that Labour would negotiate for entry to the EC, but joining would be dependent on British and Commonwealth interests being safeguarded.[41] This rather bland statement belied the tension in the party over membership of the EC. Wilson wrote that during his thirteen years as leader of the Labour Party, his most difficult task was keeping the party together on the issue of EC membership, particularly during the opposition years of 1970 to 1974.[42] That the issue of membership of the EC was a difficult one for the party was demonstrated by the actions of its NEC. Acting against Wilson's wishes, the NEC held a special conference on 17 July 1971 just to decide on the procedure for agreeing on how to respond to the Heath government's bid to join the European Community. The NEC proposed that the procedure should be that it would agree at its next meeting a 'definitive resolution on Britain's entry into the European Communities on the terms contained in the Government's White Paper'; that this resolution would be submitted to the annual conference.[43] This procedure was agreed, and at the annual conference held in October the NEC put forward a resolution that the party 'opposes entry into the Common Market on the terms negotiated by the Conservative Government'. It further called on the Prime Minister to submit to the 'democratic judgement of a General Election' on this issue, and 'invites the Parliamentary Labour Party … to unite wholeheartedly in voting against the Government's policy'. This resolution was passed by 5,073,000 votes to 1,032,000 votes.[44]

In the 1960s a lot of the rhetoric about Britain needing to remain outside the EC focussed on protecting Britain's relationship with the Commonwealth; however during the 1970s the rhetoric was firmly along the lines of the EC being an organisation that protected the interests of big business, and would hamper any attempts at social democracy at home. Quite simply, many on the left did not like the Common Market precisely because it was a market committed to free trade. Wilson was attempting to prevent the party from splitting on the issue by maintaining the line that Labour opposed the *terms* of entry under Heath's proposal, but not entry itself. The problem for Wilson was that there were members of his Shadow Cabinet such as Peter Shore and Douglas Jay who were opposed in principle to Britain joining the EC, and members of the Shadow Cabinet, in particular the deputy leader Roy Jenkins, who were opposed in principle to Britain staying out of the EC. Then there were those, such as Healey and Crossman, who did not have a particularly strong view either way. Wilson himself was more concerned with avoiding a rift in the Labour Party over membership of the EC than with whether joining the EC was good or bad in principle. Thus, Wilson sometimes appeared pro-EC, and sometimes more anti, depending somewhat on whom he was talking to. In particular, Wilson tended to reassure pro-Marketeers such as Roy Jenkins that they should remain within the Shadow Cabinet despite the party's shift away from support for membership as soon as Labour lost the 1970 election. Wilson's tactics were based upon his determination to preserve party unity, for even if a small proportion of the pro-Marketeers had been constrained to leave the party, 'they would have ruined its electoral prospects possibly well beyond the next election'.[45]

With Heath pushing forward Britain's bid for entry, Wilson was in a difficult position as he attempted to minimise damage and divisions within the party. Despite Labour's earlier bid, it would now have been impossible for Wilson to get all the Labour MPs to vote in favour of British entry, especially as thwarting Heath in his grand plan became in itself very attractive for Labour MPs. Added to this, joining the EC was still seen as deeply unpopular by large sections of the electorate, and so for many MPs, defeating Heath on this issue was seen to have no downside. In addition, even for some MPs who were in favour of Britain joining the EC, voting against Heath's 'terms of entry' was acceptable, as then British entry would be seen as a Conservative policy, and so if the decision proved unpopular with the public then it would be the Conservatives who would get the blame.

The first vote on the government's White Paper approving the principle of British entry to the European Community, Command 4715, was held on 28 October 1971. Heath wanted cross-party support not only to win the vote, but also to demonstrate to Britain's European partners that there was strong support in Britain for membership. He removed the government whip from Conservative MPs in the expectation that 'it would be more valuable to maximize Labour support by removing the taint of voting in a Government lobby than to minimize Conservative rebels'.[46] Harold Wilson initially thought that the Labour MPs should also have a free vote, but was then persuaded by anti-Marketeers such as Tony Benn to stick to the party line that Labour was opposed to the terms of entry, and would therefore vote against Heath's bill.[47] The debate on the Bill was lengthy, and for the Labour MPs it mostly focused on economics. Amongst the pro-Marketeers on the Labour benches, the argument for joining focused on the need to increase British economic growth to match European levels; without economic growth, there could be no redistribution of wealth, and national efforts to stimulate growth were now redundant in an interdependent world. The Labour anti-Marketeers argued that joining the EC would result in higher prices with the introduction of Value Added Tax, which would result in deflation, which would have a negative effect on the standard of living of the working class. Once Britain was inside the EC, a Labour government would then lose the ability to nationalise industries or to direct the economy, and so would lose the ability to implement socialism at home.[48] Thus, in many ways, Labour's dilemma over the EC was a dilemma over what it meant by socialism in Britain, and to a significant extent, by this point, those in favour of joining the EC were from the right of the party, and those against were from the left.

On 28 October the Commons voted by 356 to 244 in favour of the principle of Britain joining the EC. Of the Labour MPs, 200 voted against the government, twenty abstained from voting, and sixty-nine Labour MPs, led by Roy Jenkins, rejected the instruction of Conference and a three-line party whip and voted with the Conservative government for entry to the EC. This was an unprecedented rebellion against the Labour Party whip and demonstrated the depth of conviction of Labour's pro-Marketeers. As far as they were concerned, they were voting on a great historical issue, comparable with the repeal of the Corn Laws or the Great Reform Bill.[49] According to Tony Benn, the vote had been 'terribly tense', and there were rumours of fights breaking out amongst Labour MPs after the vote, but 'in fact, they were just shouting at Roy Jenkins as he went through the Lobby'.[50] The EC rebels included many of those who later went on to form the Social Democratic Party in 1981, including Bill Rogers, Shirley Williams, David Owen and David Marquand. The rebels had voted for the government's White Paper proposing entry to the EC, but this was not the same as voting for the actual legislation. The European Communities Bill was put before Parliament on 17 February 1972. Roy Jenkins, along with most of the other pro-EC rebels, voted against the bill; as he points out, 'Shamefacedly slinking through the "no" lobby made a pathetic contrast with striding through the "aye" lobby on 28 October'.[51] Then at an NEC meeting on 22 March 1972, when Wilson, Callaghan, Healey and Jenkins were absent, Tony Benn managed to pass a motion by thirteen votes to eleven committing the PLP to considering supporting an amendment to the European Communities Bill which would commit the British government to holding a referendum on British membership of the EC. On 10 May, Roy Jenkins resigned from his position as deputy leader of the party over the issue of EC membership, and on 11 May the PLP voted in favour of the policy of holding a referendum on Britain's membership of the EC.[52] This then became party policy.

At the 1972 annual conference there was a lengthy debate on Europe with an extraordinary number of delegates requesting an opportunity to speak on the issue. An NEC statement reaffirming that 'The Labour Party opposes British membership of the European Communities on the terms negotiated by the Conservative Government', and that Labour would 're-negotiate the entry terms', was carried by 3,407,000 votes to 1,802,000.[53] A resolution calling 'on any future Labour Government to withdraw from the Common Market on taking office' was lost, but only by a tiny margin, with 2,958,000 votes for the resolution and 3,076,000 votes against it.[54] A similar situation arose at the following year's annual conference, and Wilson even had to threaten to resign as party leader if the NEC recommended that the annual conference adopt a policy of withdrawal from the EC.[55]

Over the next few years the Labour Party managed to stick to the line that it was opposed to Britain's terms of entry to the EC, but was not necessarily opposed to entry itself, and that entry should be put to the electorate for a vote. Both of Labour's 1974 general election manifestos said that Labour would seek a 'fundamental renegotiation of the terms of entry' as the Heath government had made a 'profound political mistake' in accepting the terms of entry and in joining the EC without the consent of the British people. The main objectives would be to change the Common Agricultural Policy (CAP); to renegotiate a fairer method of financing the budget of the EC, i.e. a reduction in the amount that Britain contributed; a rejection of proposals for economic and monetary union, as this would mean a loss of control over British monetary policy; the retention of Parliamentary powers; and the protection of the interests of the Commonwealth and developing countries through trade access to British markets. If renegotiations were successful, then the British people would be given a chance to vote on Britain's continued membership of the Common Market.[56]

While the issue of membership of the EC caused bitter divisions within Labour, the party was able to unite in condemnation of Heath's handling of the economy as Britain's problems dramatically worsened. Inflation grew rapidly, unemployment grew to levels not seen since before the Second World War, and the balance of payments went from a surplus of £731 million in 1970 to a deficit of £3,278 million in 1974.[57] Nearly all the major industrial nations were facing economic problems at this time, but in Britain they were more severe. In particular, the rises in inflation were higher than in the rest of the European Community, while rises in economic output were considerably lower. Heath ended up implementing the very policies he had promised to jettison, rescuing a number of ailing industries, and implementing a wages and prices freeze in order to tackle rapidly rising inflation in 1972.

The economic issue that came to dominate Heath's premiership was industrial relations. Heath had promised a new approach to industrial policy and one of his first major bills on gaining office was his 1971 Industrial Relations Act. This Act was hastily put together, very lengthy, and even its authors found it confusing.[58] Under this proposed new law, trade unions would be required to register if they wanted to have legal protection from employers seeking financial damages from industrial action. The trade unions were vehemently opposed to this new legislation. Sections of the Labour Party were also vociferously critical of the Bill, even though it was not that dissimilar to the proposals contained in the *In Place of Strife* White Paper put forward in January 1969 by Barbara Castle, the then-Secretary of State for Employment and Productivity. Because of divisions within the Labour Cabinet, the proposals had not made it into law. Somewhat ironically, it was Barbara Castle who then led Labour's attack on the Conservative Bill in Parliament, saying that it was 'motivated by spite against the trade unions' and promising to 'fight any legislation based on these proposals tooth and nail, line by line, and, however long it takes, we shall destroy the Bill'.[59]

On coming to power, Heath and the rest of his Cabinet had been committed to tackling union power, but they had no experience of dealing with trade unions. The unions were growing in militancy, especially in the energy sector, and felt threatened by Heath's massively unpopular, confusing and widely misunderstood Industrial Relations Act. They were also determined to secure high pay settlements for their members given the rapidly rising price inflation. During his time as prime minister, Heath announced a State of Emergency as a result of striking workers an unprecedented five times; because of striking dock-workers in July 1970, electricity workers in December 1970, miners in February 1972, dockworkers again in August 1972, and miners and electricity workers in November 1973. The number of working days lost as a result of industrial action rose from 6,846,000 in 1969 to 10,980,000 in 1970, and peaked at 23,909,000, the highest figure since the General Strike of 1926.[60] Heath introduced a three-day week in January 1974 to deal with the power shortages caused by the strikes in the coal, power and transport industries.

The Yom Kippur War exacerbated these fuel shortages. On 6 October 1973, Egypt and Syria launched a co-ordinated attack on the Israeli-occupied territories in the Golan Heights and the east bank of the Suez Canal. While the Israelis were initially taken by surprise, they were quickly able to retake the Golan Heights, and Israeli forces advanced to within thirty-five miles of Damascus and then managed to trap the Egyptian Third Army east of the Suez Canal. In order to put pressure on Israel and the West, the Arab oil-producing states announced that they would reduce production of oil, increase the price of oil, and place an embargo on the sale of oil to the US and any European country supporting Israel. Both the US and the Soviet Union were keen to prevent the conflict from escalating and managed to get Israel, Egypt and Syria to agree to UN Security Council Resolutions 338 and 339, which called for a ceasefire after three weeks of fighting. However, by January 1974, the price of oil had quadrupled to nearly $12 per barrel, and this oil price shock caused significant problems for many industrialised countries dependent on oil as the main source of energy for both industry and consumers. It meant that when the British miners went on strike in the winter of 1973–74, the high price of oil and subsequent energy crisis greatly strengthened the NUM's bargaining position. Heath, beleaguered with the industrial conflict, called a general election for 28 February. Heath went to the polls with the theme of '*who governs Britain?*' dominating the election. Heath argued for the over-riding need for a strong government to counter the power of the trade unions and tackle the problems of wage inflation.[61] He hoped to win, giving his government a renewed mandate and thus the ability to restore authority over industrial rela-tions. Unfortunately for Heath, he lost. Whereas the Heath govern-ment had been beset by industrial unrest, the Labour minority government elected in February 1974 settled the miners' strike fairly amicably and within a few days of taking office. Indeed, the incoming Wilson/Callaghan government was not beleaguered by industrial unrest until its final months with the 'winter of discontent'.

Wilson's return to power

The February 1974 Conservative manifesto emphasised the dangers that Britain faced both internally and externally, and warned that 'The Labour Party today faces the nation committed to a left-wing programme more dangerous and more extreme than ever before in its history'.[62] The Labour Party's manifesto focused on the economic and political crisis that Britain faced as a result of the Conservative government. It promised that Labour would renegotiate Britain's terms of entry to the EC and that the British people would have an opportunity to vote on membership. Labour's foreign policy would be 'dedicated to the strengthening of international institutions and global co-operation', and Labour would reduce defence costs to bring them in line with Britain's European allies while supporting détente and multilateral disarmament. Controversially, a Labour government would 'seek the removal of American Polaris bases from Britain' while it worked towards the objective of 'the mutual and concurrent phasing out of NATO and the Warsaw Pact'.[63]

Labour won the February 1974 election with 301 seats, with the Conservatives on 297 seats and the Liberals on fourteen seats. However, Labour had not won an outright majority. Heath was reluctant to leave 10 Downing Street and as the sitting Prime Minister he approached the leader of the Liberals, Jeremy Thorpe, and suggested that they form a Conservative-Liberal coalition government. The Labour leadership was outraged and 'thought that Heath should have resigned forthwith'.[64] Heath's negotiations to establish a coalition government failed, and he resigned four days after the election. Labour, with only four more seats than the Conservatives, formed a minority government. In order to attempt to gain an overall majority, the Labour government held another election on 10 October 1974. This time Labour did get an overall majority, but only of three seats.

Wilson's return to power in 1974 was problematic. He had a strong team to support him, with James Callaghan as Foreign Secretary, Denis Healey as the Chancellor of the Exchequer, Roy Jenkins as Home Secretary, and Roy Mason as Defence Secretary. However, Labour's electoral victories in 1974 were very different from those of the 1960s and, in particular, having Harold Wilson as party leader was no longer seen as an advantage. Indeed, Tam Dalyell noted to Richard Crossman after campaigning in Scotland that 'In North Edinburgh, it was sadly clear that Harold Wilson, who in the past has been an electoral asset to us all, is now an electoral albatross'.[65] There were also rumours that MI5 was investigating Wilson in order to undermine his authority and bring down his government. One conspiracy theory was that the Soviet Union's KGB was blackmailing Wilson over his relationship with Marcia Williams. However, Roy Jenkins, who was Home Secretary at the time, said that there was never any evidence that MI5 regarded Wilson as a security risk, or that they planned to destabilise his government.[66] Other Labour insiders have also said that there was no plot.[67] What we can take from these rumours and stories is a sense that while the MI5 plots were overblown gossip and innuendo, Wilson did feel under siege. According to his biographer, 'Wilson himself became rattled … irritated, baffled, and a little apprehensive about what might be going to happen next'.[68]

The overall significance of these events is that while Wilson came into power in 1964 on the crest of a wave of enthusiasm for office, the 1974 government under Wilson did not have the energy, the policies or the capacity to bring about major change. The party had moved leftwards while in opposition and Wilson had to work hard to keep his party together. Between the February and October elections he had to govern without a parliamentary majority, and even after the October 1974 election only had a tiny majority to rely upon to pass his government's legislation. While the government, at least to start with, was not beset with the same level of industrial unrest that the Heath government had been, it did have to deal with intractable economic problems; unemployment doubled between August 1974 and December 1975 and then continued to increase; the value of the pound plummeted to unprecedented levels creating a massive balance of payments problem; inflation rose to unprecedented levels; and economic growth remained sluggish. It also had to deal with Northern Ireland, where the situation had deteriorated to the extent that the Heath government had suspended the Northern Irish constitution, dissolved the Stormont government, and imposed direct rule from London. In all, the 1970s were not a successful decade for either of the main political parties, and Britain no longer appeared as a great power on the world stage. In terms of foreign policy, Wilson took far less of a direct interest than he had in the 1960s. According to Callaghan, when he became Foreign Secretary, Wilson told him that 'he would not want a meticulous account of my handling of foreign policy with the exception of two areas – Israel and South Africa, the latter because of his honourable detestation of apartheid'.[69] Callaghan became Wilson's closest advisor on both government policy and the Labour Party. Indeed, he 'emerged as all-purpose operator to fill any gaps and give direction to the government. He was almost an alternative prime minister.'[70]

Southern Africa was a region that caused particular concern to the Labour government. The general election manifestos had pledged support for liberation movements and promised to seek to end the South African occupation of Namibia. At the 1973 annual conference a resolution had been passed that committed the next Labour government 'to take urgent action to reduce drastically British economic involvement in South Africa', a radical change in Britain's foreign policy towards South Africa.[71] In 1974, after a nine-month review, Jim Callaghan announced the Labour government's policy on economic links with South Africa. This promised humanitarian, financial and material aid to the liberation movements and contributions to the International Defence and Aid Fund; the prohibition of further British investment in South Africa; and an end to the military links with the apartheid regime. Wilson did not continue with the arms sales to South Africa reintroduced by Heath, instead adhering to the UN embargo on the sale of weapons and military equipment to the apartheid regime. On Namibia the Labour government's policy was to support the South West Africa People's Organisation (SWAPO) and accept without reservation all UN decisions regarding Namibia, terminating all economic, political and social links with Namibia until South Africa ended its occupation of the territory, and free and fair elections were held under the control and supervision of the UN.[72]

Right-wing regimes in Latin America also caused great concern in the Labour Party. In 1973 the democratically elected Allende regime in Chile was overthrown by a military coup that had backing from the US Central Intelligence Agency (CIA). President Allende was found dead. This appalled the Labour Party, and seemed symptomatic of US support for dubious regimes. Labour's NEC issued a statement on 30 September urging the government to recall the British Ambassador from Santiago in protest, and that the Labour Party would oppose all British aid or trade designed to sustain the military regime in power.[73] At the 1973 Labour conference, Allende's ambassador spoke movingly of events in Chile and received full public support from Labour leaders for his call to resist the Junta. Yet six months later, when the new Labour government had been in power for only six weeks, the Labour

Foreign Secretary allowed British-built warships to be handed over to the new Chilean authorities. It did make some concessions to the campaign waged by the Labour Party's General Secretary, left-wing junior ministers and trade union leaders: the government refused to sell spare parts or to overhaul engines for military aircraft and opposed plans by a major engineering consortium to build a copper smelting plant for the new military regime.

Labour, the EC and the referendum

The issue with the most potential to derail Wilson's government at this point was Europe. Wilson only had a tiny majority and his party was still deeply divided over Britain's membership of the EC. Labour's 1974 manifestos had promised that a Labour government would renegotiate better terms of entry and would then hold a referendum on whether to remain within the EC based on these terms. On 1 April the Foreign Secretary James Callaghan formally asked the EC for a renegotiation of Britain's terms of membership. These focused on four issues: the British contribution to the EC budget; the Common Agricultural Policy; access for the products of Commonwealth countries to EC markets; and a guarantee that Britain would retain autonomy over regional development within the UK. These renegotiations lasted nearly a year, with Callaghan – who by this time was taking a pragmatic approach towards EC membership – assisted by the Europe Minister, Roy Hattersley, who was an active pro-Marketeer, and Peter Shore, the Secretary of State for Trade, who was a passionate campaigner against membership of the EC. This rather incongruous team – an agnostic, a believer and a sceptic – represented all three Labour Party perspectives towards EC membership at this time. Fortunately for Wilson, an agreement was reached for new terms of British entry to the EC. On 11 March 1975 the terms were completed at a summit in Dublin. Wilson and Callaghan gave an upbeat press conference pronouncing that the renegotiations had been a success. Interestingly, during the process of the renegotiations Callaghan had shifted from being an agnostic to being firmly convinced that it was in Britain's economic interests to remain within the EC. Callaghan then led the Cabinet in declaring the new terms acceptable, but agreement was only reached after a lengthy discussion over the course of two days during which Tony Benn denounced the EC as a capitalist club.[74] On 9 April 1975 the House of Commons voted by 398 votes to 172 votes to endorse the continuation of Britain's membership of the European Community based on these new terms. The EC referendum was then held on Thursday 5 June 1975. The public were asked to vote yes or no on the question, 'Do you think the United Kingdom should stay in the European Community (Common Market)?' The result was a solid 'yes', with 67.2 per cent of the votes, while 32.8 per cent voted 'no', based on a turnout of 64.5 per cent.[75]

The 1975 national referendum on whether Britain should remain in the EC was significant not only because of its result on British-EC policy, but also because of the way that it so publicly highlighted the depth of the split within the Labour Party over the EC. At a Labour Party conference on 26 April 1975, the party had voted against continuing membership of the EC by almost two to one. Because of this split and the problem of maintaining party unity, Wilson took the extraordinary step of suspending the constitutional convention of Cabinet collective responsibility and allowed ministers to campaign publicly against each other. This was the first time that there had been official acceptance of a public Cabinet split within a one-party government. Wilson, Callaghan and the majority of the Labour Cabinet campaigned for a 'yes' vote along with Conservative and Liberal politicians. The government officially endorsed the 'yes' campaign, sending out a pamphlet to every household recommending that people vote 'yes' to staying in the European Community. It said that although Britain had not got everything it wanted with the renegotiations, 'we did get big and significant improvements on the previous terms. We confidently believe that these better terms can give Britain a New Deal in Europe.'[76] However, seven of the twenty-three members of the Cabinet, including Peter Shore, Tony Benn, Barbara Castle and Michael Foot, accompanied by many Labour Party activists, campaigned for the 'no' vote. The fact that Wilson managed to renegotiate Britain's terms of entry and manage his party during the ensuing referendum is testament to his political skill.

On the 16 March 1976, a few days after his sixtieth birthday, Wilson stunned his party by announcing his resignation as Prime Minister. Wilson had spent some time drafting a private statement that he gave to his Cabinet colleagues. In it he said that he had decided in March 1974 that he would remain in office for no more than two years. The reasons he listed for leaving were vague: he had been leader of the party for thirteen years; it was his duty not to deny the chance for others to lead; his successor would need the opportunity to impose his or her style; there was a danger of facing reruns of earlier decisions and therefore not considering alternative courses of action. He said that he was proud of his achievements over the past two years, and that the timing of his decision to resign was his own.[77] The resignation came as a shock to the Cabinet. For a serving Prime Minister to resign voluntarily was very unusual, and Wilson had never publicly stated that he did not expect to serve a full term.

It is difficult to know the exact combination of reasons that made him take this step. One likely reason was that after the painful experience of losing the 1970 election, he had determined that if he became Prime Minister again, he would go at a time of his own choosing, with the 'trappings of a great man leaving office of his own will'. Another possibility is that he was already experiencing the onset of Alzheimer's disease that was to affect him in later life, and that he had 'begun to realise that one of the best minds that Oxford had produced was no longer firing on all cylinders and that the shadow of that illness was already there'.[78] Possibly he did just feel that he had given all he could to the job, having been leader of the Labour Party for over ten years, and Prime Minister for eight years. James Callaghan won the ensuing election for the leadership of the Labour Party, and became Prime Minister just twenty days after Wilson's announcement. Wilson had unofficially endorsed Callaghan as his successor; he had come to rely greatly on him and treated him almost as Prime Minister in waiting. Unfortunately for Callaghan, the Labour government's problems were exacerbated by the fact that soon after he had taken over from Wilson, Labour lost its tiny majority in the House of Commons due to by-elections and defections from Labour. This meant that he needed the support of other parties in order to pass legislation. In the spring of 1977, Callaghan negotiated a Lib-Lab Pact with David Steel, the leader of the Liberals, with the agreement being that he would consult with the Liberals on future legislation in return for their support in the House of Commons. This pact lasted until October 1978.

Foreign and defence policy under Callaghan

Callaghan appointed Tony Crosland as his successor at the Foreign Office. Crosland was not particularly associated with foreign affairs but that was part of his appeal, as he had not played a major role in the party debates over membership of the EC, and so Callaghan felt that he would not arouse much suspicion when he took decisions that would link Britain more closely with the EC.[79] Crosland was keen to do his job well while at the same time not alienating the party and so undermining support for himself personally within the Labour Party. This was a difficult task given the party's shift to the left on foreign policy during the 1970s.

Consequently, Crosland was given a great deal of advice from his colleagues on how to deal both with the Foreign Office and with the Labour Party. At a meeting of Crosland's 'supporters', it was argued that if he wanted to win support from the Labour Party then he must appear 'to have taken control of the Department', to appear willing to reject traditional Foreign Office views and sometimes to 'stand up to the Americans'.[80] Tom McNally, Callaghan's political advisor, warned Crosland that there was a great deal of tension between the National Executive of the Party and the government, with resolutions routinely being passed at NEC meetings that were critical of some aspect of government foreign policy. The position of the constituency parties was increasingly left-wing, which also created tension. He also warned that the Labour Party's International Committee, which was now under the chairmanship of Ian Mikardo, a left-winger, was 'getting madder and madder'. However, on the plus side, the PLP was 'very quiet on Foreign Affairs at the moment'.[81] As the September party conference approached, Crosland was told in a confidential memo on the political situation by his advisor, David Lipsey, that 'The intra-party situation seems more likely to mean real difficulties for the Government than the Parliamentary situation'.[82] At the end of 1976, Lipsey wrote Crosland a note on his role as an advisor at the Foreign Office, which included liaison with the party: 'A bore given that the NEC is particularly mad on these issues, but on the whole successful in that your relations and the FCO's relations with the Party are, by all accounts, far better than they were in the PM's day.'[83]

Despite these dire warnings, Crosland had some success at the Foreign Office. In dealing with the antagonism between Britain and Iceland over fishing rights (the 'cod wars'), the UK permanent representative at NATO told Crosland that he and others had been told 'how well you had handled things and what a very good impression you had made on the Icelanders'.[84] Crosland also built up a particularly close relationship with Henry Kissinger, who wrote to Crosland as he was leaving his post as Secretary of State in January 1977, saying that 'In less than a year, we have established an intimate, constructive and rewarding friendship'. Crosland had 'brought a flash of enthusiasm and brilliance to an otherwise tedious occupation'.[85]

Crosland died suddenly in February 1977, less than a year after taking up his post. Callaghan wanted to bring in a new face rather than appoint one of the existing Cabinet members to the job of Foreign Secretary. He decided to replace Crosland with David Owen, who had been a Minister of State at the Foreign Office since September 1976, and had worked at the Ministry of Defence (MOD) before this. Owen was only thirty-eight and so this was quite a bold choice. From the right of the party, he was a committed Atlanticist, and was by instinct very suspicious and critical of the Soviet Union. His views were out of step with large sections of the party, who by this time had shifted significantly to the left on defence policy.

The early 1970s had heralded an era of détente and a new approach to the Cold War. Nixon took an unexpectedly flexible and conciliatory approach to the two communist superpowers, China and Soviet Union, while taking a belligerent approach to Marxist governments in secondary theatres, especially Latin America and Southeast Asia.[86] Progress was made on arms control for the first time. Bilateral negotiations between America and the Soviet Union resulted in 1972 in the Strategic Arms Limitations Talks (SALT I) interim agreement, which aimed at providing stability by placing a ceiling on the number of ballistic missiles that each side could have, and the Anti-Ballistic Missile (ABM) Treaty which limited ABM deployment to two sites. In June 1979 the SALT II agreement was signed, and this conceded the principle of parity on the total number of missiles, and placed ceilings on the number of warheads including multiple independent targetable re-entry vehicles. While SALT I was of limited impact, and SALT II was never actually ratified, the fact that the negotiations took place at all was important and did signify a breakthrough in East-West relations.

This era of détente in turn had an impact on Anglo-American relations. Up until the 1970s, Britain had been present at superpower discussions and had acted as an intermediary between the US and the Soviet Union when direct discussions were not possible. With détente, Britain was no longer needed as a go-between, and was no longer party to discussions between the two superpowers. Indeed, in general, during the 1970s the Anglo-American relationship was not particularly 'special'. It had deteriorated under Heath, who was by instinct much closer to Europe than to the US. While the US had been urging Britain to take a more active role within Europe, West Germany was becoming an increasingly important US partner, and was seen as an alternative American route to influence in Europe. Britain was also overtaken by West Germany as the main European contributor to NATO's conventional forces. Britain's failing economy and industrial problems highlighted the extent to which it had declined as a major power.

From the late 1940s to the early 1970s, the Anglo-American relationship, support for NATO, and the retention of a British nuclear deterrent, had been the bedrock of British defence policy, and of the Labour Party's defence policy. However, in the early 1970s this began to change. A resolution had been passed at Conference in 1972 that called for the long-term 'dissolution of NATO and the Warsaw Pact, the creation of a nuclear free zone in Central Europe, and a substantial measure of nuclear and general disarmament'.[87] Another resolution was passed that said that Conference was 'opposed to any British defence policy which is based on the use or threatened use of nuclear weapons either by this country or its allies and demands the removal of all nuclear bases in this country'.[88] These policies were reaffirmed at the 1973 annual conference, and were then fed into the two Labour general election manifestos of 1974. The February manifesto committed Labour to reducing defence costs and to working towards détente, multilateral disarmament, the removal of American nuclear bases from Britain, and the phasing out of NATO and the Warsaw Pact.[89] The October 1974 manifesto reiterated these pledges, and renounced any intention of moving towards a new generation of British strategic nuclear weapons to replace Polaris, the ageing submarine-launched independent nuclear deterrent. These were radical defence policies, and demonstrated a shift in party thinking towards that of CND and the peace movement not seen in the Labour Party since the late 1950s. The Labour Party had never previously stated as a manifesto pledge the removal of American nuclear bases from Britain, nor had it previously pledged to work towards the phasing out of NATO, even if this was phrased in terms of dissolving both NATO and the Warsaw Pact at the same time. What the Labour Party wanted was an end to the Cold War. Whereas in the 1950s and 1960s, the party had viewed British defence through the prism of the Cold War and bi-polarity, in the period of détente in the early 1970s, Labour started to view the end of the Cold War as a possibility that could be hastened by the actions of a British government. The success of the Helsinki Conference of the summer of 1975 represented a major breakthrough in terms of communications between East and West, and many in the Labour Party thought that through negotiation and a willingness of Britain to renounce its independent nuclear deterrent, it might be possible to bring about the end to the Cold War.

However, Wilson and Callaghan and their senior ministers did not agree with the sentiment of the party; or rather, they might have agreed with the sentiment, but they did not agree with these policies. Both Wilson and Callaghan were concerned that the Anglo-American relationship had deteriorated during Heath's premiership. They supported détente, but not a shift in defence policy. Consequently, both Wilson and Callaghan largely ignored Labour's defence manifesto pledges, or at least chose to interpret them very broadly.

Shortly before losing power, the Heath government had embarked upon an upgrade of Polaris with the development of the Chevaline system, which would enable Polaris missiles fired from British submarines to reach Moscow. This programme was at a very early stage and so could have been cancelled without great financial cost, and given Labour's election commitment not to develop a new generation of nuclear weapons, party members expected the Labour government to cancel it. However, the decision to go ahead with Chevaline had been made by a select and secret sub-committee of the Wilson Cabinet.[90] Wilson merely stated to his full Cabinet that Britain would lose international influence it if it gave up its nuclear deterrent, and that all that was being proposed was a 'very minor addition' to the existing nuclear weapons system, which would cost about £24 million a year.[91] The decision was not made public until 1980. In fact, Chevaline was to prove massively more expensive than anticipated, and Denis Healey later wrote that he regarded it as 'one of my mistakes as Chancellor not to get Chevaline cancelled'.[92]

In 1976 the Callaghan government agreed to a request by President Ford to deploy American nuclear-armed F-111 bombers in US bases in Britain. By 1979, with growing concerns over the Soviet Union's deployment of its new SS-20 missiles targeted on Western Europe, and the Warsaw Pact's continuing superiority in conventional forces, Callaghan had agreed in principle to NATO plans to modernise American long-range theatre weapons in Europe. At the same time, the Labour Party's NEC was looking for a new approach to defence in general, and nuclear weapons in particular, with the election to the committee of a number of people who were committed to a non-nuclear defence policy. In 1975 the NEC established a Defence Study Group under the chairmanship of Ian Mikardo. This was charged with examining the implications of reducing Britain's defence expenditure and role. The result, *Sense About Defence*, was published as a book, which advocated getting rid of some bases, cutting down on nuclear weapons, no longer commissioning new ones and cutting UK military expenditure.[93] However, *Sense About Defence* was ignored by the

Labour government. Thus, Labour developed two conflicting defence policies in the mid- to late 1970s. There was the policy of the Labour Party's NEC, which reflected resolutions passed at conference and the attitudes of the left of the party; and then there was the policy of the Labour government, which reflected the centre-right of the party. That the inconsistencies between the two were not more widely apparent helped the government at the time, but these inconsistencies reflected a battle for the future of Labour's defence policy, which were to reach their peak in the early 1980s when they proved an electoral liability for the party.

Callaghan also had to tackle the politically sensitive issue of whether to go ahead with a strategic force replacement for Britain's nuclear deterrent, Polaris. While Polaris would remain serviceable until the 1990s, Callaghan had been told that because of the long building time, any decision to replace it would have to be made by 1980. Of course, the 1974 manifestos had explicitly said that the Labour renounced any intention of moving towards the production of a new generation of nuclear weapons or a successor to Polaris. Callaghan requested Foreign Office and MOD officials carry out a study assessing the likely strategic environment in the 1990s, options for the replacement of Polaris,[94] and the alternative possibilities if Britain did not continue with its ballistic missile system. In his memoirs, Callaghan said that no decision on Polaris was needed during his premiership, and that this report was to provide necessary factual information for the *next* government.[95] The report was completed in December 1978 and circulated in secret to the Chancellor of the Exchequer Denis Healey, Foreign Secretary David Owen and Defence Secretary Fred Mulley, but not to the rest of the Cabinet. Healey, Owen and Mulley agreed to Callaghan's suggestion that he raise the question of replacing Polaris with Trident – the option they thought most likely to meet British requirements – at his forthcoming discussions with President Carter on 5 and 6 January at Guadeloupe in the West Indies. Carter and Callaghan were meeting with Giscard d'Estaing of France and Helmut Schmidt of Germany to discuss the modernisation and control of nuclear weapons in NATO. At this meeting Carter then assured Callaghan that he could see no objection to transferring the Trident technology to the UK. Callaghan wrote to Carter in March requesting that Britain's Chief Scientist in the Ministry of Defence begin exploratory talks in Washington.

Callaghan, Owen and Healey all state that Callaghan did not commit Britain to replacing Polaris and so did not break Labour's election pledge.[96] Rather, Callaghan merely asked Carter whether he might agree to let Britain have the proposed Trident C4 system, should a British government ask for it, and that he was only preparing the ground so that the next government would be in a position to make an informed decision over Britain's nuclear deterrent. However, Callaghan was certainly acting contrary to the expectations of the Labour Party at a time when relations between the government and the labour movement were breaking down. These private discussions about the possible future of Britain's nuclear deterrent were taking place against the backdrop of what came to be known as the 'winter of discontent'.

The 1974–79 Labour governments were faced with deteriorating economic conditions as Britain simultaneously experienced economic stagnation and escalating inflation. During 1976, the economic crisis in Britain worsened, and the government had to ask the International Monetary Fund (IMF) for a loan worth $3.9 billion, which would involve agreeing to more austerity measures. The Labour Party, the TUC and many of Callaghan's own Cabinet colleagues were calling for a policy of economic reflation and redistribution to deal with recessionary problems, while the IMF wanted a commitment to further deflationary measures as a condition of the loan. In the end, the Cabinet agreed to the loan and the condition of limiting public expenditure, despite their suspicions of outside interference in British economic affairs. The Callaghan government survived the immediate crisis, but the 1976 IMF loan was perceived as indicative of Britain's post-war economic decline.[97]

As part of the effort to tackle inflation the Labour government brought in an incomes policy to limit pay increases. There was meant to be a return to free collective bargaining in the second half of 1978, but instead Denis Healy introduced a 5 per cent pay limit. The TUC, which until then had supported the government in its incomes policy, voted to reject the pay limit. A resolution opposing the policy was passed at the October Labour Party conference by a massive majority, but the government was determined to continue to pursue this policy. The attempt to enforce the rule that pay increases were to be kept below 5 per cent led to strikes initially in the private sector, which then spread to the public sector. This resulted in petrol shortages as lorry drivers went on strike and petrol could not be delivered; rubbish piled up in the streets when the refuse collectors went on strike; and many hospitals only accepting emergency cases when hospital ancillary workers went on strike. Perhaps most notoriously, gravediggers in Liverpool and Tameside went on unofficial strike, and Liverpool City Council had to hire a factory to house the resulting backlog of coffins waiting burial. The resulting news headlines were particularly damaging to the government. This was made worse by Callaghan's comment when he was interviewed by the media at Heathrow as he returned from his defence summit in Guadeloupe. Intending to demonstrate that he had control over the situation in the UK, when asked about his approach to the mounting chaos at home, Callaghan said in a jocular tone that 'I don't think that other people in the world would share the view that there is mounting chaos'. The subsequent headline in the *Sun* of 'Crisis? What crisis?' made it appear that Callaghan was either in denial or simply did not care about the impact that the industrial situation was having on people. Britain's winter of discontent harmed Labour's image and its reputation for governance for years to come.

Despite Callaghan's economic difficulties, in the autumn of 1978 most opinion polls had put Labour ahead of the Conservatives. Expectation grew in early September that Callaghan would call an autumn election to take advantage of this. Callaghan allowed speculation of an election to grow to such an extent that when he did announce that there would be no election, the opposition, the media and the public felt duped, and many in his own party were astonished. Callaghan's decision to carry on proved problematic as the Liberals pulled out of the Lib-Lab pact in October, leaving Callaghan's government without a working majority. There was a further blow on 1 March 1979 at the referendums on devolution for Scotland and Wales. The vote in Scotland was in favour of devolution, though did not reach the required majority, and in Wales the result was heavily against devolution. As a consequence of this rejection of a government policy, the Conservatives tabled a motion of no confidence in the House of Commons that was passed by just one vote on 28 March. Callaghan was left with no choice to but to call a general election. His view was that under the circumstances, 'It was a miracle that we had governed as long and effectively as we had'.[98]

Whereas Callaghan had expected to win in the autumn 1978, the winter of discontent had overshadowed the government's achievements and had been a disaster for Labour's popularity. The Conservatives under Margaret Thatcher ran a successful election campaign arguing that the Labour government had become a hostage to trade union power, and advertising consultants Saatchi and Saatchi came up with the slogan 'Labour isn't working', which was seen by many as particularly apt. The election of 3 May 1979 resulted in the Conservatives winning a substantial majority with 339 seats, with Labour on 269 seats.

In conclusion, whereas the 1960s was seen as an exciting decade, when social change developed a momentum that overcame earlier taken-for-granted ways of thinking, the 1970s has been seen as a disappointing decade, characterised by strikes, inflation and economic problems. While the 1970s was certainly a gloomy period for both the main parties, for Labour, its fortunes corresponded perhaps more obviously with the zeitgeist of these years. Wilson, the energetic man of the future in the 1960s who was going to harness the 'white heat of the revolution', never seemed to have control of events, and lacked a clear a sense of direction. Wilson did not appear to enjoy his leadership role in the 1970s, and was more concerned with loss of leadership than with really exercising leadership. Then, despite James Callaghan's years in government and his previous experience as Chancellor of the Exchequer, Home Secretary and Foreign Secretary, he was faced with crises on several fronts, which seemed to cripple Britain in a way that the crises of the 1960s had not. The Wilson/Callaghan governments seemed to lack a sense of purpose and direction, and offered little in the way of policy innovation. While both leaders demonstrated political ingenuity in handling the party – Wilson with regard to membership of the EC and Callaghan over defence and the nuclear deterrent – this glossed over the growing division within the party between the Labour leadership on the one hand and the party members, activists and backbench MPs on the other. By the time of the 1979 general election, Labour had two very different external policies, and this was to become the central issue in the battle for the future of Labour Party that reached its peak in the early 1980s.

Notes

1 David Butler and Gareth Butler, *British Political Facts 1900–1985* (London: Macmillan, 6th edn, 1986), p. 227.
2 Nick Tiratsoo, 'Labour and its critics: the case of the May Day Manifesto Group', in R. Coopey, S. Fielding and N. Tiratsoo, eds, *The Wilson Governments 1964–70* (London: Pinter, 1993), p. 163.
3 Author's interview with Lord McNally, 25 July 2006.
4 *Ibid.*

5 Philip Ziegler, *Wilson: The Authorised Life of Lord Wilson of Rievaulx* (London: Weidenfeld & Nicolson, 1993), p. 355.
6 James Callaghan, *Time and Chance* (London: Collins, 1987), p. 307.
7 *British General Election Manifestos, 1959–1987*, compiled and edited by F.W.S. Craig (Aldershot: Parliamentary Research Services, 3rd edn, 1990), p. 152.
8 Labour Party archive, Museum of Labour History, Manchester, International Department, ID/1969-70/83, Resolutions received from Constituency Labour Parties and Trade Unions, September 1970, held in NEC Mins Box L, 26 September 1970.
9 *Labour Party Annual Conference Report* (hereafter *LPACR*), 1972, p. 37.
10 *LPACR*, 1973, p. 38.
11 Labour Party archive, Box on Vietnam 1957–73, news release 26 February 1973.
12 *LPACR*, 1973, p. 31.
13 Andrew Roth, *Heath and the Heathmen* (London: Routledge and Kegan Paul, 1972), p. 210.
14 Norman Tebbit, *Upwardly Mobile: An Autobiography* (London: Futura, 1989 edn), p. 120.
15 Roth, *Heath and the Heathmen*, p. 211.
16 Edward Heath, 'Realism in British foreign policy', *Foreign Affairs*, 48:1 (October 1969), pp. 41 and 48.
17 *Ibid.*, p. 50.
18 *House of Commons Debates* (hereafter *H.C. Deb.*), vol. 803, 2 July 1970, col. 79.
19 Michael Chichester and John Wilkinson, *The Uncertain Ally: British Defence Policy 1960–1990* (Aldershot: Gower, 1982), p. 33, referring to Supplementary Statement on Defence Policy 1970, Cmnd. 4521.
20 Chichester and Wilkinson, *The Uncertain Ally*, p. 40.
21 Denis Healey, *The Time of My Life* (London: Penguin edn, 1990), p. 324.
22 *H.C. Deb.*, vol. 803, 2 July 1970, col. 81.
23 These were resolution 131 of 7 August 1963; resolution 182 of 4 December 1963; and resolution 191 of 18 June 1964.
24 Edward Heath, *The Course of My Life: My Autobiography* (London: Coronet Books, Hodder & Stoughton, 1999), p. 478.
25 *LPACR*, 1970, pp. 245–53.
26 *LPACR*, 1972, p. 223.
27 Heath, *The Course of My Life*, p. 476.
28 Henry Kissinger, *White House Years* (London: Phoenix Press, 2000 paperback edn.), p. 965.
29 Author's interview with Lord McNally, 25 July 2006.
30 *LPACR*, 1971, Appendix 5, NEC statement on 'East-West Relations and European Security'.
31 *LPACR*, 1972, p. 217.
32 *LPACR*, 1972, p. 221.
33 *LPACR*, 1973, p. 301.
34 Craig, ed., *British General Election Manifestos, 1959–1987*, p. 153.
35 Heath, *The Course of My Life*, p. 495.

36 *Ibid.*, p. 472.
37 Helen Parr, *Britain's Policy Towards the European Community: Harold Wilson and Britain's World Role, 1964–1967* (London: Routledge, 2006).
38 Martin Holmes, *The Failure of the Heath Government* (Basingstoke: Macmillan, 2nd edn, 1997), p. xvi.
39 Heath, 'Realism in British foreign policy', p. 41.
40 Christopher Lord, *British Entry to the European Community under the Heath Government of 1970–4* (Aldershot: Dartmouth, 1993), p. 14.
41 Craig, ed., *British General Election Manifestos, 1959–1987*, p. 154.
42 Harold Wilson, *Final Term: the Labour Government 1974–1976* (London: Weidenfeld & Nicolson and Michael Joseph, 1979), p. 51.
43 *LPACR*, 1971, Appendix 1.
44 *LPACR*, 1971, pp. 114–15 & 144.
45 Joseph Frankel, *British Foreign Policy 1945–1973* (Oxford: Oxford University Press, 1975), pp. 32–3.
46 Lord, *British Entry to the European Community*, p. 116.
47 Tony Benn, *Office Without Power: Diaries 1968–72* (London: Hutchinson, 1988), entry for 18 October 1971, p. 379.
48 The debate lasted for the 21, 27 and 28 October. *H.C. Deb.*, vol. 823.
49 Roy Jenkins, comment in 'The Labour Committee for Europe', *Contemporary Record*, 7:2 (Autumn 1993), p. 3.
50 Benn, *Office Without Power*, 28 October 1971,p. 382.
51 Roy Jenkins, *A Life at the Centre* (Basingstoke: Macmillan, 1991), p. 338.
52 *Ibid.*, pp. 347–8.
53 *LPACR*, 1972, p. 217.
54 *LPACR*, 1972, p. 200 and p. 219.
55 Wilson, *Final Term*, p. 51.
56 Craig, ed., *British General Election Manifestos, 1959–1987*, pp. 188–9; and p. 253.
57 Butler and Butler, *British Political Facts*, p. 386.
58 Robert Taylor, 'The Heath government and industrial relations: myth and reality', in Stuart Ball and Anthony Seldon, eds, *The Heath Government 1970–1974: A Reappraisal* (London: Longman, 1996), pp. 170–1.
59 *H.C. Deb.*, vol. 807, 26 November 1970, cols 654 and 666.
60 Butler and Butler, *British Political Facts*, pp. 372–3.
61 See David Butler and Dennis Kavanagh, *The British General Election of 1974* (Basingstoke: Macmillan, 1974), pp. 61–2, 85.
62 Craig, ed., *British General Election Manifestos, 1959–1987*, p. 184.
63 Ibid., pp. 188–9 and 193.
64 Callaghan, *Time and Chance*, p. 293.
65 Modern Records Centre (MRC), University of Warwick, Crossman Files, MSS 154/3/MIS/6/4-5, Tam Dalyell to R.H.S. Crossman, 10 December 1973.
66 Jenkins, *Life at the Centre*, p. 384.
67 Author's interview with Lord McNally, 25 July 2006.
68 Ziegler, *Wilson*, p. 477.

69 Callaghan, *Time and Chance*, p. 290.
70 Kenneth O. Morgan, *Callaghan: A Life* (Oxford: Oxford University Press, 1997), p. 409.
71 *LPACR*, 1973, pp. 306–7.
72 Labour Party archive, NEC Minutes 25 February 1981, ID/1980-81/35/Dec. This NEC meeting has many reports on foreign policy that highlight not only policy in 1981 but also the policies and performance of the 1974–79 governments.
73 *LPACR*, 1973, Appendix 5.
74 Morgan, *Callaghan*, pp. 424–5.
75 David Butler and Uwe Kitzinger, *The 1975 Referendum* (Basingstoke: Macmillan, 1976), p. 263.
76 HM Government, *Britain's New Deal in Europe* (London: HMSO, 1975), downloaded from www.harvard-digital.co.uk/euro/pamphlet.htm.
77 Harold Wilson papers, Bodleian Library, Oxford, MS. Wilson c. 1350, 'Prime Minister's Statement to the Cabinet', no date but probably 16 March 1976.
78 Author's interview with Lord McNally, 25 July 2006.
79 Callaghan, *Time and Chance*, p. 399.
80 Anthony Crosland papers, British Library of Political and Economic Science, LSE, 5/12/17. Summary note of informal meeting of supporters, 16 June 1976.
81 Crosland papers, 5/12/20-23, David Lipsey note of meeting between Crosland and Tom McNally, 15 April 1976.
82 Crosland papers, 5/12/1, confidential memo on the 'Political Situation' by David Lipsey, 1 September 1976.
83 Crosland papers, 5/13/18-20, note by David Lipsey on his role as advisor, 22 December 1976.
84 Crosland papers, 5/13/6, John Killick to Crosland, 8 June 1976.
85 Crosland papers, 5/14/23, Kissinger to Crosland, 14 January 1977.
86 A. James Reichley, *Conservatives in an Age of Change: The Nixon and Ford Administrations* (Washington, D.C.: The Brookings Institution, 1981), p. 98.
87 *LPACR*, 1972, p. 217.
88 *Ibid.*, p. 221.
89 Craig, ed., *British General Election Manifestos, 1959–1987*, p. 193.
90 Peter Malone, *The British Nuclear Deterrent* (London: Croom Helm, 1984), p. 20.
91 Tony Benn, *Against the Tide: Diaries 1973–76* (London: Hutchinson, 1989), pp. 267–9; Ziegler, *Wilson*, p. 460.
92 Healey, *Time of My Life*, p. 313.
93 Labour Party, *Sense About Defence: The Report of the Labour Party Defence Study Group* (London: Quartet Books, 1977). Members of the Defence Study Group included Robin Cook, Mary Kaldor and Dan Smith.
94 Craig, ed., *British General Election Manifestos, 1959–1987*, p. 255.
95 Callaghan, *Time and Chance*, p. 553.

96 Callaghan, *Time and Chance*, pp. 557–8; Healey, *Time of My Life*, p. 456; David Owen, *Time to Declare* (London: Michael Joseph, 1991), p. 403.
97 Mark Harmon, *The British Labour Government and the 1976 IMF Crisis* (Basingstoke: Macmillan, 1997), p. 1.
98 Callaghan, *Time and Chance*, p. 564.

Chapter 5

The radicalisation of foreign and defence policy in the 1980s

The early 1980s saw a radicalisation of foreign and defence policy in Britain with the end of détente and an intensification of the Cold War. The Conservatives under Margaret Thatcher moved to the right at a time when the Labour Party was moving ideologically to the left, while the newly established Social Democratic Party (SDP) offered a middle-ground alternative to Labour. This combination meant that foreign and defence policy became a political battleground and, unusually for Britain, increasingly salient to the voters in the 1983 and 1987 elections. The Conservatives successfully labelled Labour as being weak on foreign and defence policy and asserted that Labour could not be trusted with the nation's security. At the same time, foreign and defence policy became a key part of the ideological battle within the Labour Party. Thus, Labour's foreign policy can only be fully understood if it is placed within the party context of its internal fights for the future direction of the party; the domestic context of both the main parties moving away from the political middle ground; and the international context of an intensified international political threat with the start of the 'second' Cold War.

Traditional accounts of British foreign policy emphasise a bipartisan foreign policy consensus from 1945 to the 1980s, characterised by the major members of the main political parties broadly agreeing with one another as to how foreign policy should be carried out, with a firm commitment to the Anglo-American relationship and to NATO, and the desire for Britain to play a powerful world role.[1] Any disagreement over policy therefore came from within the parties, for example from backbenchers or party activists. It is Thatcher, with her more assertive political style, who is generally credited with having brought about the end of this consensus.[2] When still in opposition, Thatcher's speeches indicated a new direction in foreign policy. She promised that if returned to power, the Conservatives would pursue Britain's interests more vigorously, in contrast to what was seen as the 'half-heartedness and implicit defeatism of much of British foreign policy in the 1970s'.[3] The 1979 Conservative Party manifesto promised a more robust response to the Soviet threat, to increase defence expenditure, and laid out Thatcher's vision of 'A strong Britain in a free world'.[4] Thatcher heralded change in that, unlike the political leaders of the 1960s and 1970s, she did not see British statecraft as the management of national decline.

Once in power, Thatcher pursued an ideological approach to foreign policy, rejecting the more traditionalist and pragmatic assumptions of her predecessors. For her, the international system was characterised by power politics and conflict, and the Soviet invasion of Afghanistan in December 1979 only served to demonstrate this. The main planks of Thatcher's foreign policy were a firm commitment to the transatlantic alliance, the strengthening of NATO and, initially at least, a more hostile approach to the Soviet Union. Thatcher provided active support for American's role in global policing and shared Reagan's fear about the Soviet threat. She reduced the value of overseas aid and its distribution was shifted to reflect British foreign policy objectives more directly. The separate Ministry of Overseas Development was abolished and placed within the Foreign and Commonwealth Office. Perhaps the major change was in her foreign policy style rather than the content of policy. The message to her overseas audience was that the Conservatives were determined to halt Britain's decline and that Britain had a new willingness to take a leading world role. Overall Thatcher heralded a change in presentation, rhetoric and aspiration, but this was not always reflected in a change in policy: some of the changes were only marginal rather than decisive. Perhaps most of all, Thatcher personalised foreign policy in terms of style. She took a more combative approach, and increasingly British foreign policy was presented as *her* policy. She projected herself as a world stateswoman and delighted in the Soviet Union's choice of nickname, the Iron Maiden.

Thatcher's more ideological approach to foreign policy was matched by a radicalisation of policy within the Labour Party. For Labour, this radicalisation was not just as a response to Thatcher or to the deepening Cold War; rather, it had its roots in the early 1970s, when the party had adopted left-wing positions on defence and nuclear policy, which were made part of the 1974 election manifestos but which were not then implemented by the Labour governments of 1974 to 1979. In the 1970s there had been a growing division between senior Labour ministers on the one hand, and party activists and backbench MPs on the other, on their attitude towards the Cold War and on defence, as détente opened up new possibilities for limiting East/West confrontation. Indeed, the Labour Party had ended up with two different defence policies, the one that was voted for by activists at the annual conference, and the one that was implemented by the Labour government. With the loss of power in 1979, these divisions became more public as the left of the party mobilised in order to try to limit the independence of Labour MPs and so prevent the possibility of this situation being repeated next time Labour was in government. In addition, the deepening Cold War made the issue of nuclear policy more imperative. In response to the Soviet invasion of Afghanistan in December 1979, President Carter withdrew the SALT II treaty from the Senate so that it could not be ratified. On 12 December 1979 NATO announced that new American medium-range Cruise and Pershing nuclear missiles would be deployed in Europe to counter the deployment of the Soviet Union's SS-20 missiles. The first Cruise missiles arrived at Greenham Common air base in Berkshire in June 1980. This decision was controversial and unpopular with the public, and the peace movement enjoyed a burst of growth and popularity. The deployment of Cruise missiles also caused massive consternation within the Labour Party, at a time when it was engaged in a fierce battle over the future direction of policy. In the summer of 1980, the Conservative government announced that it would buy the American Trident submarine-launched nuclear missile system to replace Polaris. Added to this, the Regan presidency heralded a more confrontational and bellicose approach to foreign and defence policy, and American defence expenditure increased dramatically. Whereas the 1970s had seen the hope of détente in superpower relations, the world in the early 1980s felt like a very dangerous place and the threat of nuclear war a real possibility.

Labour's internal battles, defence policy and disarmament

Labour's loss of power in 1979 was followed by a period of acute infighting between the various wings of the party as those on the left mobilised to bring about constitutional changes to restrict the power of the PLP. The work of the left-wing Campaign for Labour Party

Democracy (CLPD), which had been established in 1973, intensified. This group was committed to reforming the Labour Party constitution to ensure that policy decisions reached by the annual conference were then binding on Labour MPs. It also wanted MPs to be more accountable to the party's members – and thus to the left-wing of the party – and lobbied for mandatory reselection for sitting MPs, a policy which was adopted at the 1979 annual conference despite opposition from the Labour leadership and the PLP.[5] A total of eleven left-wing groups within the Labour Party, including the Campaign for Labour Party Democracy, the Socialist Campaign for a Labour Victory and the Militant Group, then joined forces under the umbrella grouping of the Rank and File Mobilising Committee, which was led by Tony Benn, in May 1980.[6] They succeeded in getting the 1980 annual conference to accept a resolution to extend the franchise for electing the party leader. In future, the leader of the Labour Party would not just be elected by Labour MPs, traditionally one of the least left-wing groups within the party, but by an electoral college which would also include Labour Party members and the trade unions. The annual conference could not agree on what form the new system of an electoral college should take, and so a special conference was held at Wembley on 24 January 1981. This conference endorsed a new procedure by which the leader and deputy leader should be re-elected each year at the annual conference, with 40 per cent of the votes going to the Trade Unions, 30 per cent to the Parliamentary Party, and 30 per cent to the constituency parties. These two constitutional changes were designed to limit the independence of MPs and the leader of the Labour Party.

Callaghan resigned as leader of the Labour Party in October 1980. Michael Foot, a left-winger, narrowly beat Denis Healey, who was from the right of the party, in the subsequent leadership election campaign. An election was held in 1981 for the position of deputy leader of the party, where at the second ballot Denis Healey beat Tony Benn by less than 1 per cent of the vote. The deputy leadership election was particularly bitter and vitriolic, with personal attacks being made on the integrity of the candidates. The most controversial issue within these leadership battles was the future of Labour's nuclear policy. Michael Foot and the left-wingers wanted Labour to commit to unilateral nuclear disarmament and some on the left, such as Benn, also wanted this to be accompanied by a commitment to withdraw from NATO. Those who were on the Atlanticist centre-right of the party, such as ex-government ministers Denis Healey and David Owen, still saw Britain's defence policy as based on the transatlantic alliance and were in favour of Britain retaining its independent nuclear deterrent. In an attempt to diffuse this issue in the bitter deputy leadership campaign and to appeal to party members, Healey had come out in opposition to deployment of Cruise missiles in Britain and opposition to a replacement for Polaris, Britain's independent deterrent. Once he won the election, he then had to face criticism from the media on his changed stance on defence. As Dan Keohane points out, because Healey was by far the most prominent Labour Atlanticist involved in presenting both the 'old' nuclear position and the 'new' non-nuclear policy, and because he had a somewhat combative personal style, 'he became a target for sustained questioning by critics anxious to eluci-date contradictions between his past and current postures on defence issues'.[7]

The constitutional changes to the Labour Party meant that Atlanticist MPs were operating in a very hostile environment where they were in danger of being deselected and where there was little chance of one of their own becoming party leader. The beginning of the 1980s saw the transfer of power from centre-right Atlanticists to left-winger unilateralists at the leadership level, mirroring an earlier shift within the party membership to the left. The left-wing groups within the party, which were working together to an unusual degree, were able to get resolutions passed at the 1980 annual conference which committed the next Labour general election manifesto to supporting withdrawal from the EC and the adoption of unilateral nuclear disarmament. The shifting stance of the Labour Party on foreign and defence policy was then compounded when, in despair at the policy changes over membership of the EC and the British nuclear deterrent, Roy Jenkins, David Owen, Shirley Williams and Bill Rodgers, all prominent Atlanticists, left the Labour Party to form the SDP in 1981.[8] To many within the Labour Party this was an act of betrayal that further undermined the policies being espoused by the remaining Atlanticists in the party, who were also viewed with some suspicion.

Labour's first major policy document following their 1979 defeat, *Peace, Jobs, Freedom*, was produced by the party's NEC in May 1980. While this document did not actually commit the party to unilateral disarmament, it hinted at it, and it was also strongly critical of the foreign and defence policy being pursued by the Conservative govern-ment. Despite the document espousing a new defence policy more in line with the views of the left of the party, it did not gain enough votes to be passed at the annual conference in September, where the very heated and lengthy debate on defence policy demonstrated the fault-line within the party. While a resolution committing the party to renouncing Britain's membership of NATO was overwhelmingly lost, several resolutions were passed which opposed the deployment of American Cruise missiles in Britain and rejected the replacement of Polaris, Britain's independent nuclear deterrent. One successful reso-lution also demanded that the conference call 'for a commitment in the Labour Party manifesto to unilateral nuclear disarmament'. In addi-tion, 'Conference recognises that the production of armaments is an essential feature of capitalism and super-power rivalries and that only with the victory of socialism will such rivalries and the production of weapons of mass extermination be finally eliminated'.[9]

Because these successful resolutions indicated the rejection of Labour's previous policy on nuclear weapons and the acceptance of a non-nuclear policy, the party's NEC drew up a new policy statement on nuclear weapons. This said that the next Labour government would assist progress towards multilateral nuclear disarmament by the unilat-eral initiative of closing down all nuclear bases, British or American, on British soil, and by refusing to accept Cruise missiles. The statement also affirmed Labour's strong support for a European nuclear-free zone. The statement explained that 'A British decision to remove all nuclear weapons would not require withdrawal from NATO', as Britain would join the ranks of nuclear-free NATO countries such as Norway, Denmark and Canada.[10] This, then, was the commitment to unilateral nuclear disarmament that those on the left had been fighting for. This statement was carried at the 1981 annual conference, as was a resolution by the TGWU that committed the NEC to ensure that the next election manifesto 'includes an unambiguous commitment to unilateral nuclear disarmament'. This also committed Labour to closing down all nuclear bases, reducing defence expenditure, and for all Labour-controlled councils to declare their areas as a 'nuclear weapon-free zone'.[11] Thus, the Labour Party was now committed to a non-nuclear defence policy that included the rejection of Polaris and its replacement, Trident, and the closing down of American bases.

Following the 1981 conference, the NEC asked the party's Defence Study Group to outline the nature of a future Labour defence policy, one that included the commitment to nuclear disarmament.[12] The Defence Study Group, which included Robin Cook, Mary Kaldor, Clive Soley and Mike Gapes, produced its interim report, *Defence Security and Disarmament*, in April 1982, which was then presented to conference. *Defence Security and Disarmament* reaffirmed Labour's commitment to unilateral nuclear disarmament, arguing that Labour could lead the rest of the world by its example, as 'British possession of strategic nuclear weapons has given no leverage to promote nuclear disarmament'. Instead, emphasis would be placed on conventional forces for defensive purposes. Labour would limit British arms sales and would not supply arms to countries where the chances of international conflict or internal repression would be increased, and would seek agreement on this from other arms-exporting nations.[13] The Labour Party was also concerned about the problem of cutting defence expenditure and limiting the arms trade while protecting British jobs, and the Defence Study Group produced an extensive statement on *Defence Industry Conversion and Economic Planning* dealing with this issue in March 1983.[14]

By this time, sections of the Labour Party were working closely with the peace movement. CND, which had been fairly low key during the 1970s, had seen a resurgence at the end of the decade with the heightening tensions between East and West and the introduction of new nuclear weapons in Europe. CND national membership grew from 4,287 in 1979 to 20,000 in 1981 and 110,000 in 1985.[15] The election of Michael Foot as Labour Party leader had cemented existing close relations with CND. The Labour Party officially supported the European Nuclear Disarmament (END) campaign, which had been launched on 28 April 1980, as party policy. END was committed to campaigning for a nuclear weapon free zone throughout Europe, and called for 'the people of each nation to agitate for the expulsion of nuclear weapons and bases from European soil and territorial waters' within a transcontinental movement.[16] The Labour Party was also active in mobilising public support for nuclear disarmament, organising a large demonstration against nuclear weapons in June 1980, and supporting CND's massive demonstration in October 1980. Party members were encouraged to take part in establishing and supporting local CND and peace groups in co-operation with other political organisations, religious, community, youth and student groups. It was felt that 'A strong mass movement against the Tory warmongers and Cruise and Trident will contribute greatly to the fight for a Labour Government, and a Labour Government is the only Government which will cut arms spending and get rid of nuclear weapons on British soil or in British waters'.[17]

Labour established a Labour Disarmament Liaison Committee that represented a range of peace groups, including Labour Action for Peace, Labour CND, Trade Union CND, the Bertrand Russell Peace

Foundation, END and the World Disarmament Campaign, as well as individual trade union representatives.[18] Trade Union CND had been set up as a 'specialist section of CND which works to encourage support for our policies and understanding of the disarmament issue in the trade unions'.[19] Labour CND was established as a specialist section of CND, with the aim of working to encourage support for CND policies within the Labour Party. It was open to members and supporters of CND who were Labour Party members and who wanted 'to win the whole Labour movement to the campaign for unilateral nuclear disarmament'. Committee members of Labour CND included Mo Molam, Robin Cook and Mike Gapes.[20] Labour CND organised fringe meetings at regional and national Labour Party conferences, circulated model resolutions to keep up the pressure for Labour's policies on unilateral nuclear disarmament, and liaised with other peace groups in the Labour Party and MPs in the PLP.[21] Labour CND even produced a do-it-yourself campaign kit, replete with cut-out diagrams of Tomahawk ground-launched Cruise missiles with which to decorate leaflets.[22] Richard Taylor argues that by 1983 'CND's longstanding objective of winning over the Labour Party was accomplished'.[23]

Britain's nuclear policy was not the only issue that led to divisions within the party. When Argentina invaded the Falklands, one of Britain's remaining overseas territories, on 2 April 1982, Michael Foot said that the people of the Falkland Islands were 'faced with an act of naked, unqualified aggression, carried out in the most shameful and disreputable circumstances'.[24] He endorsed the Thatcher government's decision to send a task force to recover the islands, while urging diplomatic efforts to secure an Argentine withdrawal. However, while the Labour leadership argued that it was necessary to use force against a fascist regime that had undertaken an act of aggression, the Labour Party was divided. Many on the left vociferously criticised the Labour leadership position and argued that Britain was risking lives and spending enormous sums of money defending an outpost of the British empire which, they said, consisted of a few sheep farmers. In a Commons debate on the government's decision to withdraw the latest proposal for a cessation of hostilities that had been rejected by Argentina, and which would therefore mean an acceleration of military operations, thirty-three Labour MPs, led by Tony Benn, defied the Labour whips' instructions to abstain and voted against the government.[25]

There was strong public support for the government's decision to send the task force and to take back the Falklands, and the comprehensive British victory helped portray Margaret Thatcher as a strong and decisive leader. It changed the context for Thatcher's foreign policy-making, allowing her to appoint people she felt would agree with her over the main issues. It also gave the Conservative government a boost at the general election held the following year. While Labour's divisions over the Falklands died down, it was vulnerable to attack by the press and by opponents for not being united in its support of British servicemen, 255 of whom had died. It was also uncomfortable with the public expressions of national pride generated as a result of the victory. The June 1983 Labour election manifesto complained that 'Mrs Thatcher's policy of Fortress Falklands is imposing an intolerable burden both on the British people and on the inhabitants of the Falklands themselves'. A future Labour government would restore normal links between the Falklands and the Latin American mainland, and involve the UN in finding a permanent solution to the problem.[26] This remained the line for the NEC's statement to the 1984 annual conference, which also called for an independent inquiry into the circumstances surrounding the sinking of the Argentine cruiser, the *General Belgrano*, with the loss of 370 lives, when it had been outside the exclusion zone at the time.[27]

Labour and the 1983 manifesto

The changes in Labour's foreign and defence policy were brought to prominence by the 1983 general election. Infamously dubbed the 'longest suicide note in history' by Gerald Kaufman, Labour's 1983 manifesto, *The New Hope for New Britain*, gave many new commitments, including the commitment to withdraw Britain from the EC within the lifetime of the next parliament. This was necessary, it said, because 'The next Labour government, committed to radical, socialist policies for reviving the British economy, is bound to find continued membership a most serious obstacle to the fulfilment of those policies'.[28] However, it was the manifesto's defence commitments that were seen as the most controversial, promising a 'non-nuclear defence policy' for Britain if Labour were elected. This meant the 'removal of all existing nuclear bases and weapons' in Britain and the rejection of any fresh nuclear bases or weapons in Britain, and it argued that 'The most pressing objective must be to prevent the deployment here or elsewhere in Western Europe of Cruise or Pershing missiles'. It committed Britain to cancelling the Trident programme and proposed that 'Britain's Polaris force be included in the nuclear disarmament negotiations in which Britain must take a part. We will, after consultation, carry through in the lifetime of the next parliament our non-nuclear defence policy.' The Labour government would maintain its support for NATO, but 'We wish to see NATO itself develop a non-nuclear strategy'. Labour would also cut defence expenditure in order to bring it into line with the other major European NATO countries, and would use the resources that would have gone on nuclear weapons to strengthen Britain's conventional forces.[29]

The party was far from united on the issue of unilateral nuclear disarmament, and latent disagreements and tensions over defence policy resurfaced during the election campaign. Different members of the leadership interpreted the Polaris commitment differently, much to the Conservative Party's delight. When asked what would happen to Polaris if multilateral disarmament talks were unsuccessful, Michael Foot said that it meant that Labour would decommission the existing Polaris stockpile while Denis Healey said that Polaris would be retained. Robin Cook made a speech during the 1983 election campaign in which he complained that people in the party and the media had pretended that there were alternative interpretations of Labour's manifesto on unilateral nuclear disarmament.[30] As one insider put it, 'people like Denis Healey and Roy Hattersley fought the 1983 election with their fingers crossed behind their back, assuming, quite rightly, that the party would lose and therefore it didn't really matter'.[31] The problem was that while the activists liked the policy, the voters did not. After the election the historian E. P. Thompson said that Labour's failure to say what it meant by 'non-nuclear defence' was like a 'Black Hole' in the campaign. There was concern within the Labour Disarmament Liaison Committee that 'with the public our position on defending the country is both vague and unconvincing' and that 'no one who has as yet spoken from the front bench on the question has, frankly, sounded as through they really understood the subject'.[32]

At the general election of 9 June 1983, the Conservatives won 397 seats with Labour on 209 seats. While the SDP/Liberal Alliance gained only 23 seats, it received 25.4 per cent of the vote compared with Labour's 27.6 per cent, nearly pushing Labour into third place.[33] Furthermore, the SDP/Liberal Alliance came second in 262 of the 397 seats won by the Conservatives.[34] This was a disastrous result for the Labour Party and some commentators questioned whether Labour could survive as the official opposition. Michael Foot resigned as party leader shortly afterwards. Neil Kinnock won the subsequent leadership election of 1 October, with Roy Hattersley being elected as his deputy. Kinnock was from the left of the party and was a keen supporter of unilateral nuclear disarmament, while Hattersley was from the right. It was clear that the party's structure, polices and image all needed urgent attention, and 'Kinnock realised that if Labour was to achieve electoral victory it was necessary to reorganise the Party, to make policy more acceptable to the electorate and to end the internal divisions'.[35] However, as Eric Shaw points out, 'Kinnock's predicament was that his command over the Party was insufficient to accomplish his goals'.[36] The party activists were in no mood for compromise over policy and tended to assume that 'swing door' politics would mean that Labour would be elected soon enough as the public would tire of having a Conservative government.

At the 1983 annual conference a composite resolution was passed that reaffirmed the 1983 election manifesto commitments on defence, including the non-nuclear policy, and the 'elimination of all foreign military bases on British soil'.[37] A composite resolution was proposed that demonstrated the strength of the divisions and anger in the party at this stage, which stated that 'Conference rejects and condemns those currently residing in our movement who stabbed us in the back in the general election campaign. Conference demands total support for Labour Party policy on unilateral nuclear disarmament from the party's leadership.'[38] This resolution was, fortunately for those seeking to rebuild the party, defeated. However, the strong language and overt antagonism towards the US 'foreign bases' demonstrated how far the Labour Party had shifted its position on nuclear weapons, the Atlantic alliance and Britain's role in NATO, and how hard it would be to shift the party back towards the middle ground.

The Labour Party and Europe

It was not just the issue of defence where Labour's policy was out of line with the other parties in the early 1980s. Many in the Labour Party were against Britain's continued membership of the EC, believing at that time that membership would prevent a Labour government from carrying out socialist economic strategies such as regeneration of the economy through reflationary measures. Party leader Michael Foot had been an opponent of the EC since its inception. Many in the party had been against British entry during the Heath government, and had been active in the campaign for the 'no' vote in the referendum on continued membership in 1975. Thus, as Geddes point out, between 1979 and 1983, hostility to the EC became a key feature of the party's left-wing socialist strategy.[39] At the 1980 annual conference Clive Jenkins moved a resolution stating that conference 'urges the Labour Party to include the withdrawal of the United Kingdom from the European Economic Community as a priority in the next general election manifesto'. Jenkins argued that people had supported membership in the referendum in 1975 because they had been told that jobs would be lost if Britain withdrew, but this had in fact been a lie. Despite the arguments of pro-Europeans such as Roy Jenkins and David Owen, the resolution was passed by 5,042,000 votes to 2,097,000.[40] Standing on a platform of withdrawal from the EC meant that Labour was not only out of line with both the Conservatives and the Liberals, but it was also a key reason for the defection of some of the pro-European right of the party to form the SDP in 1981. This in turn entrenched the anti-Europeanism of the Labour Party and the strength of the left. The withdrawal from the EC then became part of Labour's economic policy, which was spear-headed by the Shadow Chancellor, Peter Shore, himself a passionate campaigner against membership of the EC. Labour was aiming at the socialist transformation of the economy, which included extending public ownership of industry and controlling capital movements, and this would require the restoration of all the powers transferred to Brussels when Britain joined the EC on 1 January 1973. The 1983 Labour Party general election manifesto duly pledged British withdrawal from the EC well within the lifetime of the government, as 'the European Community, which does not even include the whole of Western Europe, was never devised to suit us, and our experience as a member of it has made it more difficult for us to deal with our economic and industrial problems'.[41]

However, this policy of definite withdrawal was short-lived. Neil Kinnock, when elected party leader on 1 October 1983, had stood on a platform of retaining nearly all the policies from the 1983 general election, arguing that Labour needed to communicate its policies better rather than ditching them. The one area where he did argue that there needed to be a policy shift was over membership of the EC. In *Statement of Values*, his leadership manifesto to the party, he argued that by 1988, the likely date of the next general election, Britain would have been in the EC for fifteen years. While this did not make withdrawal impossible, after that length of time, withdrawal should only be regarded as a last resort.[42] He argued that it would be better to reform

the EC rather than withdraw from it. By the time of the annual conference in October, Labour's position on Europe had already shifted
somewhat. An NEC policy document was passed at conference that
said 'Britain will remain a member of the EEC for the term of the next
European Parliament', which would run from 1984 to 1989, and
'Labour will fight to get the best deal for Britain within it', but
retained the option of withdrawing from the EC at a later date. It said
that Labour wanted to reform the CAP, and 'We want to see a
complete change of priorities in the EEC, with more spending on
regional and social priorities and less on agriculture'.[43] This position
was repeated in Labour's manifesto for the European elections in
1984.[44]

Kinnock gave Robin Cook, who had run his leadership campaign,
the newly created Shadow Cabinet post of European Affairs
Spokesman with the task of 'spearheading a shift in the Labour Party's
stance towards Europe'.[45] In the run-up to the European elections,
Cook began to make speeches in which he argued that far from hinder-
ing Labour's economic policies, membership of the EC could actually
help Labour to implement policies to counter unemployment, enhance
workers' rights and bring about co-ordinated reflation. At the direct
elections to the European Parliament on 14 June 1984, Labour did
credibly well, gaining 36.5 per cent of the vote and thirty-two seats,
compared with the Conservatives' forty-five seats on 40.8 per cent of
the vote. In a very short period of time, continuing membership of the
EC for the foreseeable future had become *de facto* party policy without
the anti-Marketeers being fully aware of what was happening.
According to Anderson and Mann, 'Much of the left was outraged at
the way Cook and Kinnock had bounced Labour into acceptance of
EC membership', and after the European elections, 'a steady stream of
bitter left-wing MPs and MEPs denounced the leadership's manoeuvre'.[46] However, there had been surprisingly little resistance to the shift
in policy over the EC. There were a number of reasons for this.

First, the Labour Party, especially the PLP, had been shocked by
the extent of its defeat at the 1983 election, and was concerned that it
would be pushed into third place at the 1984 European elections by
the SDP/Liberal Alliance with its pro-European standpoint. Second,
it was widely accepted that the 1975 referendum had demonstrated
that the majority of the public did support British membership of the
EC, and so to stand on a manifesto of withdrawal from the EC had
the potential to harm the party at future general elections. Third, the
party was keen to support its new leader and many accepted that

the party needed to modernise. Re-evaluating the party's policy on Europe was an integral part of the modernisation process and would demonstrate to the public that Labour had changed. Fourth, whereas in the past membership of the EC had been seen as a block on the development of socialist policies in Britain, many in the party were gradually coming to the view that because of increasing economic interdependence, a future Labour government would not be able to implement reflationary economic policies to create jobs and boost economic growth without some kind of co-ordination and economic convergence with the other EC countries. This had been demonstrated in France when the socialist government under President Mitterrand introduced a range of reflationary measures to alleviate high unemployment in 1981, which plunged the country into a severe economic crisis. Finally, with the Conservative Party so dominant in the House of Commons, the EC provided a 'new and welcome front on which to counter Thatcherism'.[47]

Thus, by 1987, the party had reversed its position on Europe, and this had been largely neutralised as an electoral issue. The 1987 election manifesto said very little about the EC, simply that 'Labour's aim is to work constructively with our EEC partners to promote economic expansion and combat unemployment. However, we will stand up for British interests within the European Community.'[48] The following year saw the conversion of the trade unions to a pro-European stance as Jacques Delores, the President of the European Commission, proposed a Social Chapter of workers' rights. When he addressed the annual conference of the TUC on 8 September, he received a standing ovation for his speech on the need for a social Europe that would improve workers' living and working conditions. Many of the TUC's objectives regarding workers' rights had been obstructed at the national level with the re-election of Thatcher in 1987, but now Delores 'held out the prospect of achieving them through action within the EC'.[49] As a consequence, Labour's policy statements on Europe became more positive. The document *Social Justice and Economic Efficiency* said that 'Britain could not withdraw from the Community without huge damage to our economy and ruined relations with key trading partners'.[50] Labour began to see that it could use Europe to its own advantage in progressing its political and economic agenda. At the 1988 conference a composite resolution was passed that stated that 'Conference recognises that Britain is politically and economically integrated into the European Community. Therefore, the Labour Party, in conjunction with the other socialist parties of the

EC, must seek to use and adapt Community institutions to promote democratic socialism.'[51] Labour also supported British membership of the Exchange Rate Mechanism (ERM), stating in its 1990 document *Looking to the Future*, that

> Joining the ERM is no panacea for Britain's economic problems. But it will provide a stable framework for long-term investment and steady growth. That is why Labour will negotiate Britain's entry at the earliest opportunity on the basis of the prudent and reasonable conditions which we have frequently outlined.[52]

By 1991, Labour was presenting itself as more pro-European than the Conservatives, arguing that 'We believe that Britain must be a leader in Europe, not a follower' and that 'Britain's future lies in the European Community. If Britain opts out, then we will lose out.'[53] By this point, it was the Conservative Party that was developing deep and bitter divisions over membership of the EC that were to damage its reputation for party unity.

The Labour Party and developing countries

Support for developing countries became a key plank of Labour's foreign policy in the 1980s and another area in which they were at odds with Conservative policy. However, unlike defence and Europe, this was a policy area where the Labour Party was almost always united. Labour supported national liberation movements, condemned intervention by either superpower, focused attention on Third World debt, and was at the forefront of the campaign in Britain to end apartheid in South Africa. The party performed the role of pressure group in terms of highlighting and propelling issues such as apartheid up the political agenda in Britain.

Labour's commitment to dealing with Third World debt, poverty and human rights was demonstrated by the activities of the NEC's International Committee in the early 1980s, which had its own subcommittees for Latin America, Asia, the Middle East and on Africa which regularly met to develop and outline party policy. It was agreed that 'The objective of a socialist foreign policy is to create the conditions necessary to free the world from poverty, inequality and war and to encourage the liberation of mankind from political and economic oppression'.[54] Because the party was 'deeply concerned at the worsening plight of the 800 million people living in absolute poverty throughout the world', the NEC set up a Development and

Cooperation Sub-Committee in 1981 to study overseas aid and development issues and to recommend policy proposals for the 1982 annual conference.[55]

Labour condemned the cuts in overseas aid carried out by the Conservatives, and declared 'its support for the poor in the Third World to eradicate hunger, disease and illiteracy'.[56] The 1983 manifesto contained a commitment to re-establish the Ministry of Overseas Development and to increase expenditure on aid, and argued 'That some 8,000,000,000 people should be condemned to a life of absolute poverty in the Third World is an affront to any version of civilised values, as well as a constant threat to international peace and stability'.[57] In 1987 Labour produced a statement on *For the Good of All: Labour's Plans for Aid and Development*. This argued that economic growth in the Third World was essential to international recovery, which would help restore prosperity in Britain. 'Most of all, it matters because we cannot tolerate a world where millions of people live out a constant struggle for survival, without hope of food or shelter.' It pledged that Labour would meet the UN aid expenditure target of 0.7 per cent of national income, rising to 1 per cent in a Labour second term, and the establishment of a Department of Overseas Development and Cooperation.[58] This was repeated in the 1987 general election manifesto. A 1988 policy document, *Democratic Socialist Aims and Values*, said that 'The division of the world into rich and poor, developed and underdeveloped, prosperous and starving nations, many of which are deprived of freedom, is equally immoral and even more dangerous for the world as a whole'.[59]

The Labour Party regularly voiced its support for liberation and progressive movements around the world. At the 1983 Annual Conference an NEC statement on Central America was passed that pledged 'its support for all those radical and democratic forces currently striving to bring dictatorship and foreign domination to an end in Central America', paid tribute to the Frente Sandinista in Nicaragua, expressed solidarity with the Revolutionary Democratic Front in El Salvador, deplored the involvement of the US in Honduras, and stated that 'Conference believes that the performance of the United States administration in Central America is damaging to democracy and to the United States itself'.[60] A resolution was also passed that 'condemns the massive and increasing United States intervention in Central America' and 'calls for the withdrawal of all United States military and financial aid to repressive regimes in Central America'.[61] The party was highly critical of America's foreign policy, more so than in previous decades. The party condemned America's 'self-appointed role as world policeman',[62] and regularly attacked US policy in Central America.[63] The 1987 manifesto said that 'We oppose United States intervention in Nicaragua and the financing and arming of the Contra rebels'.[64]

The party also supported the African National Congress (ANC) and SWAPO in South Africa and Namibia.[65] The 1983 election manifesto pledged support to the liberation movements in South Africa and Namibia, support for comprehensive UN mandatory sanctions against and economic disengagement from South Africa, opposed US policy in Central America, and expressed concern about the suppression of human and civil rights in many of the countries in Asia.[66] The policy document *Social and Economic Efficiency* in 1988 stated that 'Labour stands firmly alongside the oppressed majority in their struggle for liberation; and support comprehensive mandatory sanctions against South Africa. Labour will do everything possible to help bring about a non-racial democratic and united South Africa and a free and independent Namibia.'[67]

In terms of the Middle East, resolutions were passed at the 1982 conference that supported the Palestinian Liberation Organisation (PLO) and the establishment of a Palestinian state,[68] and opposition movements in Iran and Iraq.[69] It was felt that the Middle East's 'importance as source of oil and of petrodollars, as well as its strategic location, present particular dilemmas for socialists who support the principles of national self-determination and who favour popularly-elected democratic governments'. However, the party's NEC recognised that the Middle East 'poses a particular problem for those seeking to understand Labour's policy in Left/Right terms'. For example, 'Divisions representing often strongly held views on the Israel Arab conflict do not conform to the classic Left/Right divisions in the Party'.[70]

The Labour Party also repeatedly explicitly stated its support for human rights across the world. The 1983 general election manifesto said that 'We uphold the rights of all nations to self-determination', that 'We will protect the opponents of regimes from harassment by their government's representatives in Britain', and that 'We will also take into account human rights considerations when giving aid'. It expressed concern about human rights abuses in Turkey, in the Middle East, in Asia and Central America.[71] Labour criticised US support for repressive regimes in Central America. Labour criticised the Soviet Union over its invasion of Afghanistan in its 1983 and 1987 election manifestos, and expressed alarm over the treatment of Solidarity in Poland.[72] Labour also criticised the Soviet Union over its human rights record.[73]

The party at all levels also repeatedly stated that it was opposed to the growth of the arms trade, that Labour would limit Britain's arms sales abroad, and that arms exports to repressive regimes would be prohibited under them.[74] The 1983 election manifesto said that Labour would 'ban the supply or arms to arms to repressive regimes such as South Africa, El Salvador, Chile, Argentina and Turkey. We will not supply arms to countries where the chances of international aggression or internal repression would be increased.'[75] At the 1986 annual conference a resolution was passed that said Labour would 'adopt a policy of supplying no arms or other military equipment to countries responsible for sustained human rights abuse or involved in armed conflict.'[76] This was not included in the 1987 election manifesto, but did appear in the 1992 election manifesto, which stated that Labour would stop the sale of arms that might be used for internal repression or international aggression, and would set up a defence diversification agency.[77] The issue of arms sales of course went on to become a key plank of Labour's new approach to foreign and defence policy during the New Labour government of 1997.

While the party was united in its views on developing countries, aid and debt, and managed to neutralise Europe as lightening rod for divisions within the party, defence policy continued to be controversial. The first defence document produced by the party following the 1983 general election defeat was *Defence and Security for Britain*. This outlined Labour's non-nuclear defence policy more clearly than the 1983 manifesto had in that it said that a Labour government would decommission the existing Polaris missiles as well as cancelling Trident and closing all American nuclear bases. Instead, more money would be spent on conventional weapons. The document explained that the party resisted 'taking a sanguine view of Soviet policy ... the Soviet Union and its Warsaw Pact allies have a large military capability which could pose a potential military threat to Western Europe'. However, it repudiated the 'extreme views of Mrs Thatcher and President Reagan that the Soviet Union is "our sworn enemy" or an "evil empire" bent on world domination'.[78] Instead, it advocated the restoration of détente in order to ease military tension. During the mid-1980s the party retained its commitment to unilateral nuclear disarmament, the cancellation of Trident, the removal of all nuclear weapons from Britain, and a nuclear-free Europe.

The 1987 election and the policy review

By the time of the 1987 election, Kinnock had made progress in re-organising the party, ending internal divisions, tackling the hard left and ending the influence of Militant within Labour. Much had been done to improve the party machinery, particularly in the areas of public relations and communications. Peter Mandelson had been appointed as the party's director of communications in 1985 and early in 1986 the advertising executive Philip Gould was brought in to run the Shadow Communications Agency. The problem remained of how to present Labour's non-nuclear defence policy, which had not changed since the 1983 manifesto. Westlake says that 'By 1986 Labour strategists had largely accepted that the party's defence policy could only ever by an electoral liability'.[79] Philip Gould was commissioned to conduct research on what the public thought of the policy, and Gould found in his focus group research that the public tended to identify defence with deterrence, and thought that a strong defence policy included nuclear weapons. His suggested strategy for the coming election was to 'Position Labour as the party that puts the defence of Britain first' in contrast to the Conservatives who were running down the nation's defences 'to pay for an unusable, unaffordable and escalating nuclear arsenal.'[80] Peter Mandelson's approach was to try to minimise the likely damage caused by the non-nuclear defence policy by getting the party's leadership to say as little about defence as possible in the run-up to the 1987 general election, and failing this, to emphasise Labour's commitment to conventional forces and to the Atlantic alliance.[81]

Of course, part of the problem was that the Labour Party had never really faced up to the potential consequences for the Anglo-American alliance of Britain adopting a non-nuclear policy. Indeed, it had never actually considered whether Britain would be allowed to remain within NATO if a Labour government attempted to implement its non-nuclear policy, given that NATO's policy of flexible response meant that it was prepared to use tactical nuclear weapons in response to a Soviet attack, even if that attack used purely conventional forces, of which the Soviet Union had a preponderance. The US was hardly likely cooperate with a Labour government that was committed to unilateral nuclear disarmament, to the removal of US nuclear bases in Britain, and to changing NATO from within to create a non-nuclear zone in Europe. Furthermore, the Labour Party vociferously criticised numerous aspects of American foreign and defence policy during the mid-1980s. Kinnock personally had been very outspoken in his opposition to Reagan's proposed Strategic Defense Initiative, which would use ground- and space-based systems to protect the US by shooting down incoming strategic nuclear ballistic missiles. This scheme, according to Kinnock, represented a greater threat to NATO than the Soviet Union did.[82] Thus, the British public were not likely to be convinced of the strength of the Atlantic alliance under a possible Labour government. Added to this, Neil Kinnock's visit to the US at the end of March, just before the 1987 election, was a public relations disaster. Rather naively, Kinnock had hoped to promote Labour's non-nuclear defence policy in the US. Instead, he had a cursory meeting with Reagan, after which Reagan's press secretary, Marlin Fitzwater, outlined to the media how Reagan had informed Kinnock that the US administration disagreed with Labour's proposals for unilateral nuclear disarmament, and that it was concerned that such proposals would undercut America's negotiating position at the superpower talks on intermediate-range nuclear forces, which were due to conclude in December.[83]

The 1987 election manifesto stated that Labour would 'end the nuclear pretence' by decommissioning Polaris and cancelling Trident, and would 'ensure a rational conventional defence policy for Britain' by using the money saved to pay for improvements in conventional armed forces. This increased spending would be used for British equipment where possible, thus ensuring jobs in the British aerospace, shipbuilding and engineering industries. Labour would remove US Cruise missiles and other nuclear weapons from Britain, through international agreement between the US and Soviet Union on the removal of all nuclear weapons in Europe if possible, but through a direct request to the US if not. The manifesto said that Britain would then become the ninth out of the sixteen NATO members which did not have US nuclear weapons on their territory, and that this change would not affect the other US, British and joint defence and early warning systems in the United Kingdom.[84]

Labour was still vulnerable on a number of issues, but the most significant one was defence. In one particular interview, when Kinnock was asked to outline Labour's response to a Soviet invasion of Britain, he replied that it would be to 'make any occupation totally untenable'. The Conservatives responded with campaign posters showing a soldier with his hands up as if in surrender under the slogan 'Labour's Defence Policy'. An analysis of the Harris general election exit poll for ITN showed that when voters gave their three most important reasons for not voting Labour, 'Labour wouldn't defend Britain properly' came very high on the list.[85] In the post-election assessment, most analysts concluded that Labour's commitment to unilateral nuclear disarmament had diminished its electoral support. Despite Kinnock's attempts to modernise the party, and what was considered to be a very well-run election campaign, Labour's share of the vote at the 1987 general election was only 30.8 per cent compared with the Conservatives' 42.2 per cent. This was not much better than the disastrous 1983 election result. The conclusion that Labour's leadership reached was that if it was to have a chance of regaining power then the party would have to adopt policies that were more in tune with public opinion, rather than policies that reflected the wishes of party activists, however deeply held. This prompted Kinnock to instigate a major policy review with the aim 'to develop a programme that will match the needs and aspirations of the British people in the 1990s'.[86] The objectives were to make Labour electable and to prepare it for government.

Seven policy review groups were established with members drawn from Labour's Shadow Cabinet and the party's NEC. The aim was to produce coherent policies that were acceptable to both the party and the politicians who would have the responsibility of implementing them once Labour was in power.[87] This was significant, for it demonstrated a shift in emphasis away from developing policies that were desirable to existing party members to those that a government might actually be able to implement. The most controversial area was to be foreign and defence policy. This review group, entitled the 'Britain in the World Policy Review Group', was chaired by Gerald Kaufman, the new shadow spokesman on foreign affairs. He was from the centre-right of the party and was not a supporter of unilateral nuclear disarmament. The three main areas this group focused on were defence, the European Community, and overseas aid and development. One of the first things that this group did was to ask the Shadow Communications Agency to produce a report on polling data since the general election. Whereas previously the Labour Party had tended to be somewhat scathing about taking public opinion into account, arguing that the public was ill-informed when it came to foreign and defence policy, it now realised that it would have to consider what the public thought when developing policy. It was found that 'An overwhelming majority of the public wants to keep nuclear weapons until we persuade other countries to disarm'. The public thought a Labour government was 'unlikely to ensure Britain is adequately defended'.[88] Overall, 70 per cent of the population 'oppose what they perceive as our current policy'. Philip Gould had found from his focus group research in the run-up to the election that people felt pride and patriotism as well as fear regarding Britain's nuclear capability. Labour was regarded as being in favour of disarmament or pacifism, and were not seen a pro-defence. In particular, 'Nuclear defence' was perceived by the public to represent 'strong defence', while 'non-nuclear' was perceived as 'non-defence', and 'less defence' was perceived as 'defenceless'.[89]

This group was also keen to bring in outside expertise on a range of foreign and defence issues, and contacted a number of think tanks, pressure groups, charities, universities and individual academics invit-ing them to give evidence to the Britain in the World group on current international issues and threats.[90] Academic and specialist advisors were also invited to work with the review group, for instance Kevin Featherstone from Stirling University on the European Community, and Paul Rogers from Bradford University on defence and nuclear weapons.[91]

The problem that Labour faced was that its view of Britain's role in the world was significantly different from that of the bulk of the electorate. Kinnock and the Labour Party in the 1980s had as its start-ing point for foreign and defence policy that Britain was not a great power; rather it was a middle-ranking power which did not have the ability to change the world, and so it should act accordingly. In their view, nuclear weapons were a superpower status symbol, and it was simply not necessary for a middle power to have them. Labour's 1984 policy document *Defence and Security for Britain* had said that,

> We should no longer behave as though we were a great power or the centre of a global empire. As a medium sized Western European industrial nation we have an important role in preserving peace in Europe, defend-ing our country if we are threatened and working for security and disar-mament in Europe and internationally.[92]

As a middle-ranking power, Britain could not afford both strong conventional forces and nuclear weapons. After the 1987 election defeat, it dawned on the leadership of the Labour Party that the elec-torate did not view Britain this way. The analysis of polling data 'seems to indicate that voters overestimate Britain's power and influence – militarily, politically and economically'. The question then was, 'Do we seek to correct that view, or to live up to public aspirations? How far should public attitudes influence the priorities of our foreign policy?'[93] The answer that the Britain in the World review group came to was that Labour should do much more to live up to public aspirations.

Labour had been hindered at the 1987 election by being seen by the public as the 'unpatriotic party'. George Robertson argued that 'we should be far more positive in claiming our share of the legitimate national pride and self-confidence felt in the country as a whole'.[94]

These discussions of the future of Labour's foreign and defence policy were taking place against the backdrop of a rapidly changing international context. The success of the Intermediate-range Nuclear Forces (INF) negotiations of December 1987 between Reagan and Gorbachev marked a major breakthrough in superpower relations and heralded what was to be far more than a new period of détente. The INF treaty actually went beyond expectations, with both sides agreeing to eliminate their intermediate-range nuclear and conventional ground-launched ballistic and Cruise missiles and to allow inspections of their military installations for verification. The Labour leadership seized upon this and argued that the breakthrough in superpower nuclear arms reduction talks had changed the context for Labour's defence policy. Kinnock said in a BBC interview on 5 June 1988 that 'There is no need now for a something-for-nothing unilateralism'. He said that in the past it had been appropriate to argue that Britain should give up its nuclear weapons, as no progress had been made on nuclear arms reduction talks. Now, however, the logjam was broken, and so Britain could get 'something for something'.

Kinnock argued that international disarmament negotiations might now be the best way to achieve the decommissioning of weapons, and Britain's nuclear weapons could be included in these negotiations. However, to get the Labour Party to accept a new defence policy was not likely to be easy. At the 1987 Labour Party annual conference, a resolution reaffirming Labour's commitment to a non-nuclear defence policy was passed.[95] A resolution that sought a shift of policy away from unequivocal support for unilateralism, because 'after seven years and two general elections, the Labour Party has been unable to persuade the British people of the merits of our policy on unilateral nuclear disarmament', was defeated.[96] At the 1988 annual conference a resolution that committed the next Labour government to 'abolish the Trident programme at whatever stage of development' and to the policy of unilateral nuclear disarmament had been passed, whereas a resolution supported by the NEC which proposed taking bilateral and multilateral as well as unilateral steps towards nuclear disarmament, had been defeated.[97]

The policy review groups presented their reports to the Labour Party's NEC for approval in May 1989. The Britain in the World policy review statement on defence policy, which had been written by Gerald Kaufman, stated that while 1987 Labour government would have cancelled the Trident programme, this option would not be open to a government taking office in 1991 or 1992. Instead of decommissioning Polaris and cancelling Trident, a Labour government would build three rather than four Vanguard-class submarines to carry the Trident missiles and put British nuclear weapons into international negotiations as part of the Strategic Arms Reduction Treaty (START) II disarmament negotiations. Thus, this was a rejection of unilateral disarmament, and a return to Labour's previous policy position of working towards long-term multilateral disarmament while retaining Britain's deterrent. This was the policy review statement that was expected to cause the most controversy within the NEC, and the discussion of the new defence policy was tense. Neil Kinnock made an emotional speech in favour of the Britain in the World report in which he said that he would not support the policy of 'unilateral abandonment of nuclear weapons without getting anything in return ever again'.[98] The NEC meeting then voted on whether to endorse the final report of the Britain in the World policy review group. The report was endorsed, but Margaret Beckett, Tony Benn, David Blunkett, Eddie Haigh, Ken Livingstone, Jo Richardson, Hannah Sell and Dennis Skinner voted against it.[99]

The policy review documents were then presented to the 1989 annual conference under the title of *Meet the Challenge, Make the Change: A New Agenda for Britain*. Each of the policy documents were approved. A resolution was passed that welcomed the defence policy review and said that, 'This conference recognises that in view of the changing world circumstances and the responses of both East and West to reducing nuclear and conventional weapons, it is necessary for the Labour Party to review our existing policies on defence and disarmament'. The resolution committed a Labour government to take 'advantage of opportunities as they arise in the international situation for multilateral and bilateral negotiations and of unilateral initiatives to secure reduction of conventional and nuclear weapons'. A resolution calling for unilateral nuclear disarmament was lost on a card vote of 2,431,000 votes to 3,635,000.[100] Thus, on the third attempt, Kinnock had got the annual conference to approve a change to the commitment to unilateral disarmament, which in effect meant the end of Labour's support for unilateral disarmament.

The result of the policy review was that Labour ditched many policies that were strongly supported by party members and activists, but which were not popular with party voters who were not also members. Seyd and Whitely found in their survey of Labour supporters in 1989 that while 72 per cent of party members agreed with the statement that 'Britain should have nothing to do with nuclear weapons', only 36 per cent of people who had voted Labour in 1987 but who were not members of the party agreed with the statement.[101] The policy review effectively brought Labour into line with the existing political consensus on defence in Britain, and with the policy that had been accepted by Labour for most of the post-war period. Interestingly, the new policy was achieved with less conflict than might have been expected. By this point the majority of the party leadership, and many of the party members, were firmly of the view that if Labour was to be electable then it had to abandon the commitment to unilateral disarmament. It was helped in its quest to achieve the shift by the change in the international environment, with the willingness of Gorbachev to negotiate with the West, the success of the nuclear disarmament talks between the superpowers in 1987, and the Soviet withdrawal from Afghanistan 1988. Gorbachev's policies of economic reform (*perestroika*) and political openness (*glasnost*) in the Soviet Union led to demands for similar policies in Eastern European countries. By the end of 1989, a wave of mostly peaceful revolutions had swept across Central and Eastern Europe and the Berlin Wall, such a symbol of the Cold War division of Europe, had fallen. At the Malta summit at the beginning of December, US President George H. W. Bush and President Gorbachev of the Soviet Union declared the Cold War to be over. This meant that the public's fears of nuclear confrontation between East and West receded. In 1989, membership of CND was a little over half of that of membership in 1983.

In August 1990, Iraq invaded and formally annexed Kuwait. The UN Security Council passed a number of resolutions condemning the invasion, demanding that Iraq remove its troops from Kuwait, and imposing economic sanctions against Iraq. Resolution 678 was passed on 29 November 1990, giving Iraq an ultimatum to withdraw its troops from Kuwait by 15 January 1991, and authorising 'all necessary means', including the use of force, to enforce the withdrawal of Iraqi troops. Following Iraq's failure to respond to this ultimatum, Operation Desert Storm began on 16 January. The US-led coalition force came from thirty-four states and included troops from Afghanistan, Egypt and Saudi Arabia, and small but symbolic numbers of troops from former Eastern bloc countries of Czechoslovakia, Hungary and Poland, as well as the US and UK. Britain sent 43,000 troops.

The Labour Party leadership gave the government unqualified support throughout the Gulf War. This demonstrated the shift from the early 1980s towards a more co-operative attitude towards the US and bipartisan approach to British foreign policy. Whereas the party had been deeply troubled by the Falklands War, it was less so by the Gulf War, with only fairly small groups on the left mobilising to form a 'Stop the War in the Gulf' campaign, arguing that the conflict was fuelled by imperialist competition over oil supplies. In large part, this was because the use of force against Iraq was sanctioned by the UN Security Council and the bulk of the international community. With the end of the Cold War, the UN Security Council was able to operate in the way intended to implement a collective security system, and there emerged an optimistic expectation of the United Nations' role in maintaining post-Cold War international peace and security. A statement by the NEC in January 1991 said that while the Labour Party 'Regrets that the strategy of sanctions, blockade and military readiness to achieve the purposes of the United Nations was not pursued for a longer period', it nevertheless 'Gives full backing to the British and coalition forces being used to secure fulfilment of the United Nations resolutions'.[102] There was some rebellion in the House of Commons. Following a debate on the Gulf on 15 January, fifty-seven Labour MPs voted against government policy, while the majority obeyed the party whip and backed the government.[103]

Kinnock was determined to avoid the public divisions and criticisms that had occurred over the Labour leadership's support for the use of force to oust the Argentine invasion from the Falklands War, which had added to Labour's electoral unpopularity. Once the conflict had started, despite having previously supported the party position to support the use of force, Clare Short suddenly opposed Britain's involvement in the Gulf War. She resigned her frontbench position – the second time that she had done so – after Kinnock had told her to stick to her brief as spokesperson for Social Security. She decided to resign rather than be silenced, which antagonised her colleagues as they felt that she was being disloyal and unhelpful to the party.

Labour's position during the Gulf War received much better press coverage than it had during the Falklands War. According to an editorial in *The Times*, most commentators agreed that Kinnock had had a 'good war'.[104] It signified that Labour was perceived as having returned to a more traditional bipartisanship position when it came to foreign policy and the use of military force. That this was possible was in part the result of the end of the Cold War, in part due to the realisation amongst Labour Party activists that Labour could not simply expect to regain power every few years regardless of whether its policies were in line with public opinion, and in part due to the end of Thatcher's premiership. Thatcher was removed from power by the Conservative Party in November 1990, and replaced by John Major. He had a more conciliatory approach, and the years that followed saw a return to a less ideologically driven foreign and defence policy. In July 1992, at his last Prime Minister' questions in the Commons before the election of Kinnock's replacement, John Major thanked Kinnock 'for his support at times of crisis, for his strong support throughout the Gulf war and for the support that he has given us throughout the difficulties in Yugoslavia'.[105]

For large parts of Labour's history, foreign and defence policy has been amongst the most contentious issues facing the party. This was certainly the case in the 1980s, which saw a major shift in Labour's foreign policy stance at a time when foreign policy opinions in Britain became polarised. Labour started the 1980s already deeply divided over its external policy, and this division deepened in the early 1980s. The Conservative Party moved to the right on foreign and defence policy after Thatcher's Falklands victory in 1982, at a time when Labour had moved ideologically to the left on these issues. The Conservatives successfully labelled Labour as being weak on foreign and defence policy and not to be trusted with the nation's security. At the same time, foreign and defence policy became a key part of the ideological battle within Labour for the future direction that the party should take. It was Neil Kinnock and the modernisers that he employed who managed to overhaul the party to the point where it accepted major shifts over its attitudes to Europe and to nuclear weapons. It was of course Tony Blair who was ultimately to benefit from this in terms of actually gaining power and being in a position to implement Labour's foreign policy. However, while Labour's shift to the left on foreign and defence policy did the party immense harm electorally in the 1980s, it possibly left the party better prepared to deal with the immense changes in the international system at the turn of the 1990s with the end of the Cold War. Having already devoted attention to a new, and more modest, understanding of Britain's role in the world, and accepted that Britain was working in an increasingly interdependent world, Labour was able to accept the new tenets of globalisation in the 1990s, and to deal with the rise in transnational issues that has been a concomitant part of international relations at the end of the twentieth century, in a way that the Conservative Party had yet to grasp.

Notes

1 This is particularly the case with older accounts such as James Barber, *Who Makes British Foreign Policy?* (Milton Keynes: Open University Press, 1976), pp. 78–9, 87; Joseph Frankel, *British Foreign Policy 1945–1973* (Oxford: Oxford University Press, 1975), p. 32; David Vital, *The Making of British Foreign Policy* (London: Allen & Unwin, 1968), p. 76; William Wallace, *The Foreign Policy Process in Britain* (London: RIIA, 1975), p. 93.
2 See Michael Clarke, *British External Policy-Making in the 1990s* (Basingstoke: Macmillan, 1992), ch. 7.
3 Peter Riddell, *The Thatcher Era and its Legacy* (Oxford: Blackwell, 2nd edn, 1988), p. 230.
4 Conservative Party, *The Conservative Manifesto 1979* (London: Conservative Party, 1979).
5 See Patrick Seyd, *The Rise and Fall of the Labour Left* (Basingstoke: Macmillan, 1987), pp. 83–6 and 109.
6 *Ibid.*, p. 118.
7 Dan Keohane, *Labour Party Defence Policy Since 1945* (Leicester: Leicester University Press, 1993), p. 38.
8 See Ivor Crewe and Anthony King, *SDP: The Birth, Life and Death of the Social Democratic Party* (Oxford: Oxford University Press, 1995).
9 *Labour Party Annual Conference Report* (hereafter *LPACR*), 1980, pp. 161 and 173.
10 'Nuclear Weapons and the Arms Race', NEC statement to 1981 conference, *LPACR*, 1981, p. 301.
11 *LPACR*, 1981, pp. 145 and 157.
12 Labour Party archive, Museum of Labour History, Manchester, International Sub-Committee 1979–84, Defence Study Group, ID/1981-82/4/Nov, minutes of meeting of Defence Study Group, 16 September 1981.
13 Labour Party archive, International Sub-Committee 1979–84, Defence Study Group, 'Defence Security and Disarmament', ID/1981-82/107/April.
14 Labour Party archive, International Sub-Committee 1979–84, Defence Study Group, 'Defence Industry Conversion and Economic Planning', ID/1982-83/93/March.
15 Richard Taylor, 'The Labour Party and CND: 1957–1984', in Richard Taylor and Nigel Young, eds, *Campaigns for Peace: British Peace Movements in the Twentieth Century* (Manchester: Manchester University Press, 1987), p. 121.

16 Labour Party archive, NEC Minutes 25 February 1981, ID/1980-81/49/Dec, 'Labour's Policy on Defence and Disarmament', p. 4.

17 *Ibid.*, p. 11.

18 Labour Party archive, Labour CND 1981–82, 'Annual Labour Party Conference 1982', April 1982.

19 Labour Party archive, Labour CND 1981–82, Trade Union CND.

20 Labour Party archive, Labour CND 1981–82, Committee members of Labour CND; Labour CND 1983–84, Minutes of meeting 8 November 1983.

21 Labour Party archive, Labour CND 1981–82, 'Urgent Appeal from Labour CND to all Delegates to the Labour Party Conference 1982.'

22 Labour Party archive, Labour CND 1986–87, Labour CND Campaigning Kit.

23 Taylor, The Labour Party and CND', p. 122.

24 *House of Commons Debates* (hereafter *H.C. Deb.*), vol. 21, 3 April 1982, col. 639.

25 *H.C. Deb.*, vol. 24, 20 May 1982, col. 559.

26 Labour Party, 1983 manifesto, *The New Hope for Britain* (London: Labour Party, 1983), p. 39.

27 *LPACR*, 1984, p. 242. For a detailed account of the sinking of the General Belgrano, see Lawrence Freedman, *The Official History of the Falklands Campaign, Volume II* (London: Routledge, 2005), ch. 21.

28 Labour Party, *New Hope for Britain*, p. 33.

29 *Ibid.*, pp. 36–7.

30 Labour Party archive, Labour CND 1983–84, Press statement from Robin Cook, 26 May 1983.

31 Author's interview with Lord McNally, 25 July 2006.

32 Labour Party archive, Labour Disarmament Liaison Committee 1983–84, letter from Peter Smith to Robin Cook, 13 October 1983.

33 David Butler and Gareth Butler, *British Political Facts 1900–1985* (London: Macmillan, 6th edn, 1986), p. 228.

34 Crewe and King, *SDP*, p. 285.

35 Martin Smith and Joanna Spear, eds, *The Changing Labour Party* (London: Routledge, 1992), p. 9.

36 Eric Shaw, *The Labour Party since 1945* (Oxford: Blackwell, 1996), p. 169.

37 *LPACR*, 1983, p. 314.

38 *LPACR*, 1983, p. 153.

39 Andrew Geddes, 'Labour and the European Community 1973–93: pro-Europeanism, "Europeanisation" and their implications', *Contemporary Record*, 8:2 (Autumn 1994), pp. 370–80.

40 *LPACR*, 1980, pp. 125–6, 132.

41 Labour Party, *New Hope for Britain*, p. 33.

42 Martin Westlake, *Kinnock: The Biography* (London: Little, Brown and Company, 2001), p. 230.

43 NEC statement, *LPACR*, 1983, pp. 12–13.

44 Labour Party, *Labour's Manifesto for the European Elections, supported by the Socialist Group of the European Parliament, 1984* (London: Labour Party, 1984), p. 9.

45 John Kampfner, *Robin Cook* (London: Victor Gollancz, 1998), p. 58.
46 Paul Anderson and Nyta Mann, *Safety First: The Making of New Labour* (London: Granta, 1997), p. 121.
47 Russell Holden, *The Making of New Labour's European Policy* (Basingstoke: Macmillan, 2002), p. 6. See also Ben Rosamond, 'Labour and the European Community: Learning to be European?', *Politics*, 10:2 (1990), pp. 41–8.
48 Labour Party, 1987 general election manifesto, *Britain Will Win*, (London: Labour Party, 1987), p. 15.
49 Stephen George and Ben Rosamond, 'The European Community', in Smith and Spear, eds, *The Changing Labour Party*, p. 179.
50 Labour Party, *Social Justice and Economic Efficiency* (London: Labour Party, 1988), pp. 6 and 47.
51 *LPACR*, 1988, p. 180.
52 Labour Party, *Looking to the Future* (London: Labour Party, 1990), p. 7.
53 Labour Party, *Opportunity Britain* (London: Labour Party, 1991) p. 53; Labour Party, *Made in Britain* (London: Labour Party, 1991), p. 9.
54 Labour Party archive, NEC Minutes 25 February 1981, 'Introduction to Foreign Policy Document', ID/1980-81/97/Feb, agreed at NEC meeting of 25 February 1981.
55 Labour Party archive, NEC Minutes 25 February 1981, 'Labour's Overseas Development Policy', ID/1980-81/81.
56 LPACR, 1980, pp. 173–4.
57 Labour Party, *New Hope for Britain*, p. 37.
58 Labour Party, *For the Good of All: Labour's Plans for Aid and Development* (London: Labour Party, 1987), pp. 4 and 7.
59 Labour Party, *Democratic Socialist Aims and Values* (London: Labour Party, 1988), p. 7.
60 *LPACR*, 1983, p. 317.
61 *Ibid*.
62 *LPACR*, 1984, p. 89.
63 NEC statement on Central America, *LPACR*, 1983, p. 169; NEC statement on Central America, *LPACR*, 1984, pp. 88–9; NEC statement on Central America, *LPACR*, 1985, p. 260; NEC statement on Central America, *LPACR*, 1986.
64 Labour Party, *Britain Will Win*, p. 15.
65 *LPACR*, 1984, p. 246; NEC statement on South Africa, *LPACR*, 1985, p. 252.
66 Labour Party, *New Hope for Britain*, pp. 38–9.
67 Labour Party, *Social Justice and Economic Efficiency* (London: Labour Party, 1988), p. 47.
68 *LPACR*, 1982, pp. 131 and 133.
69 *LPACR*, 1983, p. 163; *LPACR*, 1984, p. 251; *LPACR*, 1985, p. 263.
70 Labour Party archive, NEC Minutes 25 February 1981, 'Labour's Middle East Policy (Third Draft)', ID/1980-81/69/Jan.
71 Labour Party, *New Hope for Britain*, pp. 38–9.
72 *Ibid*., p. 39; Labour Party, *Britain Will Win*, p. 15; *LPACR*, 1981, p. 129.
73 Labour Party, *Britain Will Win*, p. 15.

74 Labour Party, *New Hope for Britain*, p. 35; Labour Party, *Defence and Security for Britain* (London: Labour Party, 1984), p. 5; Labour Party, *Defence Conversion and Costs* (London: Labour Party, 1986), p. 39; NEC resolution September 1986.
75 Labour Party, *New Hope for Britain*, p. 37.
76 *LPACR*, 1986, p. 161.
77 Labour Party, *It's Time to Get Britain Working Again* (London: Labour Party, 1992), p. 27.
78 Labour Party, *Defence and Security for Britain*, p. 6.
79 Westlake, *Kinnock*, p. 377.
80 Neil Kinnock Papers, Churchill Archive Centre, Churchill College, Cambridge, Box 304, Shadow Communications Agency, Philip Gould, Provisional Defence Strategy, 13 October 1986.
81 Anderson and Mann, *Safety First*, p. 339.
82 Westlake, *Kinnock*, p. 333.
83 *Ibid.*
84 Labour Party, *Britain Will Win*, pp. 15–16.
85 Kinnock Papers, Box 1, Britain in the World Policy Review Group, PD(I):1204/December 1987, quantitative polling data.
86 Kinnock Papers, Box 1, Britain in the World Policy Review, Policy Directorate 1151B/November 1987, A note on the work of the review groups.
87 Keohane, *Labour Party Defence Policy since 1945*, p. 114.
88 Kinnock Papers, Box 1, Britain in the World Policy Review Group, PD(I):1204/December 1987, quantitative polling data.
89 Kinnock Papers, Box 1, Britain in the World Policy Review Group, Report of the 3rd Meeting, 18 January 1988, PD(I)1283: January 1988.
90 Kinnock Papers, Box 1, Britain in the World Policy Review Group, Invitations to Give Evidence, PD(I)1197: December 1987.
91 Kinnock Papers, Box 1, Britain in the World Policy Review Group, Proposed Advisors, PD(I)1198: December 1987; Report of 4th Meeting, 3 February 1988.
92 Labour Party, *Defence and Security for Britain*, p. 7.
93 Kinnock Papers, Box 1, Britain in the World Policy Review Group, Discussion on Values and Principles, 18 January 1988, PD(I)1247: January 1988.
94 Kinnock Papers, Box 1, Britain in the World Policy Review Group, Labour and Patriotism, PD(I)1344: February 1988.
95 *LPACR*, 1987, p. 169.
96 *Ibid.*
97 *LPACR*, 1988, p. 179.
98 Westlake, *Kinnock*, p. 444. See Colin Hughes and Patrick Wintour, *Labour Rebuilt: The New Model Party* (London: Fourth Estate, 1990), ch. 8.
99 Labour Party archive, NEC Minutes, Box 6 February to 28 June 1989, Minutes of Meeting of 17 May 1989.
100 *LPACR*, 1989, p. 155.
101 Patrick Seyd and Paul Whitely, *Labour's Grass Roots: The Politics of Party Membership* (Oxford: Clarendon, 1992), p. 54.

102 NEC statement, January 1991, p. 45.
103 *H.C. Deb.*, vol. 183, 15 January 1991, col. 821.
104 *The Times*, 2 March 1991, cited in Westlake, *Kinnock*, p. 503.
105 *H.C. Deb.*, vol. 211, 14 July 1992, col. 966.

Chapter 6

New Labour triumphs

Despite all of Kinnock's efforts to make the Labour Party electable and ready for government, it lost the general election of 9 April 1992, though the Conservatives were returned with the much smaller majority of only twenty-one seats. This was the fourth successive victory for the Conservative Party, but after a short period of euphoria, the Conservative government under John Major suffered a series of setbacks and for much of the next five years appeared to be lurching from one crisis to another.

The first, and perhaps most serious of these, was 'Black Wednesday'. Britain had entered the European Exchange Rate Mechanism, in October 1990. The rate at which Britain had entered proved to be too high, and as the value of sterling fell in September 1992 the Conservative Chancellor, Norman Lamont, dramatically raised interest rates in an attempt to prop up sterling. Despite raising the Bank of England interest rate to 15 per cent on Wednesday 16 September, sterling fell below its permitted level, and was forced out of the ERM. This destroyed the Conservatives' reputation for economic competence and good governance, especially as John Major had fought the 1992 election with membership of the ERM as a crucial part of his counter-inflationary strategy. As a consequence of the ERM crisis the value of the stockmarket dropped dramatically and house prices fell. Government borrowing rapidly escalated and the Conservatives increased national insurance contributions despite having promised at the 1992 election there would be no tax increases. By December 1993 Labour was leading the Conservatives in the opinion polls by about 20 per cent, a lead that it retained for the rest of the parliament. In addition, there was a loss of support for the government from newspapers traditionally sympathetic to the Conservative Party. Tabloids that had been staunchly supportive of the Conservative governments now poured scorn on John Major and his administration. By the time of the next general election in 1997, the *Sun*, Britain's biggest selling daily newspaper, had firmly switched its allegiance to New Labour.

Second, the debacle over the ERM unleashed rising hostility to European integration in the Conservative Party, which was particularly problematic for Major as the Maastricht Treaty, which had been signed in 1991 and which allowed for greater economic and political union, was due to be ratified. Major ruled out holding a referendum over the Maastricht Treaty, and so had to try to force the Treaty through Parliament, while a small number of Eurosceptic Conservative MPs very publicly did all they could to prevent this. After four successive election victories, Conservative Party MPs had lost the art of self-control, and Major found managing party divisions over Europe an insurmountable problem. In June 1995 John Major tried to reassert his authority by standing for re-election as party leader, and although he won comfortably, his Eurosceptic opponent, John Redwood, managed to gain the votes of eighty-nine MPs. The Conservatives were also split over whether Britain should take up its right to opt out of the single European currency, with the Eurosceptics trying to commit the party in the 1997 election manifesto to ruling British membership out, while key members of the Conservative government, in particular the pro-European Chancellor Ken Clarke, were favourable in principle to British joining the European single currency. The very public conflict within the Conservative Party over Europe did it a great deal of harm, while Labour, having learnt the lesson from the 1980s that the public do not vote for a divided party, benefited from the situation.

Third, allegations of 'sleaze' dogged the government. At the 1993 Conservative Party annual conference, John Major had called for a 'Back to Basics' campaign that would focus on promoting traditional law and order values. This was then widely reported as meaning he wanted a moral crusade and a return to old-fashioned family values. Consequently, journalists felt justified in investigating the private lives of Conservative politicians. This resulted in an unprecedented number of ministerial resignations due to scandals involving either extra-marital affairs or allegations of having accepted cash or favours in return for asking questions in the House of Commons. Despite Major's personal integrity, there developed widespread perceptions of government sleaze, hypocrisy and dishonesty.

All this meant that the Conservatives fared very badly in all the electoral tests they faced. On 9 June 1994 Labour won a landslide in the European elections with sixty-two seats, while the Conservatives won only eighteen seats. The Conservatives also faired very badly in by-elections and local elections and three MPs defected. Conservative Party membership dropped significantly. Disunity, poor morale and a series of misfortunes left the Conservatives looking weak and incompetent. There had been a reversal of the Conservative and Labour parties' images, and it was now the Conservatives that the public mistrusted and saw as divided and incompetent, and not the Labour Party. The Labour Party went on to triumph in the 1997 general election, winning a landslide victory.

New Labour

Neil Kinnock announced his resignation as leader of the Labour Party four days after the 1992 Labour defeat. There were only two candidates at the subsequent leadership election, John Smith and Brian Gould. Smith, who was widely regarded as the natural successor to Kinnock, won handsomely, gaining 91 per cent of Labour's electoral college. To a large extent, Smith followed a strategy of consolidating on the reforms already undertaken by Kinnock, but he succeed in getting the 1993 party conference to accept a policy of 'one member, one vote' for conference decisions, candidate selection and the leadership electoral college. This reduced the power of the trade unions in the party by removing their block vote.

John Smith died suddenly on 12 May 1994. The frontrunners to replace him were Gordon Brown, the Shadow Chancellor, and Tony Blair, Shadow Home Secretary. The two men were good friends and were both modernisers who had been impatient with the rate of change under Smith. Gordon Brown and his closest advisors saw him as Labour's leader-in-waiting, but by 1994 Blair had gained in stature with the public, the media and within the Labour Party. Blair had an easy manner, self-confidence and was a superb communicator. He was more popular with the public than Brown; he had been assiduously developing good relationships with journalists, and had made an effort to build up support with his colleagues. Brown reluctantly agreed to support Blair's candidacy in order to avoid splitting the vote amongst the modernisers in the party.[1] Blair stood against John Prescott and Margaret Beckett, and on 21 July was elected Labour leader. John Prescott then beat Margaret Beckett in the election for the deputy leadership.

At the annual conference in Blackpool less than two months later, Blair launched 'New Labour', arguing that if the party was to renew Britain, it first needed to renew itself.[2] Blair reasoned that Labour had been too dependent on the working class and trade unions, groups which were in decline, and that society had become more individualistic and aspirational. Labour needed to change its policies and ethos to take this into account and to broaden its appeal and reach out to a new and younger membership. There was also an upfront acknowledgement that the party needed to change in order to meet the current electoral preferences of the public and, in particular, to win the political centre ground. Whereas under Kinnock the party had still tended to think that perhaps it was the electorate that needed to change its ideas, rather than the party, Blair argued that 'The Tories didn't win four elections. We lost them. And we lost them because we lost touch with the people.'[3] To a large extent Blair benefited from the organisational and policy changes that had already been effected by Kinnock. There was, however, a big difference in style between the two leaders in that Blair, who was visibly impatient with sections of the party, seemed to revel in overthrowing Labour shibboleths, whereas Kinnock effected change as an end to a means and not as an end in itself. With the support of John Prescott, Blair managed to secure the repeal of the Clause IV commitment in the Labour Party constitution to the common ownership of the means of production, distribution and exchange. This for Blair was a symbolic demonstration to the electorate of the party's willingness to change from 'Old Labour' to 'New Labour'.

Blair also managed to effect a more disciplined party. He went further than Kinnock in the centralisation and professionalisation of political communications in the Labour Party. This was carried out by figures such as Peter Mandelson and Philip Gould, drawing on the expertise of outside media advisors, as well as Labour Party Members of Parliament, bureaucrats and political advisors.[4] This process of modernisation reached its peak through the establishment at the beginning of 1996 of the headquarters of Labour's permanent campaign at Millbank Tower. Headed by Mandelson, this was a state of the art campaign 'war room' by British standards. Based in part on Gould's experience of visiting Clinton's Little Rock campaign headquarters during the 1992 American presidential election, Labour created an integrated campaign team reporting to a unified command structure where emphasis was placed on media management, strategic political communications and twenty-four-hour media monitoring with a rapid rebuttal unit backed up by the Excalibur research database system.[5] Blair also worked hard to gain the support of the press, in particular wooing Rupert Murdoch, head of News International. By the time of the 1997 general election Labour had a sophisticated and 'Americanised' media and campaign operation, and once in power, it continued the media management techniques that it had used when in opposition.

Blair was assisted in all this by three changes in the party. First, since 1994 there had been an influx of new members to the Labour Party who were young and aspirational, and who did not relate to the policies and ethos of 'Old Labour', which diluted the power of the traditional leftwing members and activists. Second, between 1990 and 1997, Labour Party officials developed a new approach to policy-making that was endorsed at the 1997 annual conference. This removed policy-making from the annual conference, and replaced it with a policy forum system that worked on a two-year cycle, where members were invited to discuss and decide on policy issues at policy forums and then report back to policy commissions. These reports were then considered by the National Policy Forum and the Joint Policy Committee, which produced final policy proposals to be ratified at the annual conference. This meant that members could still have a policy input, but divisions over policy were hammered out at constituency and regional forum meetings that preceded the annual conference, rather than at the televised and closely reported annual conference.[6] This also had the effect of removing power from activists, who tended to be quite ideologically driven, while allowing ordinary members, who would not normally get to go to the annual conference, an input to the policy-making process. Third, by this point most Labour MPs desperately wanted electoral success and there was a highly unusual degree of self-restraint and self-discipline in the party as they voluntarily kept any doubts about Blair private. 'The truth is that after 1992 the party was pretty well willing to give Blair a blank cheque and say "win us power, we're fed up with being battered, get us back to power". And he delivered.'[7]

Blair's manifesto for the leadership campaign said little about foreign policy and in his speeches he tended to focus on domestic economic and social policy. He did, however, say quite a bit about Europe, on which he promised a policy of 'constructive engagement', arguing that 'If [Britain] is to maintain its historic role as a global player, Britain has to be a central part of the politics of Europe'.[8] He appointed Robin Cook as Shadow Foreign Secretary, and in 1996 the

Labour Party produced a policy document outlining foreign policy under a New Labour government, *A Fresh Start for Britain: Labour's Strategy for Britain in the Modern World*. The main thrust of this document was, first, that under the Conservatives foreign policy had been hesitant, and Britain had not been at the forefront of international diplomacy and decision-making. It argued that 'Britain can once again become influential in the world and a leading player in Europe, but Britain needs a government that is willing to accept these roles'.[9] A New Labour government would restore Britain's international status, and put it at the centre of international decision-making instead of at its margins. The second main argument was that Britain needed to focus on building a strong international community by strengthening international institutions. Labour's *Strategy for Britain in the Modern World* stated that Labour would strengthen the UN's role in maintaining international peace and security and its ability for preventive action; it would build up the Commonwealth section in the Foreign Office and strengthen the Harare Declaration on Human Rights and Democracy; and it would press for reform of the World Bank and the International Monetary Fund.[10] Third, the policy document also stated that membership of the international community 'carries with it responsibilities as well as rights', and that there was an ethical responsibility to combat poverty.[11] Labour would create a Department for International Development to be headed by a Cabinet Minister, increase aid expenditure in order to be able to meet the UN target of 0.7 per cent of GNP, and would shift aid to the poorest countries.

Many of these commitments were repeated in Labour's 1997 general election manifesto, *New Labour: Because Britain Deserves Better*, which reaffirmed the UN agreed aid target of 0.7 per cent, the establishment of a new department of International Development headed by a Cabinet Minister, that Labour would support measurs to renegotiate the debt burden, and said that 'Labour believes that we have a clear moral responsibility to help combat global poverty'.[12] In addition, it said that Labour would make the protection of human rights central to its foreign policy. However, it was the 1996 document, *A Fresh Start for Britain: Labour's Strategy in the Modern World*, which contained a more detailed overview of Labour's foreign policy than the manifesto.

In terms of defence, in the run-up to the 1997 election the Labour Party maintained consensus with the Conservative government in that it said that Britain's security would continue to be built upon NATO, and that it would retain Trident while pressing for multilateral negotiations.[13] There were some differences of policy however. First, the Labour Party promised to hold a Strategic Defence Review to reassess British interests and defence needs.[14] Second, *New Labour, New Life for Britain*, a 1996 policy document, contained a commitment to ban landmines.[15] Third, Labour gave a strong commitment to tackle the issue of arms sales. The Labour Party was not entirely comfortable with the British arms industry and with the end of the Cold War it was expected that there would be less demand for weapons. In 1995, *Strategy for a Secure Future: Labour's Approach to the Defence Industry*, repeated a commitment made back in 1991 that a Labour government would establish a Defence Diversification Agency which would diversify some of the technological processes and manufacturing skills from the defence industry into new markets. This document acknowledged that 'The export of British defence goods is vital for the long term prosperity of the UK defence industrial base as it permits British companies to lower development costs through longer production runs'. However, Labour would not sell weapons to repressive regimes. The 1996 policy document, *A Fresh Start for Britain: Labour's Strategy for Britain in the Modern World*, contained the commitment that in government, Labour would not issue export licences for the sale of arms to regimes that might use them for internal repression or international aggression.[17] The election manifesto said that 'Labour will not permit the sale of arms to regimes that might use them for internal repression or international aggression'.[18] This commitment became something of a liability once Labour was in office.

On 1 May 1997 Labour won a landslide victory with 44 per cent of the votes and 419 seats, while the Conservatives achieved just 31 per cent and lost 177 seats. Labour had an overall majority of 179 seats, which was more than the 165 remaining Conservative MPs. There was a swing of more than 10 per cent from the Conservatives to Labour across Great Britain, the largest achieved by any party since 1945. Foreign policy itself was not a major issue in the 1997 election, but Labour's successful attacks on the Conservatives during the arms to Iraq affair, when it was found that they had secretly approved the export of arms to Iraq, undoubtedly played a part in highlighting to the public Conservative hypocrisy. The rest of this chapter focuses on Labour's performance in government. It begins by outlining Robin Cook's commitment to an 'ethical dimension' in foreign policy, before turning to Blair's response to the Kosovo crises, Britain's role in Europe and an assessment of international development and aid policy.

The chapter demonstrates that, overall, New Labour did implement the policy promises made in the 1997 manifesto document.

Labour's victory and Cook's 'ethical dimension'

In the run-up to the 1997 election Robin Cook, the Shadow Foreign Secretary, had been a permanent thorn in the side of the Conservatives, using his 'forensic intelligence' and debating skills to probe the government on the arms to Iraq scandal.[19] He had humiliated Conservative ministers as they gave evidence over the secret supply of arms to Iraq to the Scott inquiry, and he 'had been feted in Opposition as one of Labour's sharpest minds, the custodian of the party's conscience from the Blairites, and the best parliamentary orator of his generation'.[20] This had made him popular with sections of the media and within the Labour Party many saw him as one of the custodians of the left. However, while admired for his abilities, he had not always been popular amongst the Labour frontbench. It is thought that Cook had wanted the post of President of the Board of Trade rather than Foreign Secretary, and that 'He was there largely at the insistence of Gordon Brown, who, resenting Cook's self-portrayal as leader of the intellectual left in the Labour leadership, had demanded that he be removed from any position of influence in domestic policy'.[21] However, unlike Blair, Cook had been active in the Labour Party's international and defence committees during the 1980s and did have an enduring interest in foreign affairs. Cook was determined to leave his mark as Foreign Secretary and this was reflected in a number of policy and institutional initiatives.

Cook had let it be known in advance that if Labour won the election, as was widely expected, he wanted to 'hit the ground running'.[22] There was a lot to get on with: Britain was due to take over the presidency of the European Union the following January; there was a forthcoming meeting of the G8; a Commonwealth Summit in Edinburgh in October; and Britain's ongoing role within NATO and on the UN Security Council to deal with. There were great expectations of what a Labour government could achieve in foreign as well as domestic policy. In the heady first days of the New Labour government, Cook invited the media, academics and diplomats to the launch of his new corporate style 'mission statement' in the Locarno Room of the Foreign and Commonwealth Office. He declared that he was going to implement a new kind of foreign policy, which 'recognises that the national interest cannot be defined only by narrow realpolitik'. The aim was 'to make Britain once again a force for good in the world'. Cook declared that,

> The Labour Government does not accept that political values can be left behind when we check in our passports to travel on diplomatic business. Our foreign policy must have an ethical dimension and must support the demands of other peoples for the democratic rights on which we insist for ourselves. The Labour Government will put human rights at the heart of our foreign policy.[23]

The media widely reported that Cook had promised an 'ethical foreign policy', rather than the more modest 'ethical dimension' to foreign policy, and this undoubtedly raised expectations for change and, much to Blair's annoyance, gave Labour's critics a prism through which to censure every foreign policy decision. Cook's mission statement was also seen by Blair and his closest advisors as an attempt to raise his own political profile. Blair preferred to speak of his new 'third way', rather than an ethical dimension, though the 'third way' really amounted to very little in terms of foreign policy, and was quietly dropped after 1999.[24]

The ethical dimension became strongly associated with the issue of human rights. The manifesto had stated that 'Labour wants Britain to be respected in the world for the integrity with which it conducts its foreign relations. We will make the protection and promotion of human rights a central part of our foreign policy.'[25] The Labour government's human rights objectives had been set out in numerous statements made both before and after the election, and the commitment to human rights was included in the Queen's Speech of 14 May 1997.[26] However, it would be wrong to assume that an interest in human rights was a New Labour creation. David Owen, Callaghan's foreign secretary from 1977 to 1979, had made a number of speeches, subsequently published as a book, on human rights and foreign policy.[27] The 1983, 1987 and 1992 Labour Party general election manifestos had also contained a commitment to promoting human rights, and the party had campaigned on this issue throughout its history. Promoting human rights had also been of concern to John Major throughout his premiership. Nevertheless, under Cook, human rights were given a higher profile in terms of FCO statements and public relations exercises, for example with the introduction of a yearly FCO report on human rights. The government announced on 21 May 1997 that it was implementing its manifesto pledge to 'ban the import, export, transfer and manufacture of anti-personnel landmines'.[28] This was ahead of the international decision taken to ban anti-personnel mines in Ottawa on 3 December, and was seen as evidence of a more ethical standpoint. Britain, unlike the US, backed the establishment of an International Criminal Court – which the Conservative government under John Major had opposed – with powers to order the arrest, trial and punishment of war criminals charged with serious human rights abuses. Throughout his tenure, Cook continued to signal his belief in human rights through speeches and through initiatives such as members of Amnesty International and Save the Children acting as advisors to the Foreign Office on human rights.[29] However, the human rights dimension proved problematic for Cook. He was criticised for his policy of engagement towards Russia and China, where the Labour government invested extensive political capital into strong bilateral relations, and was accused of failing to raise the issue of human rights more strongly. In the case of China, Cook pursued a new policy of 'quiet diplomacy', and in 1998 ended the practice of signing up to the annual resolution of the UN Commission on Human Rights condemning China's record on this issue.[30] Many commented that Cook's softening of British criticisms of China's human rights record demonstrated that the ethical dimension was 'subordinate to commercial concerns'.[31]

The other issue that came to be closely associated with the ethical dimension of New Labour's foreign policy under Cook was that of arms exports. Again, concern over British arms exports was not a New Labour creation; rather it was a topic of concern going back decades. For example, Labour had been opposed to the sale of arms to South Africa during the 1960s and 1970s. The 1983 election manifesto had pledged that 'We will not supply arms to countries where the chances of international aggression or internal repression would be increased', and a similar pledge appeared in the 1992 manifesto.[32] This was also a personal issue for Cook who had been a member of Labour's Defence Study Group in the 1970s, which had argued in its alternative defence policy, outlined in the book *Sense About Defence*, for a reduction in the arms trade.[33] In opposition, he told the 1995 Labour Conference that a 'Labour government will not license the export of arms to any regime that will use them for internal oppression or external aggression'.[34]

Soon after gaining power Cook announced that there would be a review of arms export criteria, and on 28 July 1997 he and Tony Lloyd reported on this review. They laid out the new criteria to be used in considering arms export licence applications; announced that Britain would work for the introduction of a European code of conduct for arms exports; that, in addition, to ensure transparency the government would report annually to Parliament on the application of strategic export controls; but said that it would not revoke export licenses that had been agreed by the previous administration as it would not be 'realistic or practical' to do so.[35] At the 1997 Labour Party annual conference, Cook proclaimed that Britain had been 'leading by cleaning up the arms trade', and that Labour had carried out its manifesto commitment not to give any more licences for arms exports that would 'conspire with conflict or abet repression,' and that 'brutal, megalomaniac dictators tend to be rather poor at paying their invoices on time'.[36] At the 1999 Labour Party annual conference he said 'Let's put the myth to rest: your government has not sold weapons that would suppress democracy or freedom. We rejected every licence to Indonesia when the weapons might have been used for suppression.'[37]

The decision not to revoke licenses for export granted by the Major government, including licenses for the export to Indonesia of Hawk aircraft, armoured vehicles and water cannon, was unpopular within the PLP. 136 MPs. most of them Labour, signed an early day motion attacking the decision.[38] It is inconceivable that the Labour government did not know that there was extensive evidence that these exports had been and could be used for internal repression. While Cook said that it was impossible to apply the new arms export criteria and refuse to export arms to Indonesia under pre-existing contracts, others argued that the earlier decision could have been reversed. While largely welcomed by pressure groups, the new arms export licensing criteria were said to 'have proved disappointing', as they could be interpreted with considerable flexibility. In particular, there were no guidelines to indicate how evidence of use was to be obtained, nor risks assessed, and no monitoring of the end use of the exports.[39] The commitment not to export equipment for internal repression was qualified by a statement exempting equipment judged to be for the legitimate protection of a country's security forces from violence. This too was criticised by arms control and human rights groups and experts.[40]

Despite the tightened criteria arms continued to be exported to many regimes with questionable human rights records, including Columbia, Saudi Arabia, Indonesia, Sri Lanka, and Turkey. A quadripartite committee of the four Select Committees involved in strategic export controls (Defence, Foreign Affairs, International Development and Trade and Industry) was asked to review and report on the extent to which the implementation of arms licensing matched the government's declared objectives. They found that in 1999 the proportion of all export licence applications that had been refused under the Labour government was only 0.7 per cent, compared with 1 per cent under the Conservatives.[41] In the cases of arms exports to Zimbabwe and Indonesia, policy 'did not yet reveal evidence of joined-up government. There was evidence that Whitehall baronial interests had sometimes fought each other to an unhappy compromise.'[42] It was also pointed out that all the Select Committee reports that dealt with the issue of arms export licensing had contained 'strongly worded criticism of the absence of legislation following the Scott report during this Parliament'. Indeed, 'As a result of the effort that we put in when in opposition on the issue of the Scott report, we have a legislative debt of honour to redeem the Scott recommendations in the form of legislation'. The unanimous recommendation of the four Select Committees was that they should undertake prior scrutiny of licenses, but this was rejected by the government on the grounds that it would compromise political and commercial confidentiality in the UK.[43] It was also the case that no formal mechanism existed for systematically monitoring the use that has been made of British defence equipment once it has been exported. Neil Cooper has concluded that New Labour's commitment to restricting arms exports was framed in a manner that implied 'a largely permissive attitude to UK arms exports. Judged solely on its own language, Labour's arms sales policy is less ethical than its own policy in the 1980s, less ethical than that of a number of other states, less ethical than the EU code [on arms exports] and little different from the ethically challenged approach of its Conservative predecessors.'[44] The general perception was that while Cook genuinely wished to tighten up on arms exports, he was over-ruled by the Department of Trade and Industry, which was working to a different set of priorities to that of the Foreign and Commonwealth Office.[45]

There were other foreign policy decisions that did not fit well with Cook's ethical dimension. Britain was the only European state that fully supported the US policy of sanctions over Iraq's refusal to allow the United Nations Special Commission (UNSCOM) weapons inspectors access, and the only European state to support America's use of strategic bombing to enforce the no-fly zone in northern Iraq. Cook's attempts to persuade the British public of his ethical foreign policy sometimes seemed strained to say the least, and fed the criticism that his claim to a new foreign policy was merely hype and rhetoric. This was particularly the case over the Sandline affair, when it was found that the FCO had, at some level, known about the shipment of arms to Sierra Leone (which flouted UN resolution 1132) and the intervention of mercenaries to restore President Kabbah to power. This shot a hole through Cook's attempts to present the FCO as working under a stricter regime than with the Conservatives. Cook's unhappy response to this event suggested that he considered that the upholding of UN resolutions was the ethical position to take and that officials should be punished for flouting them. Blair, on the other hand, suggested that the ends justified the means in restoring democratically elected President Kabbah, and declared somewhat confusingly that 'When people say they run an ethical foreign policy, I say Sierra Leone was an example of this'.[46] The impression given was that Cook and Blair assumed that anything Britain did in terms of foreign policy was by definition ethical.

The most dramatic crisis that the new government had to respond to was the Kosovo conflict. Here opinion was intensely divided over whether military intervention was the right thing to do, morally, legally, politically and strategically, but for Blair and Cook, Kosovo represented the apogee of the Labour government's new approach to foreign policy. British foreign policy decisions were not to be made simply in terms of what was in the national interest, but also in terms of what was in the international interest. This was a theme that had been part of the Labour Party's approach to foreign policy going back to the 1920s, but never before had a Labour government articulated it so strongly.

The Kosovo conflict

If announcing Labour's 'ethical dimension' was Cook's defining moment during New Labour's first term of office, for Blair it was Kosovo and his Chicago speech on 22 April 1999 on the 'Doctrine of the International Community'. The speech was intended to shore up American support for the use of military force in Kosovo, and in particular encourage Clinton to agree to deploy ground troops, but it was also the first time that Blair really seemed to be outlining his view of the world and the role that Britain should play within it. Quite simply, Blair argued that Britain was part of an international community that had common interests and values, and Britain should intervene when it was the right thing to do. Blair said 'We are doing what is right, for Britain, for Europe, for a world that must know that barbarity cannot be allowed to defeat justice. That is simply the right thing to do.'[47] Kosovo represented very clearly a new approach to foreign policy in terms of intervention for humanitarian reasons over-riding traditional state sovereignty. Blair argued that 'Non-interference has long been considered an important principle of international order. ... But the principle of non-interference must be qualified in important respects. Acts of genocide can never be a purely internal matter.'[48] For internationalists such as themselves, Cook and Blair argued that not to act would have been to go against their whole worldview. For critics, Blair's doctrine of the international community was a 'doctrine of ethical imperialism wrapped in the language of globalisation'.[49]

Labour's interest in Kosovo reflected earlier concerns over Bosnia. John Smith had supported the Conservative government's decision to send 1,800 troops to Bosnia in August 1992, but was concerned over the continuing human rights violations in Bosnia, and especially the siege of Sarajevo. In the Commons on 15 December 1992 he had urged John Major to join with the US and France in pressing for a new UN resolution to allow the use of military force to enforce the no-fly zone over Bosnia.[50] On the whole, the Labour leadership urged a slightly more interventionist policy in Bosnia, as did the Liberal Democrats under Paddy Ashdown. By the time that Labour was in power, there was a general sense within the party that more should have been done to protect the Bosnian population in the early and mid-1990s and that Britain and its allies were culpable in not taking firmer action more quickly to deal with the crisis of the break-up of the former Yugoslavia. In his 1995 speech to the Labour Party conference, Cook had argued that security included the international defence of Britain's values, and that those values were under attack in Bosnia. 'For the first time since the defeat of fascism, European states are being carved out behind borders drawn up by ethnic cleansing.'[51] Thus, for Cook and for Blair, when conflict flared up in Kosovo in 1997, this became an issue where Britain had to be seen to be taking a leading role in preventing a repeat of what was seen as the failure of Bosnia.

Britain's involvement in the Kosovo conflict was also institutionalised as a member of the six-nation Contact Group and through its presidency of the EU starting in January 1998. On 9 March 1998 Cook hosted an emergency meeting of the Contact Group, which denounced the use of force by both the Serb military and the Kosovo Liberation Army, and which called for an arms embargo, which was then passed by the United Nation Security Council as resolution 1160 on 31 March 1998. However, during the summer of 1998 Cook and

Blair resisted calls from the German Foreign Minister, Klaus Kinkel, for immediate military intervention.[52] Cook then co-chaired talks at Rambouillet with Hubert Védrine, the French Foreign Minister, which opened on 3 February 1999. NATO's operation Allied Force began on 24 March 1999 after Richard Holbrooke had declared that the final attempt to get Milosevic to sign the Rambouillet peace agreement had failed. As the conflict dragged on, Blair then became pivotal in getting the battle for public opinion on course, setting a military and political agenda that could be relayed to the public, and launching a massive political campaign aimed at shoring up public opinion both in Britain and abroad over NATO's intervention.[53]

Thus, the New Labour government took a much more interventionist approach to the Federal Republic of Yugoslavia than their Conservative predecessors had. This in turn was responsible for causing a shift in thinking about foreign policy on the centre-left, with a new 'warlike humanitarianism' complemented with internationalism.[54] Kosovo represented very clearly a new approach to foreign policy in terms of intervention for humanitarian reasons over-riding the traditional norm of state sovereignty, and such intervention being viewed as acting in the international interest rather than undermining it. Kosovo also set a precedent for Blair that reflected not only his political worldview but also his moralism. Following the terrorist attacks of 11 September 2001, Blair believed that the logic that had applied to the need to intervene in Kosovo – that in an increasingly globalised and interdependent world, isolationism and the principle of non-intervention had to be qualified when it came to matters of international security and acts of genocide – also applied to Afghanistan and Iraq.

The Kosovo conflict was significant for British foreign and security policy in that it was the first time in NATO's history that it had undertaken a sustained military campaign, in addition to which this campaign was aimed at preventing a humanitarian tragedy rather than a military threat to one of its member states. It was significant for Blair in that it was the most dramatic crisis that he had to respond to during his first term of office, and it seemed to highlight his new, more internationalist approach to foreign policy. However, Labour's initial reluctance to commit British ground troops, which many argued extended the length of the conflict, did not sit well with Cook's claims to the moral high-ground.[55] There were also accusations of double standards vis-à-vis Serbia's actions in Kosovo and Russia's actions in Chechnya. Kosovo did demonstrate, however, what could be achieved when the Foreign Secretary, Prime Minister, and Defence Secretary were working in harmony towards the same goal of bolstering support both internally within Britain and externally within NATO in order to carry the military campaign through. This is significant, for when Labour came to power in 1997, there was still a 'credibility gap on defence because of past policies and practice'.[56] Labour had been out of power since 1979, it had advocated unilateral nuclear disarmament for most of the 1980s, and had until recently advocated defence spending cuts. This was the first Labour government since 1945 where ministers had no direct experience of serving in the armed forces. Labour MPs were largely drawn from the liberal professions, especially law and teaching, and did not tend to have family members in the armed forces. However, Blair's election also 'came as en enormous relief to security policy-makers' as by 1997 officials at both the FCO and the MOD had 'reached their wits' end in trying to feed new security ideas into a government that simply did not want to listen'.[57]

Labour had promised in the 1997 election manifesto to hold a Strategic Defence Review (SDR) to reassess Britain's security interests and defence needs and consider how the roles, missions and capabilities of the armed forces should be adjusted to the meet the strategic realities of a post-Cold War world. This review, the government said, was to be unlike previous defence reviews in that it was to be foreign policy led rather than the usual Treasury led cost-cutting exercise. In his introduction to the SDR, Defence Secretary George Robertson called it a 'radical' review, to reflect 'a changing world in which the confrontation of the Cold War has been replaced by a complex mixture of uncertainty and instability'. It would lead 'to a fundamental reshaping of our forces', while being 'firmly grounded in foreign policy and sound military experience'. The review was not just about British national security, as 'The British are, by instinct, an internationalist people. We believe that as well as defending our rights, we should discharge our responsibilities in the world. We do not want to stand idly by and watch humanitarian disasters or the aggression of dictators go unchecked. We want to give a lead, we want to be a force for good.'[58]

The SDR was also unusual in that it consulted with a very broad spectrum of individuals and groups as part of the policy-making process, hearing from non-governmental organisations, academic defence specialists, opposition MPs, former defence ministers, serving members of the armed forces, and even received over 450 written submissions from the general public.[59] As a result of the unusually broad consultation process, the SDR took longer than expected, with the results bring presented to the Commons on 8 July 1998. Two of the largest defence procurement projects, the Vanguard-class Trident submarines and the Eurofighter, which was nearing production, were excluded from its remit.

The overall strategic conclusions were that while Britain did not face any obvious direct military threat, it should be able to respond to a major international crisis that might require a military effort and combat operations of a similar scale and duration to Britain's involvement in the Gulf War of 1990–91. Britain should also be able to undertake a more extended overseas deployment on a lesser scale, while retaining the ability to mount a second substantial deployment if this were made necessary by a second crisis. Thus, there needed to be greater emphasis on power projection and strategic mobility. The review might not have been as radical as Robertson claimed, but it did signify a shift in defence policy from previous governments.[60] On the whole, the findings were well received, though there was extensive criticism of the plan to reduce the number of Territorial Army units.

Europe

One of the most important foreign policy issues that Britain faced when Labour came to power was its relationship with, and role within, Europe. One of Blair's key foreign policy goals when he came to power – perhaps even the key goal – was to enhance Britain's role in Europe, and to be at the centre of the debate about the EU's future. This would also mean encouraging the British public to take a more positive view of the EU. In a keynote speech in April 1995 he argued that 'that the drift to isolation in Europe must stop and be replaced by a policy of constructive engagement'. This was because 'Europe is today the only route through which Britain can exercise power and influence'.[61] Labour published *A People's Europe* in 1995, which stated that 'Labour believes that we will get a better deal for Britain as a partner rather than as the odd man out'.[62] It said that there would have to be real economic convergence before Britain could enter a single currency, and 'The move towards a single currency must be based on the consent of the British people'.[63] This position on the single currency was repeated in the 1996 document, *A Fresh Start for Britain: Labour's Strategy in the Modern World*, which said that it was 'essential for Britain to reject isolation and play a positive role in Europe', because 'Today the ability of nation states to influence events unilaterally is more limited than ever before'.[64] The party's 1997 election manifesto had promised that under a Labour government Britain would have 'a fresh start in Europe' with a detailed agenda for reform, and a referendum on the single currency.[65] Labour wanted greater democratic scrutiny of the Council of Ministers and the Commission and was in favour of subsidiarity. Labour also supported the enlargement of Europe and assistance for Central and Eastern Europe.[66]

The New Labour government did appear to take a more positive approach to Europe compared with its Conservative predecessors. Certainly officials in the FCO were breathing a sigh of relief that they had a government and a minister who got on well with Britain's European partners,[67] and much was made of a new a 'new negotiating climate' with the election of the Labour government.[68] The Amsterdam Summit in June 1997 gave Blair and Cook their first opportunity to put into practice their new positive attitude towards Europe. They came away having signed up to the European Social Chapter, thus ending the British 'opt-out' that John Major had secured at Maastricht in 1991, and having signed the Amsterdam Treaty. This strengthened the power of the Commission President and the European Parliament against member state governments, and agreed to negotiations on the provision of a common European defence policy. However, Blair demonstrated a continuation of the policies pursued by their Conservative predecessors by blocking Franco-German proposals for the eventual merger of the EU and its defence arm, the Western European Union; retaining the right of each member state to the power of veto over home affairs and foreign policy in the Council of Ministers; and retaining a British opt-out from any agreement to abolish frontier controls.

When Labour was first elected, Blair was committed to shifting public opinion towards a greater understanding and acceptance of the EU, partly as it would be rather difficult for Britain to take a new leadership role in Europe given that the British population tended to be rather hostile to European initiatives, and partly in order to soften up public opinion in advance of a referendum on the single currency. Cook and other ministers at the FCO were instructed to lead public opinion on Britain's relationship with Europe by giving numerous speeches around the country on the importance of the EU to British foreign, domestic and economic policy.[69] Pro-Europeans within the government were under the impression that Blair was committed to Britain joining the single currency, though this was unlikely to happen during the first wave in 1999. However, on 18 October 1997 Gordon

Brown gave an interview in which he was perceived as saying that Britain would not join during the lifetime of the current government, which indicated a shift in policy. In the subsequent media furore it appeared that the only person who knew what was going on was Charlie Whelan, Brown's personal press secretary, who was briefing journalists on the new government policy from the Red Lion pub in Whitehall. In an attempt to clear up the ambiguities caused by Brown's comments on such a crucial issue, Blair allowed Brown to make a statement to the Commons on 27 October in which he announced that five economic tests would have to be met before the government would recommend joining the single currency. Possibly without realising it at the time, Blair had yielded control over the decision of whether to join to Gordon Brown and a markedly euro-sceptic Treasury.[70] This to some extent neutralised this highly controversial issue by presenting the decision as a purely technical and economic one rather than a political one. However, it meant that when the euro was launched in January 1999, the chances of Britain joining it were more remote than Blair had envisaged.

While Blair continued to talk of Britain playing a leading role in Europe, it was not necessarily in a good position to do so as it remained outside of the single currency, and the Labour government, like its predecessors, tended to present summit negotiations as a victory for Britain in resisting the encroachment of the EU. Furthermore, Blair's almost careless sense of superiority, for example lecturing his European counterparts on the virtues of free trade and the Anglo-Saxon economic model, rankled amongst European leaders whose countries had been managing the EU without the need for Britain's leadership. However, one area where the Blair government did show a distinguishable policy difference from its predecessors, both Conservative and Labour, was over the issue of the development of a military capability for the EU.

Despite initial reservations at the Amsterdam Summit, in late 1998 Blair decided to support the development of a military capacity for the EU. At the joint Anglo-French summit at St Malo on 3–4 December 1998, a declaration was released that said that 'The European Union needs to be in a position to play its full role on the international stage.' In order to do this, 'the Union must have the necessary capacity for autonomous action, backed by credible, military forces, the means to decide to use them, and a readiness to do so, in order to respond to international crises … acting in conformity with our respective obligations to NATO'.[71] The aim was to develop a capability that could deal with situations such as peacekeeping or peace-enforcement, conflict resolution and humanitarian relief. EU member states agreed at Helsinki in December 1999 that by 2003 the EU should be able to deploy 60,000 troops within sixty days to a crisis zone and that this force should be able to remain in theatre for twelve months. Anne Deighton has said that Blair's decision to champion the development of an EU military capability 'represents the greatest change that New Labour had made in EU policy'.[72] Others have pointed out that the outcome has been patchy at best, with disagreements over the deployment of troops and a general failure to develop a common European security and defence policy.[73] Nevertheless, Blair's position did signify a break with previous governments, where the policy had been to obstruct the development of an EU military capability for fear that this could undermine NATO and possibly lead to a disengagement by the US in Europe in the longer term.

There were a number of reasons for pushing ahead with the development of the European defence capability. First, when Blair had been briefed in mid-1998 on Europe's capacity to react to a hypothetical crisis in Kosovo, he had been 'appalled'.[74] The inability of the EU to respond to Bosnia and then Kosovo without first gaining US support and working through NATO demonstrated that the EU needed a military capability that could operate independently of the US if necessary in order to support EU foreign and security policy. Second, it provided an opportunity for Blair to demonstrate that Britain was forging a new identity with a more positive role in Europe and display the leadership that he had repeatedly spoken of. Third, it was possibly part of a 'British attempt to break into the core France-German alliance' in the EU through the use of bilateral initiatives.[75] Lastly, according to Williams, it provided an opportunity to demonstrate to Washington that Europe was serious about taking more responsibility for its own security, and 'the shift in policy represented a change of tactics rather than a rejection of the UK's traditional Atlanticist strategy'.[76] Blair viewed the development of an EU military capability as an opportunity to strengthen NATO, not to replace it, at a time when Washington was implying that Europe needed to take more responsibility for its security in order to preserve NATO. However, Washington had not been briefed in advance about the St Malo declaration, and the reaction to it was mixed. US Secretary of State Madeline Albright warned the EU against 'decoupling' within NATO, the duplication of NATO resources and capabilities, and discrimination against the NATO members who were not in the EU.[77] Throughout, Blair sought to reassure the US that NATO remained the cornerstone of European collective defence.

Apart from Blair's repeated commitment to playing a leadership role in the EU, there was one other role that he referred to repeatedly during his first period of office, and this was that Britain could act as 'bridge' between Europe and the US. Blair's first keynote foreign policy speech as Prime Minister was at the Lord Mayor's banquet in November 1997, when he said that 'We are the bridge between the US and Europe. Let us use it.'[78] He wanted to overcome the perceived dichotomy between Britain's involvement in Europe and the Anglo-American relationship, arguing that 'Britain does not have to choose between being strong with the US, or strong with Europe ... Britain can be both ... We have deluded ourselves for too long with the false choice between the US and Europe.'[79] Indeed, 'America wants Britain to be a strong ally in a strong Europe. The stronger we are in Europe, the stronger our American relationship.'[80] The 2001 election manifesto reiterated that 'Our argument is that if Britain is stronger in Europe, it will be stronger in the rest of the world. We reject the view of those who say we must choose between Europe and the USA.'[81]

However, while Blair might have been convinced that he did not have to choose between Europe and the US, other European leaders became convinced that Blair had chosen the Anglo-American relationship over Europe. Furthermore, Britain's European partners did not need a bridge as they were quite capable of having a relationship with the US without Britain acting as an intermediary. Despite the rhetoric, there was little real change on Britain's role in Europe. Thus, Riddell argues that while Blair might have regularly made pro-European speeches, 'virtually nothing changed' as a result of those speeches.[82] Blair, like all other Prime Ministers before him – with perhaps the exception of Edward Heath – viewed the Anglo-American relationship as the cornerstone of British security. For Blair, it also became the bedrock of British foreign policy following the events of 9/11, when divisions opened up between Britain and other leading European states, in particular France and Germany, over American actions in the 'war on terror'. While some European leaders saw the EU as a useful counter-balance to American power, Blair did not.

International development

When Labour came to power in 1997 it had a commitment to reforming Britain's international development policy. The party had long argued that existing policy tended to reflect strategic foreign policy goals and British commercial interests, such as the arms trade, and so benefited Britain as a donor, rather than actually benefiting the poorest countries in the world. The 1997 manifesto had stated that 'Labour believes that we have a clear moral responsibility to help combat global poverty'.[83] To this end, Blair restored an independent Department for International Development (DFID), headed by Clare Short, who was given Cabinet minister status. Harold Wilson had first established a Ministry for Overseas Development in 1964, but Thatcher had abolished it in May 1979, and the ministry had become the Overseas Development Administration, a unit within the FCO. This meant that aid and development policy had fallen within the remit and control of the FCO. The function of DFID was to promote sustainable development and eliminate world poverty, and this was far more likely to happen with an independent department with its own minister who would hold influence within the Cabinet.

DFID produced its first White Paper at the end of 1997 entitled *Eliminating World Poverty: A Challenge for the 21st Century*. That this was the first such paper outlining Britain's overseas aid strategy since 1975 demonstrated the extent to which this policy area had been marginalised. The White Paper was very ambitious and included a number of long-term strategic goals that reflected the principles agreed at the 1992 Rio Summit on sustainable development, such as the reduction by one-half of the proportion of people worldwide in living extreme poverty by 2015, and the achievement of universal primary education in all countries by 2015.[84] Britain would press for a reduction in Third World debt to sustainable levels and would direct aid towards the poorest countries to reflect recipient need and not donor interest. According to the White Paper, this was not only in the international interest, but was also in Britain's national interest due to the links between poverty, violence and human rights abuses. However, while the White Paper presented a strong strategic vision, it was short on actual specific policy recommendations.[85]

Nevertheless, Labour did undertake a number of initiatives aimed at improving the plight of the poorest countries. First, Labour ministers, particularly Chancellor Gordon Brown and Development Minister Clare Short, played a leading role in getting the international community to undertake debt relief, particularly in terms of reforming the World Bank's Heavily Indebted Poor Countries (HIPC) initiative. The government worked with Jubilee 2000, a coalition of non-governmental organisations that had been set up in April 1996, to lobby for the richest countries in the world to cancel the unpayable debts owed to them by the poorest countries in the world. Britain also agreed to cancel all of the bilateral debts owed to it by the HIPCs. Dixon and Williams question the effectiveness of the debt relief as 'New Labour's initiatives remain embedded within a neoliberal view of the global political economy with the result that debt relief remains conditional upon the imposition of neoliberal economic reforms on the debtor states in question'.[86] Nevertheless, Labour played an important role in raising debt relief up the international political agenda, especially at meetings of the G-8, and establishing the eradication of debt and of world poverty as legitimate policy goals.

Second, Labour significantly increased British aid expenditure. In 1996 funding for aid and international development was 0.26 per cent of GNP, roughly half the level at which it had stood when Labour had lost power in 1979. The 1997 manifesto reaffirmed the commitment to work towards the UN target of 0.7 per cent of GNP. Aid expenditure increased from £2.4 billion in 1996/7 to £4.1 billion in 2002/3.[87] By 2004, British aid expenditure had increased to 0.47 per cent of GNP. The 2005 election manifesto stated that under Labour aid would continue to increase, and that 'for the first time ever the UK has a clear timetable – 2013 – for achieving the UN target of 0.7 per cent of national income devoted to development'.[88] While the increase in aid in itself is evidence of Labour's commitment to international development, for Labour to need to be in power for sixteen consecutive years in order to reach a goal that had been a manifesto pledge since 1970 is not in itself quite the achievement that the 2005 manifesto suggested.

Third, Labour took a more co-operative approach to international development, rejoining the United Nations Education Scientific and Cultural Organisation (UNESCO) and reversing the decision made by John Major to leave the UN Industrial Development Organisation. DFID also consulted with a range of non-governmental organisations and academic experts working in humanitarian relief and international development. This was a different approach from that taken by the previous Conservative governments, which had largely ignored outside opinion and expertise.

In addition to these developments, the Blair government was more actively engaged in Africa than its predecessors, especially in terms of conflict prevention and resolution. Indeed, the British response to the genocide in Rwanda in 1994 from the John Major government had been a 'deeply troubling indifference' towards the victims of the genocide, apparently because they were outside the British sphere of influence on the African continent.[89] In comparison, the Blair government worked through a variety of multilateral institutions such as the UN, the EU, the G-8 and the Commonwealth to put pressure on regimes or political leaders committing large-scale human rights abuses. Labour imposed targeted sanctions such as travel bans and financial sanctions against elites, and worked to boycott or regulate the sale of goods used to finance conflicts, such as diamonds and precious minerals, drugs, oil and timber. In particular, Robin Cook played a leading role at the international level in the Kimberley Process to prevent the trade in conflict diamonds, and was involved in pushing for international agreements on the proliferation and trafficking of small arms and light weapons.[90] In May 2000, some 1300 British troops were deployed as part of Operation Palliser to Sierra Leone to protect the capital Freetown, from Revolution United Front rebels. In 2001 DFID, along with the MOD and the FCO, established a Conflict Prevention Pool for Africa, with a budget of £50 million per annum. As Williams concludes, Labour's approach to intervention in Africa has been 'highly selective both in its attempts to support peacekeeping in Africa and in the wars it sought to help manage', focusing its attention on the conflicts in Angola, Sierra Leone and Sudan.[91] However, Labour has undoubtedly been committed to taking a leading role in dealing with poverty, debt, humanitarian crises and conflict prevention, especially compared with the lack of interest demonstrated by the Conservative governments of Margaret Thatcher and John Major. During his speech to the Labour Party's annual conference in 2001, Blair argued that Africa 'was a scar on the conscience of the world' that would become 'deeper and angrier' if nothing was done to heal it.[92]

Overall, Blair did implement the policies concerning international development, foreign affairs, security and Britain's role in world contained in the 1997 general election manifesto. In addition, there were a number of fairly significant differences between Blair's foreign policy and that of his Conservative predecessors. One was an approach to policy-making, the desire to build consensus, and to bring in a range of people. This was noticeable in operations at the FCO and at DFID and the procedures adopted for the Strategic Defence Review. Second, there was a much greater emphasis placed on international development and Labour played an important role in raising debt relief up the international political agenda. Third, perhaps the key difference between foreign policy under Blair and many of his predecessors was that Blair did seek to outline what he felt Britain's role in the world should be. Douglas Hurd famously said that Britain 'punched above its weight',[93] but previous governments had been unclear as to what Britain should actually do with its power. Conservative leaders tended to talk in terms of defending the national interest as if it were immediately obvious what the 'national interest' was. The question of Britain's role in the world and of its major foreign policy goals had become more imperative with the end of the Cold War, as the collapse of the Soviet Union meant that Britain faced no immediate or obvious threat. How should Britain redefine its foreign policy goals in the changed international environment? Blair attempted to tackle this issue through policy reviews, White Papers and his speeches and statements to the Commons. On first coming to power, Blair had believed that Britain's future lay in playing a leadership role in Europe. Kosovo marked a shift in his thinking. His doctrine of the international community heralded a liberal internationalist approach which saw Britain as a leading player in an international community that had common interests and values and which required intervention and engagement. This was a more ambitious view of Britain's role in the world, and of Blair's role as a global statesman.

Notes

1 For a very good account of this episode, and whether or not a deal was agreed about Gordon Brown's role and succession to the premiership, see Anthony Seldon, *Blair* (London: Free Press, 2005), pp. 184–99.

2 Tony Blair, speech to the Labour Party conference, Blackpool, 4 October 1994, reprinted in Tony Blair, *New Britain: My Vision of a Young Country* (London: Fourth Estate, 1996), p. 50.

3 Tony Blair, *Sun*, 1 January 1996, reprinted in Blair, *New Britain*, p. 48.

4 See, for instance, Philip Gould, *The Unfinished Revolution: How the Modernisers Saved the Labour Party* (London: Little, Brown & Co., 1998); Peter Mandelson, 'Marketing Labour: personal reflections and experience', *Contemporary Record*, 1:3 (Winter 1998), pp. 11–13.

5 Gould, *The Unfinished Revolution*, pp. 175–7 and 289–99.

6 This draws on Richard Kelly, 'Farewell conference, hello forum: the making of Labour and Tory policy', *Political Quarterly*, 72:3 (2001), pp. 329–34.

7 Author's interview with Lord McNally, 25 July 2006.

8 Tony Blair, 'Britain in Europe', speech to the Royal Institute of International Affairs, London, 5 April 1995.

 9 Labour Party, *A Fresh Start for Britain: Labour's Strategy in the Modern World* (London: Labour Party, 1996), p. 1.
10 *Ibid.*, pp. 16–18.
11 *Ibid.*, p. 2.
12 Labour Party, 1997 general election manifesto, *New Labour: Because Britain Deserves Better* (London: Labour Party, 1997), p. 39.
13 *Ibid.*, p. 38.
14 Labour Party, *Labour's Strategy in the Modern World*, p. 12; *New Labour: Because Britain Deserves Better*, p. 38.
15 Labour Party, *New Labour, New Life for Britain* (London: Labour Party, 1996), p. 36.
16 Labour Party, *Strategy for a Secure Future: Labour's Approach to the Defence Industry* (London: Labour Party, 1995), pp. 3, 5 and 20.
17 Labour Party, *Labour's Strategy in the Modern World*, p. 14.
18 Labour Party, *New Labour: Because Britain Deserves Better*, p. 38.
19 Paul Anderson and Nyta Mann, *Safety First: The Making of New Labour* (London: Granta, 1997), p. 116; John Kamfpner, *Robin Cook* (London: Victor Gollancz, 1998), p. 109.
20 Andrew Rawnsley, *Servants of the People: The Inside Story of New Labour* (London: Hamish Hamilton, 2000), p. 168.
21 Kampfner, *Robin Cook*, p. 7.
22 Author's confidential interview with FCO official, London, June 1997.
23 Robin Cook, Mission statement for the Foreign and Commonwealth Office, FCO, London, 12 May 1997.
24 See Rhiannon Vickers, 'Labour's search for a Third Way in foreign policy', in Richard Little and Mark Wickham-Jones, eds, *New Labour's Foreign Policy: A New Moral Crusade?* (Manchester: Manchester University Press, 2000), pp. 33–45.
25 Labour Party, *New Labour: Because Britain Deserves Better*, p. 39.
26 *House of Commons Debates* (hereafter *H.C. Deb.*), vol. 294, 14 May 1997, col. 44.
27 David Owen, *Human Rights* (London: Cape, 1978).
28 *H.C. Deb.*, vol. 294, 21 May 1997, statement by the Prime Minister, col. 708; Robin Cook's written answer to question 1067, col. 72.
29 For example, Robin Cook, 'Human rights: making the difference', speech to the Amnesty International Human Rights Festival, London, 16 October 1998.
30 See Isobel Hilton, 'Chinese whispers: a year of quiet diplomacy ends with more arrests of dissidents', *Guardian*, 31 December 1998; Kampfner, *Robin Cook*, pp. 218–9.
31 Mark Wickham-Jones, 'Labour's trajectory in foreign affairs: the moral crusade of a pivotal power?' in Little and Wickham-Jones, eds, *New Labour's Foreign Policy*, p. 25.
32 Labour Party, 1983 general election manifesto, *New Hope for Britain* (London: Labour Party, 1983), p. 37.
33 Labour Party, *Sense About Defence: The Report of the Labour Party Defence Study Group* (London: Quartet Books, 1977), ch. 6.
34 *Labour Party Annual Conference Report* (hereafter *LPACR*), 1995, p. 191.

35 *H.C. Deb.*, 28 July 1997, Robin Cook's written answer to question 1146, cols 27–9.

36 *LPACR*, 1997, p. 133.

37 *LPACR*, 1999, p. 51.

38 Rawnsley, *Servants of the People*, p. 171.

39 Foreign Affairs Select Committee, *First Report: Foreign Policy and Human Rights* (London: TSO, 1998), Appendix 2, Memorandum submitted by TAPOL, the Indonesian Human Rights Campaign.

40 For example, in a report drawn up by the Department of Peace Studies at Bradford University and Saferworld, a campaigning group; Malcolm Chalmers, *British Arms Export Policy and Indonesia* (London: Saferworld, 1997), p. 22.

41 Defence, Foreign Affairs, International Development and Trade and Industry Committees, Special Report, *Committee's Inquiry into the 1997 and 1998 Annual Reports on Strategic Export Controls*, HC 540 (London: TSO, 1999).

42 *H.C. Deb.*, 14 December 2000, Presentation by Ted Rowlands of the reports of the four Select Committees making up the 'Quadripartite Committee' on strategic export, cols 1WH and 3 WH.

43 *Ibid.*, cols 4–5 WH.

44 Neil Cooper, 'The pariah agenda and New Labour's ethical arms sales policy', in Richard Little and Mark Wickham-Jones, eds, *New Labour's Foreign Policy*, p. 163.

45 Author's confidential interview with FCO official, London, September 2001; see, for example, Rawnsley, *Servants of the People*, pp. 170–2.

46 Tony Blair, interview on GMTV, 17 May 1998.

47 Tony Blair, speech to the nation on Kosovo, printed in the *Guardian*, 27 March 1999.

48 Tony Blair, 'Doctrine of the international community', speech to the Economic Club of Chicago, 22 April 1999.

49 Robert Skidelsky, 'The reinvention of Blair', in Anthony Seldon and Dennis Kavanagh, eds, *The Blair Effect 2001–5* (Cambridge: Cambridge University Press, 2005), p. 444.

50 *H.C. Deb.*, vol. 216, 15 December 1992, col. 290.

51 Robin Cook, speech to the 1995 Labour Party Annual Conference, *LPACR*, 1995, p. 190.

52 *Ibid.*, pp. 134–4.

53 See Rhiannon Vickers, 'Blair's Kosovo campaign: Political communications, the battle for public opinion and foreign policy', *Civil Wars*, 3:1 (Spring 2000), pp. 54–70.

54 John Lloyd, 'How the doves turned hawkish', *New Statesman*, 2 April 1999.

55 See, for example, comments by General Klaus Naumann, Chairman of the NATO Military Committee during 1999, in War in Europe, Channel 4, Episode 1, 30 January 2000; Piers Robinson, 'Ready to kill but not ready to die: NATO strategy in Kosovo', *International Journal*, 54:4 (Autumn 1999), pp. 671–82.

56 Lawrence Freedman, 'Defence', in Anthony Seldon, ed., *The Blair Effect:*

The Blair Government 1997–2001 (London: Little, Brown & Co., 2001), p. 291.

57 Jolyon Howarth, 'Discourse, ideas, and epistemic communities in European security and defence policy', *West European Politics*, 27:2 (2004), p. 220.

58 *The Strategic Defence Review*, Cm. 3999 (London: TSO, 1998), Introduction, paragraphs 2, 3 and 19.

59 *The Strategic Defence Review White Paper, 98/91*, (London, House of Commons Library, 15 October 1998), p. 11.

60 For more information, see Colin McInnes, 'Labour's Strategic Defence Review', *International Affairs*, 74:4 (1998), pp. 823–45.

61 Tony Blair, speech to the Royal Institute of International Affairs, London, 5 April 1995.

62 Labour Party, *A People's Europe* (London: Labour Party, 1995), p. 1.

63 *Ibid.*, p. 4.

64 Labour Party, *Labour's Strategy in the Modern World*, p. 3.

65 Labour Party, *New Labour: Because Britain Deserves Better*, p. 37.

66 Labour Party, *A People's Europe*.

67 Author's interview with senior foreign policy advisor to Robin Cook, London, August 2000.

68 Kampfner, *Robin Cook*, p. 137.

69 Author's interview with senior foreign policy advisor to Robin Cook, London, August 2000.

70 Seldon, *Blair*, pp. 321–8. See also Robert Peston, *Brown's Britain* (London: Short Books, 2005), pp. 207–16.

71 Joint Declaration on European Defence: British-French summit, St Malo, 3–4 December 1998, from www.fco.gov.uk.

72 Anne Deighton, 'European Union policy', in Seldon, ed., *The Blair Effect: 1997–2001*, p. 323.

73 See Paul Williams, *British Foreign Policy under New Labour, 1997–2005* (Basingstoke: Macmillan, 2005), pp. 70–4.

74 Howarth, 'Discourse, ideas, and epistemic communities in European security and defence policy', p. 221.

75 Peter Ridell, 'Europe', in Seldon and Kavanagh, eds, *The Blair Effect 2001–5* (Cambridge: Cambridge University Press, 2005), p. 364.

76 Williams, *British Foreign Policy under New Labour*, p. 61.

77 Madeleine Albright, 'The right balance will secure NATO's future', *Financial Times*, 7 December 1998.

78 Tony Blair, 'The principles of a modern British foreign policy', speech to the Lord Mayor's banquet, London, 10 November 1997.

79 Tony Blair, 'Britain's role in the EU and the transatlantic alliance', speech to the Associated Press, London, 15 December 1998.

80 Tony Blair, 'Committed to Europe, Reforming Europe', Ghent speech, 23 February 2000.

81 Labour Party, 2001 general election manifesto, *Ambitions for Britain* (London: Labour Party, 2001), p. 38.

82 Riddell, 'Europe', p. 362.

83 Labour Party, *New Labour: Because Britain Deserves Better*, p. 39.

84 DFID, *Eliminating World Poverty: A Challenge for the 21st Century* (London: TSO, 1997), paragraph 21.

85 See Ralph Young, 'New Labour and international development', in David Coates and Peter Lawler, eds, *New Labour in Power* (Manchester: Manchester University Press, 2000), pp. 259–65; Howard White, 'British aid and the White Paper on International Development: dressing a wolf in sheep's clothing in the emperor's new clothes?', *Journal of International Development*, 10:2 (1998), pp. 151–66.

86 Rob Dixon and Paul Williams, 'Tough on debt, tough on the causes of debt? New Labour's Third Way foreign policy', *British Journal of Politics and International Relations*, 3:2 (June 2001), p. 169.

87 Annual Abstract of Statistics, UK Gross public expenditure of aid, 1994/95 to 2002/03, downloaded from http://www.statistics.gov.uk/STATBASE/ssdataset.asp?vlnk=3960.

88 Labour Party, 2005 general election manifesto, *Britain: Forward not Back* (London: Labour Party, 2005), p. 90.

89 See Linda Melvern and Paul Williams, 'Britannia waived the rules: the Major government and the 1994 Rwandan genocide', *African Affairs*, 103 (2004), p. 1.

90 Williams, *British Foreign Policy under New Labour*, p. 80. See also Tom Porteous, 'British government policy in sub-Saharan Africa under New Labour', *International Affairs*, 81:2 (2005), pp. 281–97.

91 Williams, *British Foreign Policy under New Labour*, p. 79.

92 Blair's speech to the Labour Party Annual Conference, 2001.

93 Douglas Hurd, 'Making the world a safer place', *Daily Telegraph*, 1 January 1992.

Chapter 7

Labour's foreign policy in the twenty-first century

At the turn of the twenty-first century there was a renewed confidence in Britain's role in the world and optimism about global politics. Tony Blair felt that he had resolved one of the traditional dilemmas in British foreign policy, namely whether to focus on the Atlantic relationship or Britain's role within Europe. The Cold War was firmly in the past and for Blair, his liberal internationalist approach to the world seemed to be vindicated with the success of Kosovo, and his strategy of intervention and engagement seemed to be reaping rewards. He had embraced globalisation as a positive force for gradually expanding shared norms and values. Robert Cooper, Blair's special advisor on foreign affairs, argued that with peace being the natural order in the developed world, in the future the use of force might become rare, and that 'International affairs will be dull'.[1]

9/11 changed all that. Fear and pessimism replaced the optimism of the 1990s. The globalised interdependent world, far from bringing new benefits, now seemed to bring new threats: al Qaeda and transnational terrorist groups; the threat of the proliferation of weapons of mass destruction; failed states and humanitarian crises. For Blair these problems were all part of a whole, and not individual issues, and they all thrived on instability and disorder. Blair's overall approach of intervention and engagement was now directed with grim determination at fighting these threats. He still believed that the 'concept of an international community, based on core, shared values, prepared actively to intervene and resolve problems, is an essential pre-condition of our future prosperity and stability'.[2] But now sections of the international community were being threatened by instability, and Blair's view was that 'Instability is contagious'.[3] In the end, Blair staked his legacy on the way his government responded to a disordered world.

9/11 and the war on terror

It is difficult now to describe just how shocking the terrorist attacks of 9/11 were. Before 9/11, the general public had not heard of al Qaeda or Osama bin Laden and had not thought of themselves as a major terrorist target. To Americans, the attacks on New York and Washington were a second Pearl Harbour, and the loss of civilian life following the collapse of the twin towers of the World Trade Centre and the damage to the Pentagon was an atrocity that demanded an immediate response. In his address to the nation that evening, Bush declared that America would not only go after the terrorists involved but also those who harboured them.[4] Thus, the response to 9/11 would not just be the expected targeted retaliatory air strikes at known terrorist camps, but what was to be known as the 'Bush Doctrine', which was to dominate international affairs for the rest of Blair's premiership.

At the time of the 9/11 attacks Blair was preparing to give a speech to the Trades Union Congress' annual conference in Brighton. As he hurried back to London he told his aides that 'whatever else happened, America should not feel isolated'.[5] Thus, from the beginning, Blair spoke of 9/11 not as an attack on America, but an attack 'on us all'. When he gave a statement to the press that evening outside 10 Downing Street, he said that:

> [T]his mass terrorism is the new evil in our world. The people who perpetrate it have no regard whatever for the sanctity or value of human life, and we the democracies of the world must come together to defeat it and eradicate it. This is not a battle between the United States of America and terrorism, but between the free and democratic world and terrorism. We, therefore, here in Britain stand shoulder to shoulder with our American friends in this hour of tragedy, and we, like them, will not rest until this evil is driven from our world.[6]

In his statement to the House of Commons, Blair emphasised that 'The attack was an attack not on the west or the United States alone. It was an attack on civilized values everywhere.' It was an attempt 'to see the world run by the chaos consequent on terrorist outrage, rather than by disciplined and calm debate'. Blair also linked the defeat of those responsible for it directly to British national interests: 'We in Britain have the most direct interest in defeating such terror. It strikes at the heart of what we believe in. We know that, if not stopped, the terrorists will do it again, possibly this time in Britain.'[7]

Much to the relief of the British government, the Bush administration did not immediately retaliate by launching air strikes. Instead, Bush took some time to develop his response to 9/11. In a brief radio address to the American people on 15 September he said that America was planning to 'eradicate the evil of terrorism'. He warned that 'Victory against terrorism will not take place in a single battle, but in a series of decisive actions against terrorist organizations and those who harbor and support them'.[8] In an emergency speech to Congress on 20 September, at which Blair was present, Bush launched a 'war on terror' in response to the 'act of war against our country'. He said 'Our war on terror begins with al Qaeda, but it does not end there. It will not end until every terrorist group of global reach has been found, stopped and defeated.' The US would direct every source at its command to the 'defeat of the global terror network'. In addition,

> We will starve terrorists of funding, turn them one against another, drive them from place to place, until there is no refuge and no rest. And we will pursue nations that provide aid or safe haven to terrorism. Every nation, in every region, now has a decision to take. Either you are with us, or you are with the terrorists. From this day forward, any nation that continues to harbor or support terrorism will be regarded by the United States as a hostile regime.[9]

The Bush Doctrine – which included the right for the US to take preemptive force and to use force to prevent a threat form even emerging – was beginning to take shape. This heralded a new assertiveness in American foreign policy that had not been seen since the early years of the Cold War.

Bush's immediate target was the Taliban regime in Afghanistan, which allowed al Qaeda to recruit, train and organise on its territory. During his address to Congress, Bush gave the Taliban an ultimatum to deliver all the al Qaeda leaders located in Afghanistan to close all the terrorist training camps and to give the US access to them so that it could verify their closure, and to hand over every terrorist to appropriate authorities.[10] The Taliban regime responded through their embassy in Pakistan, asserting that they had no evidence linking al Qaeda to the 9/11 attacks, and that bin Laden was a guest in their country, and that as a guest they had to grant him hospitality and asylum.

Blair was an early advocate of the use of force in Afghanistan should the Taliban fail to hand over the al Qaeda leader Osama bin Laden. Blair justified the support of his government for war in

Afghanistan through a rubric that combined the rationale of combating terrorism with a powerful case for acting against the 'cruel, dictatorial and oppressive' Taliban regime, which had an appalling human rights record. He said that 'We are a principled nation, and this is a principled conflict'. There was a moral imperative that the modern world should act against those in Afghanistan who were 'the sworn enemies of everything the civilised world stands for'.[11] Not unexpectedly, the Taliban failed to hand over the terrorist leaders. It quickly became accepted within NATO – and more gradually in the international community – that the Taliban were a legitimate target for attack. Approval for the use of force was not sought in the UN Security Council. Instead, the US presented any military action in Afghanistan as an act of self-defence provided for under Article 51 of the UN Charter.

Operation Enduring Freedom began on 7 October 2001, with the US and UK leading an aerial bombing campaign in Afghanistan focusing on the capital Kabul and the Taliban heartland of Kandahar. The aims were to capture Osama bin Laden, destroy the al Qaeda network, and overthrow the Taliban regime. Ground forces were primarily supplied by the Afghan Northern Alliance, along with US Special Forces who mounted a major military expedition to find and capture the al Qaeda leaders. In 2002, infantry from America, Britain and Canada were committed, along with Special Forces from several allied nations. Later, NATO troops were added.

There was opposition from a small number of Labour backbench MPs over the initial bombing campaign. Particular concern was expressed over the use of cluster bombs, which were known to have a particularly harmful impact on the civilian population. Labour ministers defended government policy, condemning opposition to the conflict in Afghanistan and likening the threat of terrorism to that which had been posed by Nazism, and anti-war MPs to Nazi appeasers.[12] Some military analysts forecast that the military campaign would be likely to fail and extensive concerns were expressed at the danger to British troops.

Government critics were undermined by the unexpected capitulation of the Taliban regime in November 2001. Northern Alliance troops took Kabul on 13 November and the Taliban were forced back to their heartland in southeastern Afghanistan around Kandahar. Regime change had occurred more quickly than expected. Ministers argued that military action had been both necessary and justified and that there had been a duty to act against the Taliban. The al Qaeda network was ousted from its territorial stronghold, though Osama bin Laden remained at large. On 20 December 2001 the UN Security Council passed resolution 1386, authorising the creation of an International Security Assistance Force (ISAF), with authority to take all measures necessary to fulfill its mandate of assisting the Afghan Interim Authority in maintaining security. Command of the ISAF passed to NATO on 11 August 2003.

Regime change in Iraq

By the time that Bush gave his State of Union address in January 2002, the focus of the 'war on terror' was shifting away from Afghanistan and from terrorist organisations and towards the 'axis of evil', namely Iraq, Iran and North Korea, states that Bush said were 'arming to threaten the peace of the world'.[13] UN resolution 687 had been passed following the end of the Gulf War in 1991, and this had imposed economic sanctions on Iraq until it could prove that it had got rid of its chemical weapons, that it did not possess biological weapons, and that it was not developing it own nuclear capability. Saddam Hussein repeatedly interfered with the work of the UN weapons inspectors deployed to verify this, and in November 1998 the UN withdrew them from Iraq. After 9/11 the Bush administration repeatedly linked Saddam Hussein with the support of terrorist groups, including al Qaeda, and argued that Iraq could provide such groups with weapons of mass destruction (WMD). On 20 March 2003, having failed to gain UN support, the US launched pre-emptive military action against Iraq, not just to disarm its supposed WMD, but in order to secure regime change through the ousting of Saddam Hussein. This was part of Bush's rationale of taking the war to the enemy, arguing that America must 'confront the worst threats before they emerge', and that 'our best defense is a good offense'.[14] Britain contributed 46,000 troops to Operation Iraqi Freedom, joining approximately 248,000 troops from America, 2,000 from Australia, 1,300 from Spain, 500 from Denmark, and 194 from Poland. Kurdish militia troops were also deployed in northern Iraq.

The decision to invade Iraq was extremely controversial and was strongly opposed by some of America's traditional allies, including France and Germany. The UN had passed resolution 1441 in November 2002 that gave Iraq 'a final opportunity to comply with its disarmament obligations', and UN weapons inspectors had returned to

Iraq. In February 2003 the UN's chief weapons inspector, Hans Blix, reported to the UN Security Council some progress in Iraq and that inspections 'may yield results'. Blix noted that inspections based on intelligence tip-offs had found 'no evidence' of WMD. Many countries argued that the weapons inspectors were making progress and should be given more time, and that there was no justification to invade Iraq. On Saturday 15 February there was a co-ordinated worldwide protest against the invasion of Iraq in sixty countries, including a rally of three million people in Rome. In London, up to two million people took part in a 'Stop the War' rally, the biggest demonstration in British history. Blair, shocked by the scale of the protest, argued that the protesters did not represent the silent 'moral majority', and that there was a moral case for removing Saddam Hussein.[15]

Blair had initially claimed that Iraqi disarmament, not regime change, would be the reason for military action against Iraq. However, by the autumn of 2002 Blair was arguing the case for the overthrow of Saddam Hussein. He gave three main reasons: first, the imminent threat posed by Saddam's possession of weapons of mass destruction; second, Saddam's terrorist links, in particular with al Qaeda; third, concern over Saddam Hussein's record of human rights abuses and the suffering of Iraqi citizens. According to Blair, these three issues meant that Iraq was a security threat both regionally and internationally. However, no evidence was ever found of co-operation between Iraq and Osama bin Laden, and in March 2005, the CIA released a report saying that no WMD had been found in Iraq. Blair was subsequently accused of lying over the existence of weapons of mass destruction and of spinning intelligence information in order to boost his case for war, in particular in the case of the government's September 2002 so-called 'dodgy dossier' on *Iraq's Weapons of Mass Destruction*, with its erroneous claim that Iraq could deploy weapons of mass destruction within forty-five minutes.

There was no incontrovertible evidence that Saddam was progressing with the production of weapons of mass destruction, and, as Robin Cook said to the House of Commons Foreign Affairs Select Committee on 17 June 2003, 'the absence of evidence is a bloody thin ground on which to build a war'.[16] But neither was there clear evidence that Saddam had got rid of all his stockpiles of weapons from the early 1990s, or ceased in his programme to develop weapons of mass destruction. By refusing full co-operation with UN weapons inspectors, Saddam Hussein gave the impression that he had something to hide, especially after resolution 1441 had been passed by the UN in

November 2002. Saddam Hussein then behaved in a way that was counter-intuitive to thinking in Britain and the US. This is because Blair and Bush assumed that if Saddam really had no WMD, then when faced with an ultimatum by the UN, backed-up by the possibility of US military action, he would immediately and fully comply with any weapons inspections or requests for information regarding the destruction of weapons in the 1990s. However, it appears that after 1991, Saddam had stopped developing weapons of mass destruction, but he did not want people to know that this was the case. This was because his power relied on the threat of the potential use of weapons of mass destruction both domestically against his own people and regionally in terms of Iraq's relationship with its neighbour and rival, Iran.

While Blair's conviction that Iraq was still developing weapons of mass destruction can be explained, what is more perplexing is his conviction that Saddam had links with al Qaeda, and that his weapons of mass destruction might fall into the hands of terrorists. Soon after 9/11 the US administration starting describing Iraq as a rogue state that harboured terrorists. This claim was made by the Bush administration throughout the run-up to the invasion of Iraq. On this issue, Britain was relying very much on US intelligence. However, there was no clear evidence of links with al Qaeda, and Saddam did not have a track record of working with terrorist organisations or allowing them to operate in Iraq. Indeed, Saddam Hussein was a ruthless, megalomaniac dictator, and was hardly likely to allow religious opponents of his secular regime free rein in his country. And, if it were the case that Saddam was developing weapons of mass destruction, he would want to keep them for himself, rather than sharing them with potential regional rivals for power.

One of the government's opponents to the invasion of Iraq was Robin Cook. Cook was not against the use of force as such: he had publicly supported the bombing of Iraq in November 1998 in operation Desert Fox, aimed at degrading Iraq's weapons capability. He had felt that it was 'absolutely right' to take military action over Kosovo in 1999, not least because 'If Milosevic had got away with it then he might well have ended up a hero and had another ten years in power'.[17] However, Cook went on to become one of the government's most high-profile critics of the decision to go to war against Saddam Hussein. Resigning from the government on the eve of the vote in the House of Commons on military action, he said that he 'cannot support a war without international agreement or domestic support', and pointed out the paradox at the heart of the argument of the security threat posed by Saddam Hussein: 'Ironically, it is only because Iraq's military forces are so weak that we can even contemplate its invasion.'[18] The Conservative Party supported Blair's stance on Iraq and it was left to the Liberal Democrats to make the most clearly outlined opposition to the war. The Liberal Democrat leader, Charles Kennedy, while calling for definitive evidence linking Iraq with al Qaeda and 9/11, raised concerns over the notion of regime change, arguing that it did not fall to the US (or even the UN) to decide what government should be installed in which state. Similar questions were raised by Labour backbench MPs, where there was considerable unease about the legality, legitimacy, morality and consequences of invading a sovereign state in order to overthrow its government, as well as concerns that it would make the West *more* of a target for terrorist attack, not less. Even the Attorney General, Lord Goldsmith, had apparently thought that invasion was illegal. On 7 March 2003, he gave Blair a thirteen-page memo on the legality of the war, only twelve days before the start of the war. According to news reports in the *Independent* on 24 April 2005, Goldsmith gave six reasons why he feared the war in Iraq was illegal, but he then changed his mind after a quick trip to the US where he had a series of meetings in the White House, and an informal meeting at Downing Street. On 17 March, the day before the scheduled vote in the House of Commons on the use of force against Iraq, he provided a 337-word written reply to a question in the House of Lords. This stated that 'authority to use force against Iraq exists from the combined effect of Resolutions 678, 687 and 1441'. Military action was therefore legal. This House of Lords statement was given to the Cabinet that day. Cabinet was not shown the Attorney General's earlier memo where he had outlined his concerns over the legality of invading Iraq. Admiral Sir Michael Boyce, then Chief of Defence Staff, asked for unequivocal assurances that the war would be legal, which he was given.

On 18 March Blair moved the government motion that the UK 'should use all means necessary to ensure the disarmament of Iraq's weapons of mass destruction'. He argued that:

> [T]he outcome of this issue will now determine more than the fate of the Iraqi regime and more than the fate of the Iraqi people who have been brutalised by Saddam for so long, important though these issues are. It will determine the way in which Britain and the world confront the central security threat of the 21st century, the development of the United Nations, the relationship between Europe and the United States, the relations within the European Union and the way in which the United States

engages with the rest of the world. So it could hardly be more important. It will determine the pattern of international politics for the next generation.[19]

After an eight-hour debate, the motion was passed by 412 votes to 149. Eighty-five Labour MPs voted against the government.

Blair's decision to join Bush in the invasion of Iraq not only affected how Britain was seen, but it also affected how people viewed Blair and his government. The major domestic legacy of Blair's decision that British troops would join with American troops in the invasion of Iraq in March 2003 was a widespread and growing erosion of trust in the honesty of the Labour government in general, and of Tony Blair in particular. The British Prime Minister was the focus of much dismay over the inadequate nature of the intelligence used to justify action against Saddam, the troop deployments themselves, subsequent British fatalities and the controversy evoked by the suicide of Dr David Kelly.[20] Blair's support for President Bush's war in Iraq led not just to criticism at home but also to a far less positive perspective of British foreign policy within the European Union. The deployment of British troops was of particular political importance because it had given the US military action the appearance of international legitimacy and provided very obvious proof that Bush was not acting in isolation. Blair's seeming enthusiasm and commitment to war against Saddam evoked much journalistic and academic comment.[21] It was Blair's most controversial decision in his ten years as premier.

Contrary to media reports at the time, Blair did not decide to deploy British troops because of pressure from the US. He repeatedly said that he believed that overthrowing Saddam was the correct path to follow. In an interview in the *Guardian* on 1 March 2003, the Blair was asked explicitly why he was going along with Bush's policy on Iraq. Blair answered, 'It's worse than you think. I believe in it. I am truly committed to dealing with this irrespective of the position of America.'[22] Blair supported the doctrine of pre-emptive action, arguing that there could be little point in waiting for something to happen before responding. He actually shared the crusading impulse of Bush and the neo-Conservatives, their lack of self-doubt and their insular 'groupthink' when it came to Iraq.[23] It was Blair's missionary zeal to make the world a better place that led him to believe his own propaganda about Iraq. Blair also believed that the logic that had applied to the need to intervene in Kosovo – that in an increasingly globalised and interdependent world, isolationism and the principle of non-intervention had to be qualified when it came to matters of international

security and human rights abuses – also applied to Iraq. The subsequent success of the allied Anglo-American effort in Kosovo, and the
way that public opinion swung in favour of the action after it was seen
to have been a success, in many ways acted as a powerful precedent, at
least for Blair, in dealing with Saddam Hussein. As he said in a speech
at the George Bush Senior Presidential Library on 7 April 2002,
people hesitated to support intervention in Kosovo: 'we were told: it's
not our fight, why bother? There's nothing we can do; if we try to stop
him, the region will explode; we will strengthen his hand, he will win;
or he'll lose but be succeeded by someone worse. Sound familiar?' Blair
argued that intervention in Kosovo had worked: Kosovo had held its
first elections, Milosevic was on trial charged with war crimes, and
there was a democratic government in Belgrade.[24] For Blair, those who
were arguing that intervention in Iraq would destabilise the region,
that overthrowing the regime would or could bring worse problems,
were the same misguided critics who said that intervention in Kosovo
and in Afghanistan would not work; he had proved them wrong before
and would prove them wrong again. Blair was convinced that regime
change in Iraq would be successful, and that over time both domestic
and international public opinion would swing in favour of the invasion
of Iraq. For Blair, invading Iraq had become the internationalist
option, and critics of military action were taking a narrow, isolationist
perspective, which had no place in a globalised, interdependent world.
He did not reflect on the fact that all three cases were very different.
Air strikes in Kosovo were undertaken as a result of an immediate
humanitarian crisis and not to implement regime change. Military
action in Afghanistan, which involved Afghani ground forces, was seen
by many as legitimate as the Taliban regime were giving safe haven to
al Qaeda who had just committed the 9/11 terrorist attack. The situation with Iraq was very different from either Kosovo or Afghanistan,
but Blair saw the three cases as comparable. Blair also tended to dismiss
those within the Labour Party who did not support the invasion of
Iraq as taking this position because they were anti-Bush or anti-
American.

When it came to foreign affairs, Blair demonstrated his greatest
strengths and his greatest weaknesses in terms of competence and
judgement. While Blair's belief in the invasion of the Iraq was explica-
ble, his lack of grasp of detail, his failure to question more strongly
the basis of the intelligence and – perhaps even more startlingly – the
plans for reconstruction in Iraq, was not. Blair focused on the big
picture and failed to ask basic questions about specific plans. There was

a negligent lack of planning for the post-war reconstruction period, especially with regard to the safety of the Iraqi population. The Bush administration's decision to disband the 400,000 to 500,000-strong Iraqi army, thus creating a huge supply of unemployed men trained in warfare and counter-insurgency, was disastrous. The ensuing chaos and conflict in Iraq and the immense suffering and loss of life did not improve regional or international security. Neither did it help British security nor Britain's standing in the world.

On Thursday 7 July 2005, four bombs exploded between 8.51am and 9.47 am in London's public transport system. Two were in tunnels on the underground system near King's Cross and Aldgate, two were on board buses at Edgware Road and Tavistock Square. This happened while the G-8 was meeting at Gleneagles in Scotland. Tony Blair insisted that while he would return to London, the G-8 meeting would continue as 'It is important ... that those engaged in terrorism realise that our determination to defend our values and our way of life is greater than their determination to cause death and destruction to innocent people in a desire to impose extremism on the world'.[25] George Bush said that this was 'a war on terror for us all'. Fifty-two people were killed in the '7/7' attacks, as were the four suicide bombers, and about 700 people were injured. More people were killed in this event than in any single terrorist act during the Troubles with Northern Ireland. The bombings were carried out by British Islamist extremists. In a videotape aired by the al Jazeera television network on 1 September 2005, the ringleader of the group, Mohammad Sidique Khan, said he had been motivated by what he saw as the brutality with which Britain treated Muslims, and that 'until we feel security, you will be our targets ... We are at war and I am a soldier. Now you too will taste the reality of this situation.' The video was released with a statement by Ayman al-Zawahiri, an al Qaeda leader, in which he said that the attacks had occurred because of British action in Iraq and Afghanistan.[26] For Blair, though, this terrorist act was yet more evidence of the need to engage in an all-out war against extremism.

On 1 August 2006, Blair gave a major foreign policy speech to the Los Angeles World Affairs Council in which he spoke of the dangers of an 'arc of extremism across the Middle East'. He called for a 'complete renaissance' in foreign policy to combat this 'Reactionary Islam' in favour of 'Moderate, mainstream Islam'. 'To defeat it will need an alliance of moderation that paints a different future in which Muslim, Jew and Christian; Arab and Western; wealthy and developing nations can make progress in peace and harmony with each other.'[27] Blair's 'arc of extremism' speech held many echoes with Churchill's 'iron curtain' speech. The West had its new global contest, and Britain would be at the forefront of the fight against the spread of terrorism/communism. What Blair had not learnt from history was that the US and Britain had been wrong to treat all communist countries as Soviet satellites, that there was not one cohesive enemy but a range of different groups with different aims, which needed to be tackled as individual problems and not lumped to together as one homogenous threat.

Blair and Brown: the succession

Blair's role in the war on terror was eroding support for his government and he came under increasing pressure from within sections of the party to give a date for his departure. Blair had stated before the general election on 5 May 2005 that he intended to serve a full third term as Prime Minister if Labour were re-elected. However, this was not to be the case. Blair spent much of the 2005 general election defending his decision-making over Iraq and denying that he lied to Parliament and to the public over Iraq's supposed WMD. While the Labour Party won its third consecutive victory, it lost forty-seven seats, and only polled 35.2 per cent of the vote, the lowest share of the vote ever recorded for a winning party at a UK general election. One of Blair's problems was that it was nearly thirty years since 'Old Labour' had been in power and so the term 'New Labour' was losing its meaning. More ominously for his successor, confidence in Labour's handling of the economy dropped after the 2005 election, with the public no longer crediting Gordon Brown with Britain's economic growth. More importantly for the Conservatives, trust in their economic ability was increasing and they appeared to have finally put behind them the ignominy of Black Wednesday. Blair faced increasing pressure from supporters of Gordon Brown to stand down and allow Brown the chance he had long been waiting for to lead the Labour Party and the country.

Indeed, by May 2006, the Labour government was looking increasingly beleaguered. It was racked by factionalism as a result of the slow-motion power struggle between Blair and Brown over Blair's departure, mired in sleaze over the cash-for-peerages scandal, embarrassed by the revelation of John Prescott's affair with his diary secretary, and it was left looking weak and incompetent over the fiasco of the release of foreign prisoners into the community. For the first time since he came to power, Blair's approval rating was below that of the leader of the Conservative Party, David Cameron, who had replaced Michael Howard following the 2005 election. While Blair had personified what people liked about 'New Labour' in 1997, it seemed that he had come to personify what people disliked about the Labour government by 2006. Blair's electoral strategy of dominating the centre-ground of politics was being undermined by Cameron's determination to challenge him with centrist policies. Cameron was learning from Blair's electoral success and Labour's assumption that the Conservatives would oppose them by moving further to the right was no longer working.

Following disappointing local election results of 4 May 2006 when Labour lost 300 council seats, Blair launched a major cabinet reshuffle. Foreign Secretary Jack Straw, largely seen as an astute operator at the FCO, faced the same ignominy as Robin Cook by being demoted to Leader of the House Commons. He was replaced by Margaret Beckett. There was surprisingly little interest in Britain's first female Foreign Secretary, just a perplexed silence from journalists and pundits. Beckett had not been associated with any debates on foreign policy and had little in the way of international standing, and perhaps this was why Blair appointed her as it enabled him to assert himself as both Prime Minister and Foreign Secretary. Beckett's first challenge was to attend crisis talks in New York on Iran's nuclear programme, where she admitted that she had been thrown in at the deep end and was 'flying by the seat of my pants'.[28] There were also growing complaints that Beckett was not up to the job, with Foreign Office officials apparently saying that 'the Israel-Lebanon war has exposed Margaret Beckett's inadequacies as foreign secretary'.[29] Israel had launched massive air attacks and a blockade against the south of Lebanon in response to a cross-border raid by Hezbollah in which two Israeli soldiers were abducted and three were killed. In interviews on the *Today Programme* on Radio 4 Beckett sounded defensive and angry and out of her depth. In addition to her weak position, much of Blair's contact with politicians in the Middle East was through his fundraiser and special envoy, Lord Levy. Blair had been bypassing the Foreign Office by using Levy, but there were concerns that he was not a credible peace envoy in the Middle East given that his background was as an accountant in the music industry. In early August, more than 100 Labour MPs backed a call for the Commons to be recalled from its summer break to debate the crisis in Lebanon.

Brown's interminable wait for Blair to go and Blair's resistance to be pushed out of office, increasingly affected the party. The interregnum of the succession became tedious to all but Whitehall insiders and did little to help the government's fortunes. It was quite clear to everyone that Blair and Brown could not stand each other and that Blair wanted to resist giving way to Brown for as long as possible while Brown brooded in the background, Blair's would-be nemesis. In early September 2006 there was what was described as an attempted coup to get rid of Blair when a number of MPs wrote to him urging him to resign. On 7 September Blair announced that he would step down within a year. A leaked memo from a Downing Street spin-doctor talked of 'Tony's farewell tour', of how he should leave the electorate wanting more. This memo also talked of Iraq as the 'elephant in the room', the issue that had destroyed Blair's popularity and overshadowed his government's successes. Some Labour Party activists had come to detest Blair over what they felt was the subordination of British foreign policy to the White House. Even the general population saw Blair as compromised by his support for Bush in the face of worldwide concern over the situation in Iraq, the belligerent American approach to Iran, the failure to press for a ceasefire early on in the conflict between Israel and Lebanon, and lack of support for human rights and the Geneva Convention. Labour MPs hoped that by getting rid of Blair, British foreign policy would change track and that Brown would take a more independent approach. However, Brown never stated that this would be the case. It was actually left to David Cameron to make the case for a more independent foreign policy. In a speech on foreign policy and national security on the fifth anniversary of 9/11, Cameron emphasised his belief in the importance of the Anglo-American relationship, but said that 'we will serve neither our own, nor America's, nor the world's interests if we are seen as America's unconditional associate in every endeavour'. He argued that by slavishly following America, Britain had risked combining 'the maximum of exposure with the minimum of real influence over decisions'. Over the last five years, foreign policy had been too warlike, and had lacked 'humility and patience', which were 'two crucial qualities which should always condition foreign policy-making'.[30] This was the message that the Labour Party wanted to hear from Gordon Brown, not from the leader of the opposition.

On 10 May 2007 Blair went to his constituency of Sedgefield to announce his decision to stand down from the leadership of the Labour Party, and said that on 27 June he would resign from the office of Prime Minister. He had been in power for just over ten years. Blair's

resignation speech was illuminating. Speaking to his constituency
Labour Party members as though they were the British public, he said
that expectations had been high when he came to power, 'Too high.
Too high in a way for either of us.'[31] Of his foreign policy, he said in
the cases of Sierra Leone and Kosovo, 'I took the decision to make our
country one that intervened, that did not pass by, or keep out of the
thick of it.' Then came 9/11, when he decided to stand 'shoulder to
shoulder with our oldest ally', and intervened in Afghanistan and Iraq.
For the first time, Blair publicly acknowledged that there had been a
price to pay in terms of British security because of the invasion of Iraq,
for 'the blowback since, from global terrorism and those elements that
support it, has been fierce and unrelenting and costly'. He said that
whatever people thought of him, 'I ask you to accept one thing. Hand
on heart, I did what I thought was right.'[32] The next day, Gordon
Brown announced that he would be a candidate to be leader of the
Labour Party. He gave little indication about any specific foreign
policy, but did say that he had 'a belief that Britain can lead the world,
the compassion of each of us contributing to the well being and security of all'. He finished by saying that 'I want to lead a government
humble enough to know its place – where I will always strive to be –
on the people's side'.[33] In the ensuing leadership election, only one
MP, John McDonnell, stood against Brown, but he failed to achieve
enough nominations to get on to the ballot and so conceded defeat to
Gordon Brown, who had been nominated by 313 MPs, including
Blair. Brown was duly elected leader of the Labour Party. The competition for deputy leader, which was more intense, was won by Harriet
Harman. Despite a decade of friction between Tony Blair and Gordon
Brown, the transition was orderly, as Blair had been promised it would
be. Each man was gracious to the other.

In his final Prime Minister's questions, Blair began as usual by
paying tribute to fallen soldiers, two killed in Iraq, and one in
Afghanistan. He then went on to praise the armed services, saying that:

> I have never come across people of such sustained dedication, courage and
> commitment. I am truly sorry about the dangers that they face today in
> Iraq and Afghanistan. I know that some may think that they face these
> dangers in vain. I do not, and I never will. I believe that they are fighting
> for the security of this country and the wider world against people who
> would destroy our way of life. But whatever view people take of my deci-
> sions, I think that there is only one view to take of them: they are the
> bravest and the best.[34]

It was a bravura performance and at the end of Blair's comments he received an unprecedented two-minute standing ovation from all sides of the House of Commons. He then travelled by train to tell his Sedgefield constituency that he would be standing down as MP in order to take up the post of special envoy for the Middle East negotiating Quartet, consisting of the US, Russia, the UN and the EU. In a statement the Quartet announced that his role would be to mobilise and co-ordinate international aid for the Palestinians, to help them build their own governing institutions and reform the Palestinian policy, and promote economic development. Russia had had some reservations about Blair's appointment, but had acquiesced after changes they had demanded to the terms of Blair's remit were made. Gordon Brown was described as angry that he had been presented with a *fait accompli* that would make it difficult for him to formulate his own Middle East policy.[35]

In his first speech as Prime Minister, given on the steps of Number 10 Downing Street, Brown gave a characteristically solemn promise that 'I will be strong in purpose, steadfast in will, resolute in action in the service of what matters most to the British people, meeting the concerns and aspirations of our whole country'. He said that he would be forming a government of all talents beyond narrow party interests, and spoke of the need for change.[36] He then announced a major Cabinet reshuffle in what was seen by the media as an attempt by Brown to draw a line under the Blair premiership, and appointed critics of the Iraq war to his government. Most notably, David Miliband – who had, according to the media, privately regarded the invasion of Iraq as a grave error, and privately criticised Blair's support for Israel during the crisis in Lebanon the previous summer – became Foreign Secretary.[37] At the age of forty-one, he was the youngest Foreign Secretary since David Owen. According to press reports, diplomats hoped that under Brown the FCO would once again take the lead role in foreign policy, and that important decisions would not be confined to the Prime Minister and his top advisors as they had with Blair.[38] Brown also announced that he would publish a national security strategy and establish a National Security Committee; that MPs would get to ratify treaties, rather than the decision to do so being made by ministers; and that MPs would have the opportunity to vote on whether to go war. This last change had actually been promised by Blair, and nothing was said about when such a vote would be put to Parliament. As one journalist put it, 'Call me cynical, but Parliament simply wouldn't dare vote for peace when the battle engine was already roaring'.[39] Blair had of course given the Commons the chance to vote on the eve of the invasion of Iraq.

Terrorism immediately became the major challenge for Brown. On 29 June, just two days into his premiership, a Mercedes car was found packed with sixty litres of petrol, nails and gas canisters outside a night-club in London's West End. Another car bomb was found in a Mercedes that had been towed to an underground car park. The discovery of the bombs confirmed the fears of counter-terrorist officers that Islamic fundamentalist terrorist groups would bring Iraqi-style tactics, where vehicle-borne improvised explosive devices went off daily, to Britain. Two days later, a Jeep Cherokee also packed with gas canisters was rammed into the doors of the main terminal at Glasgow airport and set on fire. The two men inside, one of them wearing a suicide belt, then tried to detonate it, but were overpowered and arrested by police with the assistance of bystanders. The national threat level was raised to the maximum 'critical'. Just a few days into his premiership, Gordon Brown was dealing with the most dangerous situation since the July 2005 attacks in London. In a televised address from Downing Street, a sombre Brown urged people to be vigilant. He said 'I know that the British people will stand together, united, resolute and strong'. The following morning in an interview with Andrew Marr, he again spoke of the need for vigilance, but said that in the face of such terrorism 'we will not yield, we will not be intimidated. And we will not allow anyone to undermine our British way of life.' This would be a long-term threat that would have to be fought mili-tarily, by security, by police, by intelligence.[40] Significantly, Brown did not talk of an 'arc of extremism' or an 'evil ideology' and no mention was made of a 'war on terror'. Instead, Brown and his new Home Secretary, Jacqui Smith, stressed the need for the public to be vigilant, but for people to continue their lives as normal. The perpetrators of the bombings were described as criminals and the tone taken by Brown to describe events was different from that of his predecessor, significantly less dramatic and less emotional.

Brown's foreign policy

There was a flurry of activity over the summer of 2007 as Brown and his new foreign policy team sought to outline their approach to foreign affairs and to the immediate issues facing them. There was an early blunder when Lord Malloch Brown, a newly appointed junior minister at the Foreign Office, gave a speech suggesting that Britain would no longer be 'joined at the hip' to the US. The Foreign Secretary, David Miliband, tried to quash the media speculation that Britain would distance itself from the US in an interview with the BBC, saying that 'Our commitment to work with the Americans in general and the Bush administration in particular is resolute.' He went on that Britain wanted to be a 'serious player' in the world, and 'You do that with the US, not against'.[41] During a keynote speech to the Royal Institute of International Affairs, Chatham House, on 19 July 2007, Miliband made a point of saying twice that Britain's single most important bilateral relationship was with the US. 'The US is the world's largest economy. Engaged – whether on the Middle East Peace Process or climate change or international development – it has the greatest capacity to do good of any country in the world.'[42] This was interpreted by the media as a 'rousing defence of Britain's special relationship with America', aimed at reassuring the White House that there would be no rift under Brown.[43] Miliband only referred to Iraq once, and there was no mention of the 'war on terror'. Brown also sought to dispel fears in Washington that he would adopt a more arms length approach to the relationship with the US. At his first regular press conference as Prime Minister on 23 July he said that 'the American relationship for Britain is our strongest bilateral relationship and I am determined to do everything in my power to make sure that it is strong and effective in the work that it does, not just between our two countries but for the whole world'.[44]

The media excitement over the nature of the Anglo-American relationship was quickly displaced by the developing rift with Russia. On 16 July 2007 Miliband announced that the Foreign Office was ceasing co-operation with Moscow on a range of issues, starting with the imposition of restrictions on visas issued to Russian government officials visiting the UK and the expulsion of four Russian intelligence officers. This action was in protest at the Kremlin's refusal to extradite Andre Lugovoi, the prime suspect in the murder of Alexander Litvinenko. He had died from poisoning on 23 November 2006 due to the ingestion of radioactive polonium-210, a substance that would be very difficult to get hold of without the co-operation of a nuclear weapons producing state. The story of Litvinenko's murder had gripped the British media with its connotations of a Cold War spy story and it was widely argued that Russian intelligence agencies must have been involved in the murder. The Russian Foreign Ministry condemned the move as 'immoral and provocative', and said that it reflected the 'Russo-phobic sentiment' in British society.[45] In retaliation, on 19 July the Russian Foreign Ministry announced that it was expelling four British diplomats and that Russia would stop issuing visas to British officials. It also said that it would no longer co-operate on counter-terrorism and intelligence sharing with Britain. This was not seen as a major blow for British intelligence services as there was little information flow between the UK and Russia on terrorism; the relationship was not nearly as important as the British intelligence relationships with the US, Saudi Arabia or Pakistan.

While this marked the lowest point in Anglo-Russian relations since the end of the Cold War, there had been concerns about Russia's internal and external political behaviour since Putin's re-election as President four years previously. These included his increasingly authoritarian behaviour and Russia's human rights record, its use of its energy supplies to exert political influence across Europe, and its capture of gas fields in the Arctic Ocean. Russia's relationship with the US had also been strained and Putin had been particularly angry about the proposed extension of the US missile defence system to Poland and the Czech Republic. Russia's withdrawal in July 2007 from the post-Cold War treaty restricting the deployment of forces in Europe was seen as a response to this.

Gordon Brown made his first Prime Ministerial visit to America at the end of July, meeting with George W. Bush at Camp David. This was a long-awaited meeting of the leaders and many on the left of the Labour Party, who had been hoping that Brown would distance himself from Bush, would have been both reassured and disappointed. At their joint press conference on 30 July, Brown said that America remained Britain's key ally and that they had a 'shared destiny'. Brown praised America, focusing on the historic links between the two countries and recalling comments that Winston Churchill made about the US. He did not praise Bush. Bush on the other hand delivered an unequivocal endorsement of Brown, praising him as 'a principled man who really wants to get something done', a 'glass half-full man', a 'humorous Scotsman'. Bush even said that the relationship with the UK was America's 'most important bilateral relationship', a comment that Presidents usually avoid making in public as it might cause offence to all the other countries that the US has key partnerships with, such as Israel, Saudi Arabia, Mexico and Canada. Brown looked statesmanlike while signalling a subtle change of tone in the transatlantic relationship. He only referred to Iraq once, saying that he would make a Commons statement in October on the future of the 5,500 British troops in Basra, and that any decision would be based on the military advice from its commanders on the ground. This was seen in the media as Brown indicating to Bush that he would not delay the withdrawal of British troops in order to show unity with the US. Brown referred to Afghanistan, not Iraq, as the 'front line against terrorism', and said that 'Terrorism is not a cause but a crime – a crime against humanity'. In contrast, President Bush spoke of 'this war against extremists and radicals'.[46] Thus, Brown avoided the 'war on terror' rhetoric of his predecessor, and continued to categorise terrorism as a criminal act rather than an all-out global war.

The following day Brown addressed the UN in New York where he focused on the crisis in Darfur. He had already agreed at a meeting with the French President, Nicolas Sarkozy, that they would begin a new push to end the conflict in Darfur by jointly sponsoring a UN resolution calling for an African Union and UN hybrid peacekeeping force. In his speech to the UN, Brown began by referring to Darfur as 'the greatest humanitarian disaster the world faces today', with over 200,000 people dead and two million displaced.[47] He urged the UN Security Council to agree to the Anglo-French resolution, which by this point had American support, proposing to send a 26,000-strong international force consisting of UN and African Union soldiers and police to Darfur to stop the fighting between government and rebels. The vote was passed unanimously after China, the Sudanese government's main supporter in the UN, dropped its objections to the resolution. According to British officials, China's oil interests in Sudan had been outweighed by its concern about a possible international human rights backlash over Darfur at the 2008 Olympic Games to be held in Beijing.[48] Getting the resolution passed by the UN Security Council was seen as a 'foreign policy victory' for Gordon Brown, who had made Darfur a priority since becoming Prime Minister.[49] And it was a victory, even if a limited one, as the UN had not been able to agree on action previously. The international force was to be dispatched under Chapter 7 of the UN charter, giving them the right to use force to protect civilians as well as themselves. China had been urging for any deployment to be under Chapter 6 of the UN charter, which would have meant that troops would not have been able to use force. This new international force was to take over from the 7,000 African Union force in western Sudan, which had been seen as ineffectual at best. Thus, overall, Brown's first visit to the US as Prime Minister was seen in the media as a resounding success. He had managed to get a concrete policy decision while signalling some differences with Bush but without having offended the US administration.

Brown's first keynote foreign policy speech was at the Lord Mayor's banquet in November 2007, which tradition dictates should focus on the international situation. Brown described his approach to the world as 'hard-headed internationalism', and he defended interventionism. He talked about the global forces that were changing the world and the subsequent unexpected level of disorder and uncertainty since the end of the Cold War. In these respects, his vision of the world, and of Britain's role in it, was much the same as Blair's. His speech highlighted three themes that he believed should be higher on the world agenda. First, he emphasised the need to speed up reform of international institutions, including the UN, the World Bank, G-8 and the IMF. Second, he spoke of the need to think about new ways in which nuclear states could enforce non-proliferation without depriving the developing world of nuclear energy. He declared that Britain would lead the international campaign to stop Iran's nuclear programme by calling for new sanctions on oil and gas investments if Iran continued to ignore UN Security Council demands to suspend uranium enrichment. Third, he emphasised the importance of reconstruction that needed to take place alongside peacekeeping efforts. In an implicit acknowledgement that the planning of post-war reconstruction in Iraq had been inadequate, he said that 'In future, Security Council peacekeeping resolutions and UN envoys should make stabilisation, reconstruction and development an equal priority'.[50]

There were two major differences between the approach being outlined by Brown and that of his predecessor. First, whereas Blair's approach to foreign affairs was to place emphasis on the efficacy of the use of force, Brown's approach instead placed faith in the use of economic measures: aid and economic development for Africa, economic reconstruction for conflict zones in the Middle East, and sanctions against transgressors such as Iran. Second, Brown mentioned Iraq only briefly, and said nothing about radical Islam or 9/11. Brown was signalling very clearly that Britain had moved on from the immediate post-9/11 era that had been defined by the 'war on terror', a phrase that Brown was careful not to use. Brown's foreign policy was to be slightly less ambitious in its expectations of changing the world than Blair's had been. With Brown's premiership, Britain had left the immediate post-9/11 era behind. Instead, Britain entered an era of unprecedented financial uncertainty and the threat of global recession.

Gordon Brown and the credit crunch

There had been a small increase in the popularity of the Labour government immediately after Brown became Prime Minister, but this honeymoon period was to be very short lived. A mood of fear and anxiety engulfed the electorate with the onset of a global financial crisis and credit crunch triggered by problems in the US housing market. Many banks and financial institutions stopped lending to each other. Britain's fifth biggest mortgage lender, Northern Rock, which gained an unusual amount of its funding from the financial markets rather than relying on money provided by savers, dramatically ran into trouble in August 2007. News that it had gone to the Bank of England for emergency funding triggered the first run on a British bank in more than a century, and images of people queuing to get their money out of Northern Rock flashed around the world. It was not until February 17, six months after the crisis, that Brown announced that Northern Rock would be nationalised. The first nationalisation since the 1970s, this would require emergency legislation to be passed in Parliament, and a £24 billion state loan. The delay had caused confusion in the banking sector; Gordon Brown's record for economic competence came under attack, and he was accused of dithering over what to do with Northern Rock. Then there was the fiasco in September over whether to hold a snap general election.

Having spent ten years as Chancellor of the Exchequer, Brown was more experienced in governing than most incoming British Prime Ministers. Because of this experience the general public had high expectations of Brown. There were also very high expectations of a Brown premiership from the left of the Labour Party. During his time as Chancellor, Brown had talked of his 'moral compass', which the left had interpreted to mean that he would focus on alleviating poverty once he became Prime Minister. Initially, Brown's colleagues, the Labour Party, the media and the public were impressed with his calm and steady approach and the apparent lack of media manipulation. The briefings from Blair's camp of Brown's 'psychological flaws', the rumours of his brooding, bullying personality, were forgotten. Many of Brown's closest advisors urged him to cash in on his popularity and call a snap election. They stoked election speculation to a fever-pitch during the Labour Party conference in early September 2007, thinking that it would undermine the Conservatives at their conference the following week. However, it did the opposite, galvanising the

Conservatives behind their leader, David Cameron. The polls started to record a drop in Brown's popularity and the media became increasingly strident in their request for Brown to say definitely whether or not he was calling an election. On 6 October Brown announced in an interview with the BBC's Andrew Marr that he would not be calling an election as he wanted time to show people how the government was implementing his vision for change in Britain. The media and the public felt that they had been tricked by Brown as the election speculation had gone on for so long, and the opposition accused him of showing weakness and indecision. Brown went from being seen as a man of conviction, a statesman above petty party-political interests, to one who dithered and took a self-serving approach to politics. It appeared that Brown was not the straight-talking conviction politician that he had claimed. Vince Cable, acting leader of the Liberal Democrats, made a quip that 'The house has noticed the prime minister's remarkable transformation in the past few weeks – from Stalin to Mr Bean'.[51] A great howl of laughter went up. It was cruel, but the comment seemed to many observers to be rather apt.

As the credit crunch persisted house prices fell at a rate not seen since the property crash of the early 1990s, with a drop of 7 per cent between January and May 2008. Whereas banks and building societies had previously competed for customers by offering the lowest mortgage rates and arrangement fees, the credit crunch led to a complete reversal. Lenders competed to offer the least attractive deals in order to limit the number and type of customers taking out their mortgages. Homeowners found that they were paying more for their mortgage at the same time as their home was falling in value, and in many parts of the country house sales ground to a halt. This was combined with rising food and energy prices which meant that people's purchasing power dropped, as did their confidence in Labour's ability to run the economy. After a decade of easy credit, people suddenly found that they could not get good mortgage deals or loans and many lenders failed to pass on cuts in interest rates. One of the problems that Brown faced was that unlike other new Prime Ministers, he could not blame economic problems on the opposition, or even on the previous Chancellor. Brown had previously boasted that he had abolished the 'boom and bust' business cycle. Instead, he inherited the consequences of his own economic policies of easy credit and light-touch regulation of financial institutions. Another problem that Brown faced was that the talents required to be a Prime Minister are somewhat different from those of being a successful Chancellor. In particular, Brown lacked the political skill of Blair. His handling of the ten-pence tax rate row was particularly poor.

In his last year as Chancellor, Brown had financed a cut in the basic rate of tax by abolishing the ten-pence rate, and this came into effect in April 2008. As the realisation dawned that this meant that some very low-paid workers would now be paying more tax, and higher paid workers less tax, many of those who had fought so hard to replace Blair with Brown felt appalled. Brown refused to accept that any low-paid workers would be worse off, even though the Treasury released figures demonstrating that those without children of school age would be hit by a tax increase. At a meeting of the PLP, angry backbenchers ended up shouting at Brown as he kept repeating that there would be no losers because of his tax credit policy. As Cameron denounced Brown over this decision, the Conservatives were able to present themselves as the defenders of the poor. Brown came across as obdurate, out of touch and lacking in empathy with the public. Rather than having a strong 'moral compass' he seemed detached from the values associated with his party, and which his supporters had expected him to implement when he came to power. This was compounded by hat-trick of electoral setbacks the following month. On 2 May Labour lost the London mayoral election, with Boris Johnson winning for the Conservatives, and Labour came third in the local elections, losing an astonishing 331 council seats and gaining just 24 per cent of the vote, compared with the Conservatives' 44 per cent. In the Crewe and Nantwich by-election on 22 May the Conservatives overturned a 7,000 Labour majority to win with their own majority of nearly 8,000. The 17.6 per cent swing to the Conservative Party occurred despite the fact that the Labour candidate was Tamsin Dunwoody, the daughter of Gwyneth Dunwoody who had held the seat for the past thirty years. Afterwards, David Cameron said that the result was clear evidence of 'the end of new Labour'.

The problem was not just the credit crunch. The Northern Rock fiasco smacked of bad governance, while Brown had been the author of his own political misfortune over the snap election fiasco. Despite working extraordinarily long hours, Brown seemed unable to prioritise, and in his desire to avoid offending anyone, he managed to please no one. This happened at the international level as well as domestic. Brown refused to bow to pressure from Eurosceptics to hold a referendum on the Lisbon Treaty on the grounds that it was not a constitutional treaty, but then appeared to be attempting to appease the Eurosceptics by turning up late to the signing ceremony and so failing to sign with the other European Prime Ministers. When the Dalai Lama visited Britain, Brown agreed to meet with him, but not to receive him at Downing Street for fear of offending China. When the Olympic torch came to London, Brown agreed to be photographed with it, but then shied away from actually holding the torch. Brown seemed unable to get anything quite right. Even his trip to Washington in April 2008 was overshadowed by the Pope's visit to the US. When George Bush made what was to be his last visit to Europe, he spent twice as long in France as he did in the UK. Britain, despite its support over Iraq, seemed to have been downgraded in importance.

During September and October 2008 the credit crunch escalated beyond anyone's expectations. The financial maelstrom of bank failures, credit crises and rollercoaster stock prices affected countries around the world. In the US, Congress approved a $700 billion bank bailout. On 3 October, Brown announced a reshuffle and the establishment of the National Economic Council to act as an economic war-Cabinet and oversee government handling of the financial crisis. Brown brought Peter Mandelson back from his post as EU Trade Commissioner to become Secretary for Business, Enterprise and Regulatory Reform. After years of loathing each other they said they were now fighting for the same cause. However, even Mandelson's dramatic return to the Cabinet was quickly superseded by the worst week for financial markets since the 1987 crash. On 8 October Brown unveiled a radical £500 billion rescue plan for the British banking system. This included a guarantee of the debt issued by banks up to £250 billion, an increase by £200 billion of the amount available to banks to borrow from the Bank of England, and a capital injection of £50 billion in eight major banks. The first details of the £50 billion capital injection were revealed the following week, when Brown announced that the government was injecting £20 billion of taxpayers' money into the Royal Bank of Scotland giving the government a 60 per cent stake in the company's ordinary shares, and £17 billion in to Lloyds TSB and HBOS, giving it a 41 per cent stake. This was state intervention on a scale that only days earlier had seemed unimaginable. Ironically, Brown, who as Chancellor had supported only light-touch regulation of financial services, was implementing policies of state intervention and regulation of the financial sector that had been jettisoned by the Labour Party back in the mid-1980s for being too left-wing.

Amongst the gloom there was great excitement in November 2008 when Barack Obama won the US presidential election. Obama

came to power repudiating Bush's foreign policy approach and promising to renew America's leadership in the world. There would be a
greater focus on diplomacy than under Bush, and he would 'rebuild
alliances, partnerships, and institutions necessary to confront common
threats and enhance common security'. He said that America would
withdraw from Iraq, which had been 'a diversion from the fight against
the terrorists who struck us on 9/11', focus its military efforts on
Afghanistan, take a tougher stance with Pakistan, and 'reinvigorate
American diplomacy' in the Middle East. Obama had a very different
perspective from Bush in that he felt that the 'The mission of the
United States is to provide global leadership grounded in the understanding that the world shares a common security and a common
humanity'.[52] He was committed to using American power differently
from Bush, in a way that focused more on the need to build consensus
and a sense of international legitimacy for American actions. Amongst
his early foreign policy initiatives on becoming President was his
promise to close the detention facility at Guantánamo Bay within a
year; his commitment to withdraw US troops more quickly from Iraq
than Bush would have done; his offer of direct diplomatic engagement
with Iran; his attempt to reach out to the Muslim world though a
number of key speeches and interviews; and his promise of action to
combat climate change.

However, despite the massive expectations of a radical new foreign
policy approach under Obama, it would be unwise to overemphasise
the extent to which Obama's election heralded a dramatic shift from
the Bush presidency. Obama's global grand strategy was very similar to
Bush's in terms of using American leadership and maintaining
American pre-eminence. Secretary of State Hilary Clinton said in a
speech at the Council on Foreign Relations that 'The question is not
whether our nation can or should lead, but how it will lead in the
twenty-first century'. Furthermore, 'We will not hesitate to defend our
friends, our interests, and above all, our people vigorously and when
necessary with the world's strongest military'.[53] Obama avoided using
the phrase 'war on terror', but having inherited the situation from
Bush, he was promising to execute the fight against extremism and
terrorism more effectively – for example by placing greater focus on
tackling the creeping Talibanisation of Pakistan – rather than withdrawing from it and ending American interventionism.

Brown's premiership continued to be dogged by misfortune.
He entered the 2010 general election campaign on the back foot, and
it was Nick Clegg, the Liberal Democrat leader, who emerged the

winner from the televised election debates. Foreign policy featured very little during the election campaign; it was almost as if all the party campaign teams were slightly worried about making commitments on Britain's foreign and security policy, and so decided to say as little as possible. Labour's manifesto promised to conduct a Strategic Defence Review; to use Britain's reach to build security and stability internationally; to 'Lead the agenda for an outward-facing European Union'; to re-energise the drive to achieve the Millennium Development Goals; and, rather glibly, it pledged to 'Reform the UN, International Financial Institutions, the G8 and G20, and NATO, to adapt to the new global challenges'.[54] Most of the information in the manifesto focused on what the government had already done and there was very little policy detail about how these goals would be achieved. With regard to the reform of international institutions, the policy was simply that 'we will make the case for' the reforms,[55] as if this was the same as actually bringing about reform. Nor was there any mention of how Britain's commitments could be carried out within the context of the financial crisis and record budget deficit, which was to change the context in which British foreign policy was made for the next government.

The election result from 6 May 2010 was inconclusive in that no one party gained the 326 seats needed to give it an overall majority, but with the election having the feel of a referendum on Labour's thirteen years in power, it was clear to many people that Labour had lost. The Conservatives won 307 seats with 36.1 per cent of the vote, Labour won 258 seats with 29.0 per cent of the vote, and the Liberal Democrats won only 57 seats with 23 per cent of the vote. Brown hoped to form a coalition with the Liberal Democrats, but Clegg had said in the campaign that in the event of a hung Parliament, he would he only form a coalition government with the party that gained the most seats and votes. In addition, Labour was out-manoeuvred by a well-prepared Conservative team who had already developed a potential coalition manifesto. After five days of tense negotiations, a Conservative-Liberal Democrat coalition was agreed. According to Peter Mandelson, Nick Clegg ended Brown's efforts to establish a coalition government and remain as Prime Minister by telling him to his face that there could be no coalition deal with Labour unless he resigned, and that the Labour Party was 'knackered after thirteen years in power'.[56] David Cameron entered 10 Downing Street on 11 May, and the following day announced the beginning of the first peacetime coalition government since the 1930s. Cameron appointed Clegg as

Deputy Prime Minister, serving as one of five Liberal Democrat ministers in the new administration.

To conclude, in terms of Tony Blair's overall policy, somewhat remarkably for a Labour politician, he came to believe in the efficacy of the use of military force as a short-cut to achieving long-term goals. Blair's premiership came to be dominated by his approach to foreign policy and the 'war on terror'; Brown's premiership was dominated by the economy, the scene of his greatest strength and greatest weakness. For both of these Prime Ministers, their period in office was characterised by features of globalisation. For Blair it was fear of global terrorism, for Brown it was fear of the collapse of the global financial system and a global economic downturn similar to the 1930s. In direct contrast to Blair, one of the defining features of Brown's approach to foreign policy was that he tended to say very little about it. He perhaps felt that Blair's very public focus on international affairs, his response to Kosovo, to 9/11 and the invasions of Afghanistan and Iraq, distracted him from the domestic agenda and caused divisions in the Labour Party. A more risk-averse approach to foreign affairs was in tune with concerns felt by the public, which had no appetite for further troop deployments to conflict zones. As the British army suffered terrible losses during Operation Panther's Claw in July 2009, a report by the Foreign Affairs Select Committee found that the UK had suffered 'significant mission creep' since deploying to Afghanistan in 2001.[57] Mike Gapes, the chair of the Committee, said that there was a 'serious risk' of the government losing public support for the mission in Afghanistan unless it better explained why British soldiers were fighting and dying there. Brown's long-awaited announcement of an inquiry into the Iraq war – from the run-up to the invasion through to the occupation – was a public relations disaster. Initially saying that evidence would be given in private, Brown then had to back-track and agree that Sir John Chilcot could hold most of the evidence sessions in public. With the inquiry not due to conclude before the general election, it meant that the Labour government would be under the spotlight in much the same way as the Major government had been with the arms to Iraq inquiry, when the party in opposition had been able to do so much to highlight the government's policy-making shortcomings. The optimism of Labour's election in 1997 had been firmly replaced by concern and pessimism, with no clear sense of Britain's role in a world hit by a global recession, and weariness from the public over the costly commitment to an open-ended conflict in Afghanistan. The interventionism of the Blair years, with his commitment to changing the world, had been replaced by a more prosaic approach to the international affairs, with the government and the public more aware of the unintended costs and consequences of intervening abroad.

Notes

1 Robert Cooper, 'The Long Peace', *Prospect*, April 1999, pp. 22–4.
2 Tony Blair, 'Terrorism must be tackled head on', speech given to the Foreign Policy Centre, 21 March 2006.
3 Tony Blair's speech at the George Bush Senior Presidential Library, 7 April 2002.
4 Bob Woodward, *Bush at War* (London: Pocket Books, 2003), pp. 17-31.
5 John Kampfner, *Blair's Wars* (London: The Free Press, 2004), p. 111.
6 Prime Minister Tony Blair, statement in response to terrorist attacks in the United States, 11 September 2001: available at www.number10.gov.uk/output/page 1596.asp.
7 *House of Commons Debates* (hereafter *H.C. Deb.*), vol. 378, 8 October 2001, column 814.
8 George W. Bush radio address, 15 September 2001, downloaded from www.whitehouse.gov/news/releases/2001/09/20010915.html.
9 George W. Bush address to Congress, 20 September 2001, downloaded from www.whitehouse.gov/news/releases/2001/0920010920-8.html.
10 *Ibid.*
11 Tony Blair's speech to the Welsh Assembly, 30 October 2001, downloaded from www.number10.gov.uk/output/page1636.asp.
12 Lucy War, 'Nazi jibe fuels Labour dissent', *Guardian*, 22 October 2001.
13 George W. Bush, State of the Union Address to Congress, 29 June 2002.
14 George W. Bush, Graduation Speech at West Point, 1 June 2002; G. W. Bush, The National Security Strategy of the United States of America, September 2002, available at www.whitehouse.gov/nsc/nss.html.
15 Kampfner, *Blair's Wars*, p. 273.
16 Foreign Affairs Select Committee, *Ninth Report: The Decision to Go to War with Iraq* (London: TSO, July 2003), downloaded from www. publications.parliament.uk/pa/cm200203/cmselect/cmfaff/813/8130 2.htm.
17 Author's interview with Robin Cook, 9 October 2001, Privy Council Office, London.
18 *H.C. Deb.*, vol. 401, 17 March 2003, cols 726–8.
19 *H.C. Deb.*, vol. 401, 18 March 2003, col. 761.
20 James Gow, *Defending the West* (London: Polity, 2004).
21 For example, David Coates, Joel Krieger, with Rhiannon Vickers, *Blair's War* (Cambridge: Polity, 2004); Robin Cook, *The Point of Departure* (London: Simon & Schuster, 2003); Kampfner, *Blair's Wars*; Peter Stothard, *30 Days: A Month at the Heart of Blair's War* (London: Harper

Collins, 2003). Then there are the select committee reports and inquiries, including Lord Butler, *Review of Intelligence on Weapons of Mass Destruction* (London: The Stationary Office, 2004).

22 Tony Blair interview, *Guardian*, 1 March 2003.
23 See Caroline Kennedy-Pipe and Rhiannon Vickers, '"Blowback" for Britain: Blair, Bush, the War in Iraq', *Review of International Studies*, 33:2 (April 2007), pp. 205–21.
24 Tony Blair's speech at the George Bush Senior Presidential Library, 7 April 2002, downloaded from www.pm.gov.uk/output/Page1712.asp.
25 Terry Kirby and Andrew Malone, 'Rush-hour bomb attacks kill dozens and injure 700', *Independent*, 8 July 2005, p. 2.
26 London bomber video aired on TV, BBC News, http://news.bbc. co.uk/go/pr/fr/-/hi/uk/4206708.stm, 2 September 2005.
27 Tony Blair's speech to the Los Angeles World Affairs Council, 1 August 2006.
28 George Jones, 'Blair is most unpopular Labour PM', *Telegraph*, 10 May 2006.
29 'Questions asked about the performance of Beckett', *Guardian*, 1 August 2006.
30 David Cameron's speech to the British American Project, 'I am not a neo-con', 11 September 2006.
31 Tony Blair's resignation speech, Sedgefield, 10 May 1997, downloaded from the Labour Party's website, www.labour.org.uk/leadership/ tony_blair_resigns.
32 *Ibid*.
33 Speech by Gordon Brown, 11 May 2007, downloaded from www.gordonbrownforbritain.com/2005/05/11/gordon-brown-launches-leadership-campaign/.
34 *H.C. Deb.*, vol. 462, 27 June 2007, col. 323.
35 'Scepticism hangs over Blair's appointment as quartet envoy', *Guardian*, 28 June 2007, p. 17.
36 'Brown day one', *Guardian*, 28 June 2007, p. 1.
37 Julian Borger and Patrick Wintour, 'War sceptic Miliband offers chance of clean state on Iraq', *Guardian*, 29 June 2007, p. 5.
38 *Ibid*.
39 Simon Carr, 'Brown's halo dims as his reforms are rumbled', *Independent*, 4 July 2007, p. 16.
40 Andrew Marr interview with Gordon Brown on 1 July 2007 for 'BBC Sunday AM', from http://news.bbc.co.uk/1/hi/programmes/ sunday_am/6258416.stm accessed on 1 July 2007.
41 Andrew Marr interview with David Miliband on 15 July 2007 for 'BBC Sunday AM'.
42 Speech by David Miliband, Foreign Secretary, 'New Diplomacy: Challenges for Foreign Policy', Chatham House, 19 July 2007, downloaded from the FCO website on 20 July 2007.
43 Richard Beeston, 'Miliband rallies support for Bush with a defence of vital alliance', *The Times*, 20 July 2007, p. 30.
44 Gordon Brown's press conference, 23 July 2007, downloaded from www.number-10.gov.uk/output/Page12590.asp.

45 'Cold War diplomacy is back as UK expels spies', *Guardian*, 17 July 2007, p. 1.
46 Transcript of Gordon Brown's press conference with President Bush at Camp David on 30 July 2007, www.number-10.gov.uk/output/Page12765.asp.
47 Gordon Brown's speech to the UN, New York, 31 July 2007, from www.number-10.gov.uk/output/Page12755.asp.
48 Julian Borger and Patrick Wintour, 'UN vote backs Brown's call for action to end Darfur conflict', *Guardian*, 1 August 2007, p. 4.
49 So said the front page of the *Guardian*, 1 August 2007.
50 Gordon Brown, Lord Mayor's banquet speech, 12 November 2007.
51 *H.C. Deb.*, vol. 468, 28 November 2007, col. 275.
52 Barack Obama, 'Renewing American leadership', *Foreign Affairs*, 86:4 (July/August 2007).
53 Secretary of State Hilary Clinton's foreign policy address to the Council on Foreign Relations, Washington DC, 15 July 2009, downloaded from www.usembassy.org.uk/forpo053.html.
54 Labour Party, 2010 general election manifesto, *A Future Fair for All* (London: Labour Party 2010), section 10.2.
55 *Ibid.*, section 10.6.
56 'Clegg the executioner', *The Times*, 12 July 2010.
57 House of Commons Foreign Affairs Committee, *Global Security: Afghanistan and Pakistan* (London: TSO, 2 August 2009).

Chapter 8

Conclusion

Labour's election victory in 1997 stimulated a new generation of academics to develop an interest in foreign policy under a Labour government. The commitments that Robin Cook and Tony Blair made back in 1997 seemed at the time to most scholars of International Relations to be novel, a product of a globalised post-Cold War era, and there was little awareness of how these commitments had developed. One of the aims of this study has been to show that the ideas at the heart of Labour's foreign policy at the end of the twentieth century had their antecedents in the ideas put forward by the various groups that made up the Labour Party at the beginning of the twentieth century. This study has argued that throughout its history, the Labour Party has been involved and interested in international policy and with Britain's role in the world. International affairs have been a major cause for concern for the Labour Party, not least because of its fundamental understanding that domestic and international politics were part of a whole that could not be treated as mutually exclusive. Because of this, Labour has tried to rethink the nature of British foreign policy. This study has argued that Labour has sought to offer an alternative to the traditional, power politics or realist approach of British foreign policy, which had stressed national self-interest. This alternative was a version of British foreign policy based on internationalism, which stressed co-operation and interdependence, and a concern with the international as well as the national interest While this concept of internationalism is very vague, at its heart is the idea that while states are sovereign entities, the peace and stability of any one state and the peace and stability of the international system as a whole are inexorably linked.

As Volume 1 of this study points out, the Labour Party developed as a loose federation of organisations rather than a party with a specified ideology. There were four main progenitors, each bringing their own influences on domestic and foreign policy to the Labour Representation Committee, which was set up in 1900 and became known as the Labour Party in 1906. These were, in no particular order of importance, the trade union movement, the Independent Labour Party, the Fabian Society, and the Social Democratic Federation and various Marxist groups. In addition to these four, there was a fifth grouping that then had a remarkable degree of influence over Labour's developing foreign policy, and this was composed of radical Liberals, epitomised by the members of the Union of Democratic Control. Each of these groups had its own particular influence over the way that foreign policy and international affairs were thought about. Each had its own particular analytical framework for understanding relations between states, and each had its own way of responding to concrete situations. These different influences provided a rich source for ideas on international politics, but also produced impulses towards Labour's appropriate response to particular foreign policy issues which were sometimes antithetical to each other. This has added to the problems of developing a typology of the British Labour Party's foreign policy, while also explaining in part the depth of the some of the intra-party conflict on international affairs.

Another reason for the depth of conflict within the Labour Party over its foreign and defence policy has been that for extensive periods in the twentieth century Labour's foreign policy has developed while in opposition rather than in power. As such, it has been developed more as a response to the internal dynamics of the party, the tensions between left and right factions, rather than as a response to international events. The result of this has been that Labour has tended to promise an alternative foreign policy when in opposition, seeking a new formulation of foreign policy based on principles that reflect party opinion. This means that Labour governments always face the problem of managing party members' over-inflated expectations of change. It then finds that once in power, the opinions of rebellious backbenchers' become rather less significant compared with the pressures that governments come under from other nations, international organisations and existing commitments, resulting in a changed foreign policy stance. As former Labour leader and Prime Minister James Callaghan pointed out,

> Foreign policy is a mixture of the old and the new. We may initiate but we also inherit; we may vote at the ballot box for changes in policy and personalities, but on acquiring office governments inherit an international

> situation on which the footprints of the past are heavily marked. We
> cannot legislate about the actions of other nations, we cannot wipe the
> slate completely clean. We become at once both instigator and recipient,
> actor and stage manager.[1]

However, that does not mean that Labour governments have not
attempted to rethink foreign policy, or that their claims to be initiating
a new foreign policy approach are simply propaganda or spin.

Despite the problems of outlining the basis of Labour's approach
to foreign policy throughout its history, this study has argued that
there have been six main principles to its internationalist outlook.
These are, first, that while states operate in a system of international
anarchy, fundamental reform of the system is possible because states
have common interests and values. This change is only likely to be
secured through the construction of international institutions to regulate economic, political and military relations between states. Second,
linked to this is a sense of belonging to an international community,
that each state has a responsibility to work towards the common good
of the international system, to work in the 'international' interest
rather than purely in what it perceives to be its national interest. Third,
that international policy and governance should be based on democratic principles and universal moral norms. Fourth, that collective
security is better than secret bilateral diplomatic treaties or balance of
power politics, which are self-defeating in terms of generating conflict.
Fifth, that armaments and arms races can destabilise the international
system; that the proliferation of arms should be limited, the arms trade
regulated, and that disarmament, in principle, is desirable. In addition
to these five largely liberal internationalist principles is one additional
socialist aspect of Labour's international thought, and this has been a
belief in international working-class solidarity and a concern to
improve working conditions and to alleviate poverty globally.

However, as this study has shown, within the Labour Party there
have always been divisions over how these internationalist principles
should be interpreted, which of these principles should be prioritised,
and which of these principles were achievable in the real world in any
particular time-period. Internationalism is an impulse that can be used
to prescribe non-intervention in the pursuit of peace, or intervention
for military or humanitarian means. The divisions over policy have at
times led to the party itself being split over the position to take, or in
an attempt to avoid appearing to being split, developing a policy so
complex that not even the party leaders themselves really understand
what it is. This has tended to happen over defence and the role of

nuclear weapons in particular. The party held two conflicting defence policies for much of the 1970s, and the leadership went into the 1983 general election with differing views on how to interpret Labour's nuclear policy. Nevertheless, this attempt to outline and deliver an alternative foreign policy, and the deep debates over particular policy issues, means that Labour has made a massive contribution to British foreign policy in terms of making politicians, the media, and the public rethink the sorts of priorities that Britain should have when it comes to foreign affairs. This contribution has included debates over the morality of owning, testing and using weapons of mass destruction, in particular nuclear weapons; the obligation that Britain has towards people in other states, given Labour's belief in international solidarity, and the extent to which Britain should intervene to help them; the strong belief in the utility of organisations such as the UN to bring about change and international peace and security; debate about the circumstances in which force should be used – especially with regard to the use of force against fascist regimes – and whether it should be used unilaterally; and debates about Britain's role in a changing world, especially with regards to Britain's moral leadership.

However, Labour's commitment to internationalism has sometimes been in conflict with its view of Britain's role as a leading international actor. Labour has been just as reluctant as its opponents to give up the trappings of a world power; indeed, apart from a short period in the 1980s, the Labour Party has not thought of Britain as just another European country, but as a great power nation. It was the Attlee government that decided to go ahead with the atom bomb, and Labour has never advocated unilateral nuclear disarmament when it has been in power. Indeed, in the 1970s, the Wilson government secretly agreed to go ahead with Chevaline, which would result in an upgrade of Polaris, and James Callaghan secretly prepared the ground with President Carter for Britain to be granted access to America's Trident C4 system so that Britain could replace Polaris. For the centre-right of the party, Britain's possession of an independent nuclear deterrent meant that it could take a leadership role as a mediator between the US and the Soviet Union during the Cold War, as well as providing for British security through its deterrent effect. It was only in the 1980s that Labour rethought this position and presented a policy based on the assumption that Britain was no longer a great power, and as such did not have the ability to change the world, nor the need for nuclear weapons which were a great power status symbol. Rather, 'as a medium sized Western European industrial nation', Britain should 'no

longer behave as though we were a great power or the centre of a
global empire'.[2] However, the Labour Party, perceived by the electorate as out of touch, unpatriotic and more interested in fighting itself
than defending Britain, was punished for this deviation from the
assumption that Britain was, and should be, at the heart of global
politics.

While Labour might temporarily have adopted a policy that gave
up one great power status, Labour has never suggested that Britain
should give up its other great power status symbols, such as its permanent seat on the United Nations Security Council. In terms of Britain's
imperial role, the Commonwealth was seen for both the left and the
right of the party as a means of continuing British influence, and
carried an implicit assumption of Britain's leadership.[3] Labour's 1931
general election manifesto argued that a Labour government would
give Britain 'the moral leadership of the world'.[4] This moral leadership
has been a recurrent theme up to the present day, with New Labour's
frequent claims to be acting as a force for good in the world.[5]
Throughout the twentieth century Labour has stressed the potential
for Britain to play a leadership role in international disarmament and
control of the arms industry. For the left of the party, unilateral nuclear
disarmament was seen as a way for Britain to exert its moral leadership
in the world, with the expectation that other countries would follow
Britain's example. During the Cold War Labour emphasised the role
that Britain could play in acting as a bridge between East and West to
resolve deadlocks between the two. This moral imperative has been
highlighted at various times by all sections of the party. Thus, Labour's
commitment to working in the international interest rather than purely
in what it perceives to be its national interest has often been based on
the idea of Britain's leadership in the world. Labour did not stop to
ponder whether the rest of the world wanted or needed Britain's moral
leadership. This belief in Britain's moral leadership role under a Labour
government not only arises from the fact that the Labour Party developed within the context of Britain as a superpower, but also reflected
the third of its principles of internationalism, namely that foreign
policy should reflect democratic principles and universal moral norms,
and because much of the Labour Party's thinking on internationalism
was shaped by liberal thinking. Elements of Gladstonian liberalism
were very visible in Blair's desire to reform and reorder the world.

It was Blair's missionary zeal to make the world a better place
that led him to believe his own propaganda about the threat that
Saddam Hussein posed and to end up breaking international norms

and violating the UN Charter in order to invade Iraq. Britain and the US broke the laws of occupation by not only bringing about regime change, but by also drastically changing the nature of the Iraqi state and political system.[6] It is ironic that one of the most controversial military actions in which Britain has been involved in recent history occurred when Labour was in power, given the extent to which it has committed itself to working through the UN. In particular, there are some interesting parallels with the Suez crisis. The Labour Party vociferously criticised Eden over the way that he handled Suez, especially for taking action without explicit UN approval. During the Parliamentary debate over the Suez crisis on 2 August 1956, Gaitskell argued that Britain had for many years avoided any international action which would be 'in breach of international law or, indeed, contrary to the public opinion of the word', and so Britain must not get into a position where it could be denounced as an aggressor.[7]

The first volume in this study argued that Labour never really came to an ideological agreement over how to be internationalist within an international system dominated by nation-states. Labour did not question the existence of a world of sovereign nation-states, but its internationalist perspective led it to look for ways to control relations between states and ameliorate the inherent conflict in the international system: to replace the system of international anarchy with a world order that could create the framework for a world society.[8] The tension between national sovereignty and internationalism lay behind many of the battles over Labour' foreign policy, and the party often found itself unable to transcend national barriers in order to meet its commitment to internationalism. However, in recent years, with the end of the Cold War and the impact of globalisation, support for multilateralism appeared to offer a solution and a way to transcend national barriers in order to meet commitments to internationalism. By the time that Labour came to power in 1997 it had come to the conclusion that on many issues – which were increasingly transnational in nature – what was in the international interest was also in Britain's long-term national interest. This provoked debate, for example from Wheeler and Dunne, about the nature of Labour's foreign policy, and they urged that Blair should reject the conventional assumption that there is necessarily a dualism between the pursuit of a national interest and a nation-state's obligation to the international community, and proposed that Britain should act as a 'good international citizen'. To a certain extent, this study would argue that Labour has done this. However, while Labour's position might have provoked debate about whose interest

Britain should act in and whether it was possible to reconcile national and international interests, one question that has not been sufficiently studied is the problem of knowing what the international interest actually is. While Chapter 1 of this volume began by pointing out that the national interest is not self-evident or value neutral, and that interests are constructed, the same could be said of the international interest. Labour governments since 1997 have tended to make the same sort of assumptions about the international interest that traditional British foreign policy made about the national interest.

Thus, just as it is not always clear what the national interest is, it is not always clear what the international interest is. In many ways, the Blair governments were the apogee of Labour's internationalist stance; British foreign policy decisions were not to be made just in terms of what was in the national interest, but also in terms of what was in the international interest, or in Blair's words, the interests of the international community. Quite simply, Blair argued that Britain was part of an international community that had common interests and values, and Britain should intervene when it was the right thing to do. This meant that the traditional norms of state sovereignty and non-intervention, which are embedded in the UN Charter, could be over-ruled, not just because a state was behaving in a way that was a threat to international peace and security, but also because a state was undermining the very idea of the international community by committing ethnic cleansing within its own borders.[9] Blair argued that 'Non-interference has long been considered an important principle of international order … But the principle of non-interference must be qualified in important respects. Acts of genocide can never be a purely internal matter.'[10] Kosovo represented very clearly a new approach to foreign policy in terms of intervention for humanitarian reasons over-riding the traditional norm of state sovereignty, and such intervention being viewed as acting in the international interest rather than undermining it. The 1998 Strategic Defence Review stated that 'The British are, by instinct, an internationalist people. We believe that as well as defending our rights, we should discharge our responsibilities in the world. We do not want to stand idly by and watch humanitarian disasters or the aggression of dictators go unchecked. We want to give a lead, we want to be a force for good.'[11] Security was to include the international defence of Britain's values.

However, the outcome has not been a happy one for the Labour Party. Kosovo set a precedent for Blair that reflected not only his political worldview about intervening in the international interest, which could be defined in very broad terms, but also his moralism. Following the terrorist attacks of 11 September 2001, Blair believed that the logic that had applied to the need to intervene in Kosovo – that in an increasingly globalised and interdependent world, isolationism and the principle of non-intervention had to be qualified when it came to matters of international security and acts of genocide – also applied to Afghanistan and Iraq. For Blair, invading Iraq had become the internationalist option, and critics of military action were taking a narrow, isolationist perspective, which had no place in a globalised, interdependent world. Blair's mistake was to believe his own propaganda and to assume that because he believed something to be in the international interest, then it must necessarily be so. What Blair had forgotten was what previous Labour leaders had tended to argue – that using force always has unintended consequences, and in particular, when force was used without the support of the international community, this tends to undermine the UN and to undermine Britain's leadership role in the world. Another unintended consequence is that at the end of writing this study, the Labour Party finds itself in a situation where it is unusually quiet about foreign policy. Only with election defeat and a new leadership is the Labour Party likely to start setting out a new foreign policy for the post- 'war on terror' era, which is likely to be defined by the attempt to scale back foreign and defence commitments due to financial constraints, rather than on exerting Britain's global role.

Notes

1 James Callaghan, *Time and Chance* (London: Collins, 1987), p. 331.
2 Labour Party, *Defence and Security for Britain* (London: The Labour Party, 1984), p. 7.
3 Caroline Knowles, *Race, Discourse and Labourism* (London: Routledge, 1992).
4 The 1931 Labour Party general election manifesto, in *British General Election Manifestos, 1900–1974*, compiled and edited by F.W.S. Craig (London: Macmillan, revised and enlarged edn, 1975), p. 97.
5 This aim was even written into the 1998 Strategic Defence Review, *The Strategic Defence Review*, Cm. 3999 (London: TSO, 1998), Introduction, paragraphs 2, 3 and 19.
6 See Russell Buchan, 'The international community and the occupation of Iraq', *Journal of Conflict and Security Law*, 12:1 (Spring 2007), pp. 37–64.
7 *House of Commons Debates*, vol. 557, 2 August 1956, cols 1613–7.

8 Labour Party, *Problems of Foreign Policy* (London: Labour Party, 1952), p. 2.

9 My thanks to Adrian Gallagher for this insight. See Gallagher, 'Genocide and its Threat to International Society', PhD thesis, University of Sheffield, 2010.

10 Tony Blair, 'Doctrine of the international community', speech to the Economic Club of Chicago, 22 April 1999.

11 *The Strategic Defence Review*, Cm. 3999, Introduction, paragraphs 2, 3 and 19.

Bibliography

The National Archives, London

Cabinet Office, CAB 128/25; Foreign Office, FO 371; FO 800 private papers collection; Prime Minister's Office, PREM 13/103-4, 222, 316, 689, 1262, 1271

US National Archives, College Park Maryland

US National Archives II, State Department RG59

Archives

Campaign for Nuclear Disarmament, Modern Records Centre, University of Warwick
International Marxist Group, British Library of Political and Economic Science, LSE, and Modern Records Centre, University of Warwick
Labour Party Archive, Museum of Labour History, Manchester
Trades Union Congress, Modern Records Centre, University of Warwick
National Security Archive at the George Washington University, Washington DC

Private papers

Arthur Bottomley, British Library of Political and Economic Science, LSE
Anthony Crosland, British Library of Political and Economic Science, LSE
Richard Crossman, Modern Records Centre, University of Warwick
George Brown (Lord), Bodleian Library, Oxford
Hugh Gaitskell, University College London
Patrick Gordon Walker (Baron Patrick Gordon-Walker), Churchill Archive Centre, Churchill College, Cambridge
Hugh Jenkins, British Library of Political and Economic Science

Neil Kinnock, Churchill Archive Centre, Churchill College, Cambridge
Jo Richardson, Museum of Labour History, Manchester
Peter Shore, British Library of Political and Economic Science
Michael Stewart (Lord Stewart of Fulham), Churchill Archive Centre, Churchill College, Cambridge
George Wigg (Baron Wigg), British Library of Political and Economic Science
Harold Wilson, Bodleian Library, Oxford

Published documents

Lord Butler, *Review of Intelligence on Weapons of Mass Destruction* (London: The Stationary Office, 2004)
Current British Foreign Policy: Documents, Statements, Speeches, 1971, ed. D.C. Watt and James Mayall (London: Temple Smith, 1973)
Defence, Foreign Affairs, International Development and Trade and Industry Committees, Special Report, *Committee's Inquiry into the 1997 and 1998 Annual Reports on Strategic Export Controls*, HC 540 (London: TSO, 1999)
Department for International Development, *Eliminating World Poverty: A Challenge for the 21st Century* (London: TSO, 1997)
Foreign Affairs Select Committee, *First Report: Foreign Policy and Human Rights* (London: TSO, 1998)
——, *Ninth Report: the Decision to Go to War with Iraq* (London: TSO, July 2003)
Foreign Relations of the United States, various vols (Washington DC: Department of State, various)
House of Commons Debates (Hansard), series 5, various vols (London: HMSO, various)
House of Commons Foreign Affairs Committee, *Global Security: Afghanistan and Pakistan* (London: TSO, 2 August 2009)
Keesings' Contemporary Archives, various vols (London: Keesings, various)
Labour Party Annual Conference Reports, various vols (London: Labour Party, various)
MacDonald, J. Ramsay, *A Policy for the Labour Party* (London: Leonard Parsons, 1920)
Presidential Directives on National Security from Truman to Clinton, ed. Jeffrey Richelson (Washington, DC: The National Security Archive and Chadwyck-Healey, 1994)
The Strategic Defence Review, Cm. 3999 (London: TSO, 1998)
The Strategic Defence Review White Paper, 98/91, (London, House of Commons Library, 15 October 1998)
Trade Union Congress Annual Reports, various vols (London: TUC, various)

Unpublished work

Gallagher, Adrian, 'Genocide and its Threat to International Society', PhD thesis, University of Sheffield, 2010

Randall, Nick, 'The Dynamics of Ideological Change in the British Labour
    Party 1951–1964 and 1983–1997', PhD thesis, University of
    Manchester, 2000
Shaw, Eric, 'British Socialist Approaches to International Affairs, 1945–1951',
    MPhil thesis, University of Leeds, 1974

Published pamphlets

CND, *Vietnam Briefing* (London: CND, no date)
Conservative Party, *The Conservative Manifesto 1979* (London: Conservative
    Party, 1979)
Duff, Peggy, *Vietnam: The Credibility Gap* (London: CND, no date)
Healey, Denis, *A Neutral Belt in Europe?* (London: Labour Party, 1957)
HM Government, *Britain's New Deal in Europe* (London: HMSO, 1975)
Labour Party, *Memorandum on War Aims* (London: Labour Party, 1918)
——, *Our First Duty Peace* (London: Labour Party, 1951)
——, *Problems of Foreign Policy* (London: Labour Party, 1952)
——, *Britain and the Common Market*, Information Series, no. 14 (London:
    Labour Party, 1960)
——, The Race Against the H-Bomb (London: Labour Party, 1960)
——, 1983 general election manifesto, *The New Hope for Britain* (London:
    Labour Party, 1983)
——, *Defence and Security for Britain* (London: Labour Party, 1984)
——, *Labour's Manifesto for the European Elections, supported by the Socialist
    Group of the European Parliament, 1984* (London: Labour Party, 1984)
——, *Defence Conversion and Costs* (London: Labour Party, 1986)
——, *For the Good of All: Labour's Plans for Aid and Development* (London:
    Labour Party, 1987)
——, 1987 general election manifesto, *Britain Will Win* (London: Labour
    Party, 1987)
——, *Democratic Socialist Aims and Values* (London: Labour Party)
——, *Social Justice and Economic Efficiency* (London: Labour Party, 1988)
——, *Meet the Challenge, Make the Change: A New Agenda for Britain*
    (London: Labour Party, 1989)
——, *Looking to the Future* (London: Labour Party, 1990)
——, *Made in Britain* (London: Labour Party, 1991)
——, *Opportunity Britain* (London: Labour Party, 1991)
——, *It's Time to Get Britain Working Again* (London: Labour Party, 1992)
——, *A People's Europe* (London: Labour Party, 1995)
——, *Strategy for a Secure Future: Labour's Approach to the Defence Industry*
    (London: Labour Party, 1995)
——, *A Fresh Start for Britain: Labour's Strategy in the Modern World*
    (London: Labour Party, 1996)
——, *New Labour, New Life for Britain* (London: Labour Party, 1996)
——, 1997 general election manifesto, *New Labour: Because Britain Deserves
    Better* (London: Labour Party, 1997)
——, 2001 general election manifesto, *Ambitions for Britain* (London:
    Labour Party, 2001)

——, 2005 general election manifesto, *Britain: Forward not Back* (London: Labour Party, 2005)

——, 2010 general election manifesto, *A Future Fair for All* (London: Labour Party 2010)

McDermott, John, *Vietnam Profile: A History of the Vietnam Conflict and its Origins* (London: CND, 1965)

MacDonald, J. Ramsay, *Labour and International Relations* (Derby: Derby and District ILP Federation, 1917)

Published work

Ali, Tariq, *1968 and After: Inside the Revolution* (London: Blond and Briggs, 1978)

Anderson, Paul, and Nyta Mann, *Safety First: The Making of New Labour* (London: Granta, 1997)

Attlee, Clement, *The Labour Party in Perspective* (London: Victor Gollancz, 1937)

Bale, Tim, '"A deplorable episode"? South African arms and the statecraft of British social democracy', *Labour History Review*, 62:1 (1997), pp. 22–40

Ball, Stuart, and Anthony Seldon, eds, *The Heath Government 1970–1974: A Reappraisal* (London: Longman, 1996)

Barber, James, *Who Makes British Foreign Policy?* (Milton Keynes: Open University Press, 1976)

Barder, Brian, 'Britain: still looking for that role?' *Political Quarterly*, 72:3 (2001), pp. 366–74

Bartlett, C.J., *"The Special Relationship": A Political History of Anglo-American Relations Since 1945* (London: Longman, 1992)

Baylis, John, *Anglo-American Defence Relations 1939–1980* (London: Macmillan, 1981)

Beer, Samuel, *Modern British Politics: Parties and Pressure Groups in the Collectivist Age* (London: Faber, 2nd edn. 1969)

Benn, Tony, *Out of the Wilderness: Diaries, 1963–67* (London: Hutchinson, 1987)

——, *Office Without Power: Diaries 1968–72* (London: Hutchinson, 1988)

——, *Against the Tide: Diaries 1973–76* (London: Hutchinson, 1989)

Blake, Robert, *A History of Rhodesia* (New York: Alfred Knopf, 1978)

Blair, Tony, *New Britain: My Vision of a Young Country* (London: Fourth Estate, 1996)

Bogdanor, Vernon, and Robert Skidelsky, eds, *The Age of Affluence 1951–1964* (London: Macmillan, 1970)

Boren, David, 'The Trident missile and Britain's 1981 Defence Review', in Richard Aldrich and Michael Hopkins, eds, *Intelligence, Defence and Diplomacy: British Policy in the Post-War World* (London: Frank Cass, 1994), pp. 100–30

British General Election Manifestos, 1900–1974, compiled and edited by F.W.S. Craig, revised edn, (London: Macmillan, 1975)

British General Election Manifestos, 1959–1987, compiled and edited by F.W.S. Craig (Aldershot: Parliamentary Research Services, 3rd edn, 1990)

Brivati, Brian, *Hugh Gaitskell* (London: Richard Cohen Books, 1996),

Brown, George, *In My Way. The Political Memoirs of Lord George-Brown* (London: Victor Gollancz, 1971)

Buchan, Russell, 'The international community and the occupation of Iraq', *Journal of Conflict and Security Law*, 12:1 (Spring 2007), pp. 37-64

Busch, Peter, *All the Way with JFK? Britain, the US and the Vietnam War* (Oxford: Oxford University Press, 2003)

Butler, David, and Gareth Butler, *British Political Facts, 1900–1985* (London: Macmillan, 6th edn. 1986)

Butler, David, and Dennis Kavanagh, *The British General Election of 1974* (Basingstoke: Macmillan, 1974)

Butler, David, and Dennis Kavanagh, *The British General Election of 1997* (London: Macmillan, 1997)

Butler, David, and Anthony King, *The British General Election of 1964* (Basingstoke: Macmillan, 1965)

Butler, David, and Uwe Kitzinger, *The 1975 Referendum* (Basingstoke: Macmillan, 1976)

Byrd, Peter, ed., *British Foreign Policy Under Thatcher* (Oxford: Philip Allen, 1988)

Cairncross, Sir Alec, 'The Heath government and the British economy', in Stuart Ball and Anthony Seldon, eds, *The Heath Government 1970–1974: A Reappraisal* (London: Longman, 1996), pp. 107–38

Callaghan, James, *A House Divided: The Dilemma of Northern Ireland* (London: Collins, 1973)

——, *Time and Chance* (London: Collins, 1987)

Callaghan, John, *British Trotskyism: Theory and Practice* (Oxford: Basil Blackwell, 1984)

Carlton, David, *Anthony Eden: A Biography* (London: Allen Lane, 1981)

——, *Britain and the Suez Crisis* (Oxford: Basil Blackwell, 1988)

Castle, Barbara, *The Castle Diaries 1964–1970* (London: Weidenfeld & Nicolson, 1984)

Catterall, Peter, 'Foreign and Commonwealth policy in opposition: the Labour Party', in Wolfram Kaiser and Gillian Staerck, eds, *British Foreign Policy 1955–64: Contracting Options* (Basingstoke: Palgrave, 2000)

Chalmers, Malcolm, *British Arms Export Policy and Indonesia* (London: Saferworld, 1997)

Chichester, Michael and John Wilkinson, *The Uncertain Ally: British Defence Policy 1960–1990* (Aldershot: Gower, 1982)

Clarke, Michael, *British External Policy-Making in the 1990s* (Basingstoke: Macmillan, 1992)

Coates, David, *The Labour Party and the Struggle for Socialism* (Cambridge: Cambridge University Press, 1975)

——, *Labour in Power? A Study of the Labour Government, 1974–1979* (London: Longman, 1980)

Coates, David, and Peter Lawler, eds, *New Labour in Power* (Manchester: Manchester University Press, 2000)

Coates, David, and Joel Krieger, with Rhiannon Vickers, *Blair's War* (Cambridge: Polity, 2004)

Coates, Ken, *The Crisis of British Socialism: Essays on the Rise of Harold Wilson and the Fall of the Labour Party* (London: Spokesman Books, 1971)

Cockerell, Michael, Peter Hennessy and D. Walker, *Sources Close to the Prime Minister* (Basingstoke: Macmillan, 1984

Cole, G.D.H., *A History of the Labour Party from 1914* (London: Routledge, 1948)

Collins, Canon L. John, *Faith Under Fire* (London: Leslie Frewin, 1966)

Cook, Robin, *The Point of Departure* (London: Simon & Schuster, 2003)

Cooper, Neil, 'The pariah agenda and New Labour's ethical arms sales policy', in Richard Little and Mark Wickham-Jones, eds, *New Labour's Foreign Policy: A New Moral Crusade?* (Manchester: Manchester University Press, 2000), pp. 147–67

Cooper, Robert, 'The Long Peace', *Prospect*, April 1999, pp. 22–4

Crewe, Ivor, and Anthony King, *SDP: The Birth, Life and Death of the Social Democratic Party* (Oxford: Oxford University Press, 1995)

Crosland, Anthony, *The Future of Socialism* (London: Cape, 1956)

Crossman, Richard, *Diaries of a Cabinet Minister, vol. 1, Minister of Housing, 1964–66* (London: Hamish Hamilton and Jonathan Cape, 1975)

——, *The Diaries of a Cabinet Minister, vol. 2, Lord President of the Council and Leader of the House of Commons, 1966–68* (London: Hamish Hamilton and Jonathan Cape, 1976)

——, *The Diaries of a Cabinet Minister, vol. 3, Secretary of State for Social Services, 1968–70* (London: Hamish Hamilton and Jonathan Cape, 1977)

Curtis, Mark, *Web of Deceit: Britain's Real Role in the World* (London: Vintage, 2003)

Daddow, Oliver, ed., *Harold Wilson and European Integration: Britain's Second Application to Join the EEC* (London: Frank Cass, 2003)

——, 'Anthony Crosland, 1976–77', in Kevin Theakston, ed., *British Foreign Secretaries Since 1974* (London and New York: Routledge, 2004), pp. 67–91

——, 'Playing games with history: Tony Blair's European policy in the press', *British Journal of Politics and International Relations*, 9:4, (2007), pp. 582–98

Darby, Philip, *British Defence Policy East of Suez 1947–1968* (London: Oxford University Press for the RIIA, 1973)

Deighton, Anne, 'European Union policy', in Anthony Seldon, ed., *The Blair Effect: The Blair Government 1997–2001* (London: Little, Brown & Co., 2001), pp. 307–30.

Dixon, Rob, and Paul Williams, 'Tough on debt, tough on the causes of debt? New Labour's Third Way foreign policy', *British Journal of Politics and International Relations*, 3:2 (June 2001), pp. 150–72

Dobson, Alan, *The Politics of the Anglo-American Economic Special Relationship 1940–1987* (Brighton: Wheatsheaf, 1988)

——, 'The years of transition: Anglo-American relations 1961–1967', *Review of International Studies*, 16:3 (1990), pp. 239–58

Dockrill, Saki, 'Britain's power and influence: dealing with three roles and the Wilson government's defence debate at Chequers in November 1964', *Diplomacy and Statecraft*, 11:1 (2000), pp. 211–40

Donoughue, Bernard, *Prime Minister: The Conduct of Policy under Harold Wilson and James Callaghan* (London: Jonathan Cape, 1987)

Donoughue, Bernard, and George Jones, *Herbert Morrison: Portrait of a Politician* (London: Weidenfeld & Nicolson, 1973)

Dorril, Stephen, *MI6: Fifty Years of Special Operations* (London: Fourth Estate, 2001 edn)

Dorril, Stephen, and Robin Ramsay, *Smear! Wilson and the Secret State* (London: Grafton, 1992 edn)

Douglas, R.M., *The Labour Party, Nationalism and Internationalism, 1939–1951* (London: Routledge, 2004)

Doyle, Michael, 'Kant, liberal legacies and foreign affairs', parts 1 and 2, *Philosophy and Public Affairs*, 12:3 (Summer 1983), pp. 205–35; and 12:4 (Autumn 1983), pp. 323–53

Driver, Christopher, *The Disarmers: A Study in Protest* (London: Hodder and Stoughton, 1964)

Duff, Peggy, *Left, Left, Left. A Personal Account of Six Protest Campaigns, 1945–65* (London: Allison and Busby, 1971)

Dumbrell, John, 'The Johnson administration and the British Labour government: Vietnam, the pound and east of Suez', *Journal of American Studies*, 30:2 (1996), pp. 211–31

Dumbrell, John, and Sylvia Ellis, 'British involvement in Vietnam peace initiatives, 1966–1967: marigolds, sunflowers and "Kosygin Week"', *Diplomatic History*, 27:1 (2003), pp. 113–49

Dunne, Tim, and Nicholas Wheeler, 'Blair's Britain: a force for good in the world?', in Karen Smith and Margo Light, eds, *Ethics and Foreign Policy* (Cambridge: Cambridge University Press, 2001), pp. 167–84

——, 'Moral Britannia: Evaluating the Ethical Dimension in Labour's Foreign Policy', published by The Foreign Policy Centre (April 2004), pp. 1–40

Edmunds, June, 'The evolution of British Labour Party policy on Israel from 1967 to the Intifada', *Twentieth Century British History*, 11:1 (2000), pp. 23–41

Ellis, Sylvia, '"A demonstration of British good sense?" British student protest during the Vietnam War' in Gerard DeGroot (ed.), *Student Protest: The Sixties and After* (London: Longman 1998), pp. 54–69

Evans, Martin, *Afghanistan: A New History* (London: RoutledgeCurzon, 2002)

Fielding, Steven, *The Labour Party: Socialism and Society since 1951* (Manchester: Manchester University Press, 1997)

Finnemore, Martha, *National Interests in International Society* (Ithaca, New York: Cornell University Press, 1996)

Flower, Ken, *Serving Secretly: An Intelligence Chief on Record. Rhodesia into Zimbabwe 1964 to 1981* (London: John Murray, 1987)

Foot, Michael, *Aneurin Bevan: A Biography, vol. 2, 1945–1960* (London: Davis-Poynter, 1973)

Frankel, Joseph, *British Foreign Policy 1945–1973* (Oxford: Oxford University Press, 1975)

Freedman, Lawrence, 'Defence', in Anthony Seldon, ed., *The Blair Effect: The Blair Government 1997–2001* (London: Little, Brown & Co., 2001), pp. 289–305

——, *The Official History of the Falklands Campaign, Volume II* (London: Routledge, 2005)

Gati, C., 'Imre Nagy and Moscow, 1953–56', *Problems of Communism*, 35:3 (May/June 1986), 32–49

Geddes, Andrew, 'Labour and the European Community 1973–93: pro-Europeanism, "Europeanisation" and their implications', *Contemporary Record*, 8:2 (Autumn 1994), pp. 370–80

George, Stephen, and Ben Rosamond, 'The European Community', in Martin Smith and Joanna Spear, eds, *The Changing Labour Party* (London: Routledge, 1992), pp. 171–85

Good, Robert, *UDI: The International Politics of the Rhodesian Rebellion* (London: Faber, 1973)

Gordon, Michael, *Conflict and Consensus in Labour's Foreign Policy 1914–1965* (Stanford, CA: Stanford University Press, 1969)

Gordon Walker, Patrick, 'The Labor Party's defense and foreign policy', *Foreign Affairs*, 42:3 (April 1964), pp. 391–8

Gordon Walker, Patrick, edited with an introduction by Robert Pearce, *Political Diaries 1932–1971* (London: Historian's Press, 1991)

Gorst, Anthony, and Lewis Johnman, *The Suez Crisis* (London: Routledge, 1997)

Gould, Philip, *The Unfinished Revolution: How the Modernisers Saved the Labour Party* (London: Little, Brown & Co., 1998)

Gow, James, *Defending the West* (London: Polity, 2004)

Groom, A.J.R., *British Thinking about Nuclear Weapons* (London: Pinter, 1974)

Haines, Joe, *The Politics of Power* (London: Jonathan Cape, 1977)

Hanning, Hugh, 'Britain east of Suez – facts and figures', *Review of International Studies*, 42:2 (April 1966), pp. 253–60

Harmon, Mark, *The British Labour Government and the 1976 IMF Crisis* (Basingstoke: Macmillan, 1997)

Harrison, Martin, *Trade Unions and the Labour Party since 1945* (London: Allen and Unwin, 1960)

Healey, Dennis, *The Time of My Life* (London: Penguin, 1990)

——, *When Shrimps Learn to Whistle* (London: Penguin Books, 1991)

Heath, Edward, 'Realism in British foreign policy', *Foreign Affairs*, 48:1 (October 1969), pp. 39–50

——, *The Course of My Life: My Autobiography* (London: Coronet Books, Hodder & Stoughton, 1999)

Hill, Christopher, 'Foreign Policy', in Anthony Seldon, ed., *The Blair Effect: The Blair Government 1997–2001* (London: Little, Brown & Co., 2001), pp. 331–53

——, 'The historical background: past and present in British foreign policy', in Michael Smith, Steve Smith and Brian White, eds, *British Foreign Policy: Tradition, Change and Transformation* (London: Unwin Hyman, 1988), p. 28

——, 'Britain's elusive role in world politics', *British Journal of International Studies*, (1979), pp. 249–59

Henderson, Arthur, *Consolidating World Peace* (London: Burge Memorial Lecture, 1931)

Hinton, James, *Protests and Visions: Peace Politics in Twentieth Century Britain* (London: Hutchinson, 1989)

Holden, Russell, *The Making of New Labour's European Policy* (Basingstoke: Macmillan, 2002)

Holmes, Martin, *The Failure of the Heath Government* (Basingstoke: Macmillan, 2nd edn, 1997)

Horne, Alistair, *Macmillan, 1957–1986: Volume II of the Official Biography* (London: Macmillan, 1989)

Howard, Michael, 'Britain's strategic problem east of Suez', *Review of International Studies*, 42:2 (April 1966), pp. 179–83

Howarth, Jolyon, 'Discourse, ideas, and epistemic communities in European security and defence policy', *West European Politics*, 27:2 (2004), pp. 211–34

Hughes, Colin, and Patrick Wintour, *Labour Rebuilt: The New Model Party* (London: Fourth Estate, 1990)

Jefferys, Kevin, *The Labour Party Since 1945* (London: Macmillan, 1993)

——, ed., *Leading Labour: From Keir Hardie to Tony Blair* (London: I.B. Tauris, 1999)

Jenkins, Roy, *A Life at the Centre* (Basingstoke: Macmillan, 1991)

Johnson, Lyndon Baines, *The Vantage Point: Perspectives of the Presidency 1963–1969* (London: Weidenfeld & Nicolson, 1971)

Jones, Jack, *Union Man: The Autobiography of Jack Jones* (London: Collins, 1986)

Jones, Peter, *America and the British Labour Party: The 'Special Relationship' at Work* (London: I.B. Tauris, 1997)

Jones, Roy, *The Changing Structure of British Foreign Policy* (London: Longman, 1974)

Jones, Tudor, *Remaking the Labour Party: From Gaitskell to Blair* (London: Routledge, 1996)

Kampfner, John, *Robin Cook* (London: Victor Gollancz, 1998)

——, *Blair's Wars* (London: The Free Press, 2004)

Katzenstein, Peter, ed., *The Culture of National Security. Norms and Identity in World Politics* (New York: Columbia University Press, 1996)

Kavanagh, Dennis, 'The fatal choice: the calling of the February 1974 election', in Stuart Ball and Anthony Seldon, eds, *The Heath Government 1970–1974: A Reappraisal* (London: Longman, 1996), pp. 351–70

Kelly, Richard, 'Farewell conference, hello forum: the making of Labour and Tory policy', *Political Quarterly*, 72:3 (2001), pp. 329–34

Kennedy, Paul, *The Realities behind Diplomacy: Background Influences on British External Policy, 1865–1980* (London: Allen and Unwin, 1981)

Kennedy-Pipe, Caroline, *The Origins of the Present Troubles in Northern Ireland* (London: Longman, 1997)

Kennedy-Pipe, Caroline, and Rhiannon Vickers, '"Blowback" for Britain: Blair, Bush and the War in Iraq', *Review of International Studies*, 33:2 (April 2007), pp. 205–21

Keohane, Dan, *Labour Party Defence Policy Since 1945* (Leicester: Leicester University Press, 1993)

Kissinger, Henry, *White House Years* (London: Phoenix Press, 2000 paperback edn.)

Knowles, Caroline, *Race, Discourse and Labourism* (London: Routledge, 1992)

Kyle, Keith, 'Britain and the Crisis, 1955–1956', in Wm. Roger Louis and Roger Owen, eds, *Suez 1956: The Crisis and its Consequences* (Oxford: Clarendon Press, 1989), pp. 103–30

'The Labour Committee for Europe', *Contemporary Record*, 7:2 (Autumn 1993), pp. 386–416

Labour Party, *Sense About Defence: The Report of the Labour Party Defence Study Group* (London: Quartet Books, 1977)

Lapping, Brian, *The Labour Government 1964–70* (Harmondsworth: Penguin, 1970)

Little, Richard, and Mark Wickham-Jones, eds, *New Labour's Foreign Policy: A New Moral Crusade?* (Manchester: Manchester University Press, 2000)

Logevall, Fredrik, *Choosing War: The Lost Chance of Peace and the Escalation of War in Vietnam* (Berkeley, LA: University of California Press, 1999)

Lord, Christopher, *British Entry to the European Community under the Heath Government of 1970–4* (Aldershot: Dartmouth, 1993)

McInnes, Colin, 'Labour's Strategic Defence Review', *International Affairs*, 74:4 (1998), pp. 823–45

Malone, Peter, *The British Nuclear Deterrent* (London: Croom Helm, 1984)

Mandelson, Peter, 'Marketing Labour: personal reflections and experience', *Contemporary Record*, 1:3 (Winter 1998), pp. 11–13

Marquand, David, 'Bombs and scapegoats', *Encounter*, 16:1 (January 1961), pp. 43–8

Martin, Laurence, and John Garnett, *British Foreign Policy: Challenges and Choices for the 21st Century* (London: Royal Institute of International Affairs, 1997)

Mason, Roy, *Paying the Price* (London: Robert Hale, 1999)

Mayhew, Christopher, *Britain's Role Tomorrow* (London: Hutchinson, 1967)

Melvern, Linda, and Paul Williams, 'Britannia waived the rules: the Major government and the 1994 Rwandan genocide', *African Affairs*, 103 (2004), pp. 1–22

Miller, Kenneth, *Socialism and Foreign Policy: Theory and Practice in Britain to 1931* (The Hague: Martinus Nijhoff, 1967)

Minkin, Lewis, *The Labour Party Conference: A Study in the Politics of Intra-Party Democracy* (Manchester: Manchester University Press, 1980)

Morgan, Austen, *Harold Wilson* (London: Pluto, 1992)

Morgan, Janet, ed., *The Backbench Diaries of Richard Crossman* (London: Hamish Hamilton and Jonathan Cape, 1981)

Morgan, Kenneth O., *Labour People: Leaders and Lieutenants, Hardie to Kinnock* (Oxford: Oxford University Press, 1987)

——, *The People's Peace: British History 1945–1990* (Oxford: Oxford University Press, 1992 edn)

——, *Callaghan: A Life* (Oxford: Oxford University Press, 1997)

Nailor, Peter, 'Denis Healey and rational decision-making in defence', in Ian Beckett and John Gooch, eds, *Politicians and Defence: Studies in the Formulation of British Defence Policy 1845–1970* (Manchester: Manchester University Press, 1981), pp. 154–77

Obama, Barack, 'Renewing American leadership', *Foreign Affairs*, 86:4 (July/August 2007)

Owen, David, *The Politics of Defence* (London: Jonathan Cape, 1972)

——, *Human Rights* (London: Jonathan Cape, 1978)

——, *Time to Declare* (London: Michael Joseph, 1991)

Parkin, Frank, *Middle Class Radicalism: The Social Bases of the British Campaign for Nuclear Disarmament* (Manchester: Manchester University Press, 1968)

Parr, Helen, *Britain's Policy Towards the European Community: Harold Wilson and Britain's World Role, 1964–1967* (London: Routledge, 2006)

Parr, Helen, and Melissa Pine, 'Policy towards the European Economic Community', in Peter Dorey, ed., *The Labour Governments 1964–1970* (London: Routledge, 2006), pp. 1-8-29

Peston, Robert, *Brown's Britain* (London: Short Books, 2005)

Phythian, Mark, *The Politics of British Arms Sales Since 1964* (Manchester: Manchester University Press, 2000)

Pimlott, Ben, ed., *The Political Diary of Hugh Dalton, 1918–40, 1945–60* (London: Jonathan Cape, 1986)

——, *Harold Wilson* (London: Harper Collins, 1993 edn)

Ponting, Clive, *Breach of Promise: Labour in Power 1964–1970* (London: Hamish Hamilton, 1989)

Porteous, Tom, 'British government policy in sub-Saharan Africa under New Labour', *International Affairs*, 81:2 (2005), pp. 281–97

Rawnsley, Andrew, *Servants of the People: The Inside Story of New Labour* (London: Hamish Hamilton, 2000)

Reichley, A. James, *Conservatives in an Age of Change: The Nixon and Ford Administrations* (Washington, D.C.: The Brookings Institution, 1981)

Riddell, Peter, *The Thatcher Era and its Legacy* (Oxford: Blackwell, 2nd edn. 1988)

——, 'Europe', in Anthony Seldon and Dennis Kavanagh, eds, *The Blair Effect 2001–5* (Cambridge: Cambridge University Press, 2005), pp. 362–83

Robinson, Piers, 'Ready to kill but not ready to die: NATO strategy in Kosovo', *International Journal*, 54:4 (Autumn 1999), pp. 671–82

Rodgers, Bill, *Fourth Among Equals* (London: Politicos, 2000)

Rosamond, Ben, 'Labour and the European Community: Learning to be European?', *Politics*, 10:2 (1990), pp. 41–8

Roth, Andrew, *Heath and the Heathmen* (London: Routledge and Kegan Paul, 1972)

Schneer, Jonathan, 'Hopes deferred or shattered: the British Labour left and the Third Force movement, 1945–49', *Journal of Modern History*, 56:2 (1984), pp. 197–226

Seldon, Anthony, *Blair* (London: Free Press, 2005)

——, ed., *The Blair Effect: The Blair Government 1997–2001* (London: Little, Brown & Co., 2001)

Seldon, Anthony, and Kevin Hickson, eds, *New Labour, Old Labour: The Wilson and Callaghan Governments, 1974–79* (London: Routledge, 2004)

Seldon, Anthony, and Dennis Kavanagh, eds, *The Blair Effect 2001–5* (Cambridge: Cambridge University Press, 2005)

Seyd, Patrick, *The Rise and Fall of the Labour Left* (Basingstoke: Macmillan, 1987)

Seyd, Patrick, and Paul Whitely, *Labour's Grass Roots. The Politics of Party Membership* (Oxford: Clarendon, 1992)

Shaw, Eric, *The Labour Party since 1945* (Oxford: Blackwell, 1996)

Short, Edward, *Whip to Wilson: The Crucial Years of the Labour Government* (London: MacDonald, 1989)

Shultz, George, *Turmoil and Triumph* (New York: Macmillan, 1993)

Singham, A.W., 'Immigration and the election', in David Butler and Anthony King, *The British General Election of 1964* (London: Macmillan, 1965), Appendix III, pp. 360-3

Skidelsky, Robert, 'The reinvention of Blair', in Anthony Seldon and Dennis Kavanagh, eds., *The Blair Effect 2001–5* (Cambridge: Cambridge University Press, 2005), pp. 439–44

Smith, Martin, and Joanna Spear, eds, *The Changing Labour Party* (London: Routledge, 1992)

Smith, Michael, Steve Smith and Brian White, eds, *British Foreign Policy: Tradition, Change and Transformation* (London: Unwin Hyman, 1988)

Sopel, John, *Tony Blair: The Moderniser* (London: Bantam, 1995)

Snyder, William, *The Politics of British Defense Policy, 1945–1962* (Bowling Green: Ohio State University Press, 1964)

Steininger, Rolf, '"The Americans are in a hopeless position": Great Britain and the war in Vietnam, 1964–5', *Diplomacy and Statecraft*, 8:3 (November 1997), pp. 237–85

Stewart, Michael, *Life and Labour: An Autobiography* (London: Sidgwick and Jackson, 1980)

Stothard, Peter, *30 Days: A Month at the Heart of Blair's War* (London: Harper Collins, 2003)

Taylor, Ian, and Paul Williams, 'The limits of engagement: British foreign policy and the crisis in Zimbabwe', *International Affairs*, 78:3 (2002), pp. 547–65

Taylor, Richard, 'The Labour Party and CND: 1957 to 1984', in Richard Taylor and Nigel Young, eds, *Campaigns for Peace: British Peace Movements in the Twentieth Century* (Manchester: Manchester University Press, 1987), pp. 100–30

Taylor, Robert, 'The Campaign for Nuclear Disarmament', in Vernon Bogdanor and Robert Skidelsky, eds, *The Age of Affluence 1951–1964* (London: Macmillan, 1970), pp. 221–53

——, 'The Heath government and industrial relations: myth and reality', in Stuart Ball and Anthony Seldon, eds, *The Heath Government 1970–1974: A Reappraisal* (London: Longman, 1996), pp. 161–90

Tebbit, Norman, *Upwardly Mobile: An Autobiography* (London: Futura, 1989 edn)

Tiratsoo, Nick, 'Labour and its critics: the case of the May Day Manifesto

Group', in R. Coopey, S. Fielding and N. Tiratsoo, eds, *The Wilson Governments 1964–70* (London: Pinter, 1993)

Twitchell, N.H., *The Tribune Group: Factional Conflict in the Labour Party 1964–1970* (London: Rabbit Publications, 1998)

Urban, Mark, *Big Boys' Rules: The SAS and the Secret Struggle against the IRA* (London: Faber and Faber, 1992)

Verrier, Anthony, 'British defence policy under Labor', *Foreign Affairs*, 42:2 (January 1966), pp. 282–92

Vickers, Rhiannon, 'Blair's Kosovo campaign: political communications, the battle for public opinion and foreign policy', *Civil Wars*, 3:1 (Spring 2000), p. 5470

——, 'Labour's search for a Third Way in foreign policy', in Richard Little and Mark Wickham-Jones, eds, *New Labour's Foreign Policy: A New Moral Crusade?* (Manchester: Manchester University Press, 2000), pp. 33–45

——, *The Labour Party and the World, Volume 1: The Evolution of Labour's Foreign Policy 1900–1951* (Manchester: Manchester University Press, 2004)

——, 'The new public diplomacy in Britain and Canada', *British Journal of Politics and International Relations*, 6:2 (Spring 2004), pp. 182–94

——, 'Robin Cook, 1997–2001', in Kevin Theakston, ed., *Foreign Secretaries since 1974* (London: Routledge, 2004), pp. 247–67

——, 'Harold Wilson, the British Labour Party, and the war in Vietnam', *Journal of Cold War Studies*, 10:2 (Spring 2008), pp. 43–72

Vital, David, *The Making of British Foreign Policy* (London: Allen & Unwin, 1968)

Wallace, William, 'World status without tears', in Vernon Bogdanor and Robert Skidelsky, eds, *The Age of Affluence 1951–1964* (London: Macmillan, 1970), pp. 192–220

——, *The Foreign Policy Process in Britain* (London: Royal Institute of International Affairs, 1975)

Waltz, Kenneth, *Foreign Policy and Democratic Politics: The American and British Experience* (London: Longmans, 1968)

Weart, Spencer, *Nuclear Fear: A History of Images* (Cambridge, MA: Harvard University Press, 1988)

Westlake, Martin, *Kinnock: The Biography* (London: Little, Brown & Co., 2001)

Wheeler, Nicholas, and Tim Dunne, 'Good international citizenship: a Third Way for British foreign policy', *International Affairs*, 74:4 (1998), pp. 847–70

White, Howard, 'British aid and the White Paper on International Development: dressing a wolf in sheep's clothing in the emperor's new clothes?', *Journal of International Development*, 10:2 (1998), pp. 151–66

Wickham-Jones, Mark, 'Labour's trajectory in foreign affairs: the moral crusade of a pivotal power?', in Richard Little and Mark Wickham-Jones, eds, *New Labour's Foreign Policy: A New Moral Crusade?* (Manchester: Manchester University Press, 2000), pp. 3–32

Wigg, Lord, *George Wigg* (London: Michael Joseph, 1972)

Williams, Paul, *British Foreign Policy under New Labour, 1997–2005* (Basingstoke: Macmillan, 2005)

Williams, Philip, *Hugh Gaitskell* (London: Jonathan Cape, 1979)

——, ed., *The Diary of Hugh Gaitskell, 1945–1956* (London: Jonathan Cape, 1983)

Wilson, Harold, *The Labour Government 1964–1970: A Personal Record* (London: Weidenfeld & Nicolson, 1971)

——, *Final Term: The Labour Government 1974–1976* (London: Weidenfeld & Nicolson and Michael Joseph, 1979)

——, *Memoirs: The Making of a Prime Minister 1916–64* (London: Weidenfeld & Nicolson and Michael Joseph, 1986)

Woodhouse, C.M., *British Foreign Policy since the Second World War* (London: Hutchinson, 1961)

Woodward, Bob, *Bush at War* (London: Pocket Books, 2003)

Woolf, Leonard, *Foreign Policy – The Labour Party's Dilemma* (London: Labour Party, 1947)

Wrigley, Chris, 'Now you see it, now you don't: Harold Wilson and Labour's foreign policy 1964–70', in R. Coopey, Steven Fielding and Nick Tiratsoo, eds, *The Wilson Governments 1964-70* (London: Pinter, 1993)

Wright, Peter, with Paul Greengrass, *Spycatcher: The Candid Autobiography of a Senior Intelligence Officer* (New York: Viking Penguin, 1987)

Young, John W., 'The Wilson government and the debate over arms to South Africa in 1964', *Contemporary British History*, 12:3 (Autumn 1998), pp. 62–86

——, 'Britain and "LBJ's war", 1964–68', *Cold War History*, 12:3 (April 2002), pp. 63–92

——, *The Labour Governments 1964–1970, vol. 2: International Policy* (Manchester: Manchester University Press, 2003)

Young, Kenneth, *Rhodesia and Independence: A Study in British Colonial Policy* (London: Eyre and Spottiswoode, 1967)

Young, Ralph, 'New Labour and international development', in David Coates and Peter Lawler, eds, *New Labour in Power* (Manchester: Manchester University Press, 2000), pp. 254–67

Ziegler, Philip, *Wilson: The Authorised Life of Lord Wilson of Rievaulx* (London: Weidenfeld & Nicolson, 1993)

Index